The Three Lives of the Kaiser

The Three Lives of the Kaiser

A BIOGRAPHY OF FRANZ BECKENBAUER

Uli Hesse

**SIMON &
SCHUSTER**

London · New York · Sydney · Toronto · New Delhi

First published in Great Britain by Simon & Schuster UK Ltd, 2023

3 5 7 9 10 8 6 4 2

Simon & Schuster UK Ltd
1st Floor
222 Gray's Inn Road
London WC1X 8HB

www.simonandschuster.co.uk
www.simonandschuster.com.au
www.simonandschuster.co.in

Simon & Schuster Australia, Sydney
Simon & Schuster India, New Delhi

A CIP catalogue record for this book
is available from the British Library

Hardback ISBN: 978-1-4711-8910-4
eBook ISBN: 978-1-4711-8911-1

Typeset in Bembo by M Rules
Printed and Bound using 100% Renewable
Electricity at CPI Group (UK) Ltd

MIX
Paper | Supporting
responsible forestry
FSC
www.fsc.org   FSC® C171272

Is this the way to the World Cup?

TONY CHRISTIE

Better a diamond with a flaw than a
pebble without

CONFUCIUS

CONTENTS

INTRODUCTION

Headbutting at the Sugar Club

The story of this book begins in the autumn of 2014 at the Sugar Club in Dublin. I had been invited to an event called 'An Evening with The Blizzard Football Quarterly', which consisted of three football writers sharing a stage and chatting amiably about the game while fielding the occasional question from a capacity audience. I was sitting alongside Jonathan Wilson, the founder and editor of *The Blizzard* magazine, and the French journalist Philippe Auclair, while RTÉ Sport's Damien O'Meara compèred the proceedings.

Since football is the only walk of life in which hipsters and traditionalists are one and the same, we were mostly stuck in the past in a delightful way, sharing anecdotes about reckless tackles or great players of our long-gone youths and listening to jokes about Sunderland, which everybody got but me. Then, almost twenty minutes into the second half, Damien suddenly went off on a tangent by announcing: 'Coming to a *Blizzard* event and not hearing us talk about FIFA and Qatar is like going to see the Eagles and they don't perform "Hotel California".' While I was still trying to collect the deplorably few thoughts I entertained about FIFA, Qatar and the Eagles, Jonathan looked me in the eye and said: 'Uli, how is Franz Beckenbauer perceived in Germany? It seems to me that in a pretty contested field, he might be the most loathsome football politician in Europe.'

It was the journalistic equivalent of a headbutt. Beckenbauer? Loathsome? I had never met the man but knew many who had – and they invariably described him as courteous, pleasant and infinitely more humble than a living legend had any right to be. There were a few scattered laughs after Jonathan's quip, signalling I now had to come up with some repartee. Unfortunately, all I could think of was: 'Err, why's that?' A man who during a long playing career counted only Pelé and Johan Cruyff as his equals – abominable? Arguably the only footballer who invented an entirely new position on the field – abhorrent? One of only three men who won the World Cup as both a player and a coach – detestable?

Jonathan went on to explain that Beckenbauer's role in Germany being awarded the 2006 World Cup was, to put it mildly, somewhat unclear. 'Let's not forget Charles Dempsey, for whatever reason, abstained at the last minute,' he added by way of an explanation, referring to the fact that the Scottish-born New Zealand delegate had crucially refused to cast a vote at the final moment, despite unmistakable instructions to the contrary. This remark prompted Philippe, a seasoned swimmer in the muddy waters of football politics, to join the discussion. His was a most welcome intrusion because I was now well and truly absent-minded. How did Germans perceive Beckenbauer? What an intriguing question.

Remember, this was November 2014, a full eleven months before *Der Spiegel* magazine broke the story about 10 million Swiss francs nobody could or would properly account for, which cast Germany's celebrated World Cup bid in a highly unfavourable light. (The money was sent, via a circuitous route, from the German World Cup organising committee to Mohammed bin Hammam, a former Qatari football administrator who was banned for life by FIFA in 2012 and who had been the subject of a *Sunday Times* exposé only a few months before the Sugar Club event.)

This revelation would do the unthinkable: namely blemish Beckenbauer's reputation at home. But as I said, this was almost a year in the future. Despite Jonathan's evidently low opinion of the man, I could have told him that, by and large, Germans loved Beckenbauer unreservedly. In fact, many people had stopped calling him the Kaiser, because even this illustrious nickname – probably the most deferential in world football – seemed woefully inadequate to describe his exalted position. Instead, Beckenbauer had become 'the shining light of German football', an expression coined by none other than Berti Vogts in 1990 to explain why he would never be able to compete with the man who had preceded him as national coach.

However, I was old enough to also remember the days before Beckenbauer had become Germany's shining light. A few months after my eleventh birthday in 1977, he abruptly left the country to ply his trade across the big pond for New York Cosmos in what Germans derisively called an *Operettenliga*, a showbiz league devoid of any real value. The shock move not only curtailed his international career and annoyed national coach Helmut Schön, who had hoped Beckenbauer would be his captain at the World Cup in Argentina, it also angered the general public. What was seen as his defection even made the cover of *Der Spiegel*. The magazine spoke of a 'surge of indignation' and headlined its influential article *Libero auf der*

Flucht – 'Sweeper on the Run'. Beckenbauer was trying to escape from many things, the piece argued, among them not only the tax authorities, a dysfunctional Bayern Munich team and a disintegrating marriage, but also a country that nurtured a love-hate relationship with its greatest football player because it had never really figured out what to make of the man.

In the most famous of Beckenbauer's numerous autobiographies, published in 1975, there's a revealing passage that reads: 'I have had first-hand experience of the effect someone can have on a crowd. Even the fans in Munich never cheered me the way people in Hamburg cheered their Uwe Seeler, a player they called "Uwe" or "Fatty" and adored in a manner that was in equal parts gushing and matey.' Beckenbauer, or more precisely the ghostwriter he talked to, then deplored the fact he had never been given an affectionate nickname like that, in marked contrast to not only Seeler but also many of his own Bayern team-mates like Josef Maier (Sepp), Franz Roth (the Bull) or Georg Schwarzenbeck (known since childhood by the nonsensical moniker Katsche). 'These are men everyone can relate to,' Beckenbauer said. 'People have the impression that this player is one of them. Sadly, this is not the case with me.'

On the other hand, I had heard and read a lot about the days before people decided that Beckenbauer was not one of them. I was born a few months before he became an international star during the 1966 World Cup in England. He was young then, he was handsome, he was playing for two very popular teams (Bayern Munich had not yet become the club everybody loved to hate, and you could argue the same went for the West German side of the mid-1960s). Three months after the World Cup, he was voted Germany's Footballer of the Year, way ahead of none other than Uwe Seeler. According to his biographer Torsten Körner, one thousand letters or postcards landed on Beckenbauer's doorstep every day: love messages, requests for autographs and simple notes of admiration. A film producer from Berlin offered the twenty-one year old the role of a taxi driver who solves a murder case. While Beckenbauer let this opportunity pass by, he did use the occasion of a Bayern game away at Cologne in October 1966 to go into a recording studio and cut a pop single.

Körner says the record made the German Top Ten, while Beckenbauer would claim in 2020 that he outsold the Beatles. Both are slightly wrong. 'Gute Freunde Kann Niemand Trennen' – Nobody Can Separate Good Friends – stalled at number 31 in the charts. Still, young Franz was on everyone's lips (and in some ears) in the wake of the World Cup, and a major reason must have been precisely that he was so different from the typical German footballers, from the Seelers and the Vogtses. Yes, the backlash would come, as it always does. But there was obviously a period before my time when Beckenbauer was almost universally popular and his country's greatest promise.

Once I had chewed on all this, I was ready to tell Jonathan: 'You know, Pelé touched people's hearts and Cruyff inspired their minds. But it's really difficult to say what legacy Beckenbauer's extraordinary life will leave. The answer to your question as to how he is perceived in Germany has changed many times over the years and may tell us more about ourselves than about the man.' But just at that moment, I heard Damien utter the words: 'Money talks and World Cups walk. And now we go to the floor.' And, with that, he handed the microphone to a member of the audience who asked us a question about football's loan system. It meant I had nobody to share my ruminations with. Until now.

Sunday in Samoa

While Bayern Munich were waiting for a miracle to happen, Franz Beckenbauer was dreaming. At fifty-four years of age, he was not only the club's greatest-ever player and a Bavarian icon, but he was also officially Bayern's number-one representative, having been elected club president in November 1994. And yet Beckenbauer was not sitting in Munich's Olympic Stadium next to his fellow board members Karl-Heinz Rummenigge or Uli Hoeness on this Saturday – 20 May 2000, the last day of a turbulent and thrilling Bundesliga season. Instead, he was lying in bed, sound asleep and, on account of the temperature, stark naked.

Beckenbauer had two good excuses. The first was that he, like everybody else, knew the race was over and the title lost even though there were still ninety minutes of football left. Bayern, playing host to Werder Bremen, trailed Bayer Leverkusen by a full three points. There would have been at least a glimmer of hope if Leverkusen had been faced with a stern task – say, a game against Hamburg, Kaiserslautern or even, whisper it, 1860 Munich. Instead, the league leaders were playing away at lowly Unterhaching, a small club based just outside Munich and enjoying its first season in the top flight. A surefire relegation candidate, Unterhaching had stunned the country by somehow nestling into a comfortable tenth place, but of course you couldn't expect them to defeat a stylish Leverkusen side starring a young Michael Ballack.

Beckenbauer's second excuse was that, at least for him, it wasn't even Saturday any more. He was more than ten thousand miles away from Munich, in Apia, the capital of Samoa, where it was early Sunday morning. Beckenbauer and his right-hand man Fedor Radmann, a gifted networker since his days as an Adidas executive in charge of international relations, had travelled to Polynesia to attend a meeting of the Oceania Football Confederation and to advertise Germany's bid for the 2006 World Cup. Oceania had only a single vote, but you never know.

To be honest, it was all bit of a lost cause, born out of desperation and thus not unlike Bayern Munich's attempt to win the league. Beckenbauer and Radmann were not the only lobbyists in town. Sir Bobby Charlton and Alec McGivan had eschewed the FA Cup final at Wembley to be present in Samoa, and their job was a lot easier. That's because Oceania had more or less already decided what to do. Their representative on FIFA's executive committee, the 79-year-old Charles Dempsey, would be given a clear mandate: first vote for England and, if and when this bid is rejected, then vote for South Africa. Still, Dempsey was known as a golfing enthusiast and Beckenbauer, an excellent player with a single-figure handicap, was looking forward to enjoying a round with the Glaswegian, just for fun.

It was 4.30 a.m. when Beckenbauer was woken up by a phone call. For a brief moment, he didn't quite know where he was. In the last week alone, he had been in Nassau, then Kuala Lumpur and now Samoa. When he answered the phone, he heard the excited voice of his wife Sybille. He listened for a few minutes, incredulity slowly giving way to delight. Finally, Beckenbauer hung up, jumped out of bed and left his room, still naked. He banged on the door next to his until a bleary-eyed – and also naked – Radmann opened it.

'You're not going to believe this,' Beckenbauer said, 'but we won the league! We beat Bremen 3-1, and Leverkusen managed to lose 2-0 at Unterhaching!' Whereupon the two Germans danced down the corridor, both in their birthday suits. (One can only hope that the near-octogenarian Dempsey had not stirred from his sleep and felt inclined to step outside to see what was going on.) Suddenly, Beckenbauer had an idea. He went back into his room, grabbed the phone and dialled a number. It was close to five o'clock.

'Yes?' mumbled a tired FIFA president Sepp Blatter.

Without introduction or explanation, Beckenbauer began to sing.

'Stand up if you're Bavarian!' the man they called Kaiser belted out. 'Stand up if you're Bavarian!'

LIFE I

Chapter One

One of the most famous and oft-quoted lines about Franz Beckenbauer was written by an Englishman, the Bristol-born J. L. Manning, whom Brian Glanville once called 'a very prominent journalist, but a rather conceited sort of man'. In the summer of 1970, Jim Manning was in Mexico to report on the World Cup for newspapers at home. He was best known as a columnist for the *Daily Mail*, but the words which concern us here appeared in the *Evening Standard* on Thursday 18 June, the day after a truly epic semi-final between West Germany and Italy. Whenever Manning's sentences are quoted today, which actually happens more often in Germany than in the UK, they are reduced to six key words, so let's have a bit of context before looking at the entire paragraph.

Some sixty-five minutes into the game, Beckenbauer had been brought down just inches outside Italy's penalty area ('by cunning intent', as Glanville noted in his own account of the match). A few moments later, the West Germans used up their second substitution, which proved to be unfortunate because it soon transpired that Beckenbauer was so severely injured that his arm had to be taped to his torso to keep the pain just about bearable. With this handicap, he not only played through the rest of regulation time, but also an additional thirty minutes in the relentless Mexican heat. It was all in vain, as Beckenbauer's team eventually lost what the hosts quickly dubbed *El Partido Del Siglo* – the match of the century – 4-3.

Now, Manning. 'When the end came, players sprawled all over the pitch,' he wrote. 'Their dressing room must have been a marathon walk from where they had dropped as the whistle blew. All the players except one, that is. Franz Beckenbauer, his right arm strapped to his chest because his shoulder was dislocated, nearly one hour earlier, strode from the field as a wounded, defeated but proud Prussian officer. One of the greatest players in these Championships was cheered step by step.'

The six key words are, of course, 'wounded, defeated but proud Prussian officer'. They have proved so enduring because they seem to elegantly encapsulate what was so striking about Beckenbauer's style of play – his nonchalant grace under pressure and his almost unnaturally erect posture. Even today, roughly half a century after he all but glided across football pitches, it is astonishing to see that all the things you have heard about Beckenbauer are true. Yes, he played almost every pass with the outside of his foot, as if any other technique would have ruined his perfect pose – the stillness of his upper body – because it involved either turning a shoulder or moving an arm. And yes, he almost never looked down at his feet to see where the ball was. Actually, this is all the more impressive precisely because it happened fifty years ago, when football pitches were not the manicured carpets of today but sometimes frozen, often muddy and always bumpy, treacherous surfaces.

And yet Manning got it all terribly wrong. Beckenbauer, who never spent a day in the army even though West Germany introduced conscription for all male citizens before he turned eleven, was never officer material, as his temper and his lack of discipline were the stuff of legend at his club. And, much more importantly, the man who was so many things – a winner, an innovator, a stylist, an uncrowned monarch, a shining light and even a pop singer – was never ever anything even approaching a Prussian. In fact, a few weeks before the 1974 World Cup, he would tell the political magazine *Der Spiegel*: 'I'm not a German, I'm a Bavarian. In my opinion, that is a major difference.'

His name told you as much. No, not his given name, as Franz (which was handed down from his father) used to be as common in Germany as Francis, Francesco or François were and probably still are in other countries. But 'Beckenbauer' ... now that's a very interesting one. You sometimes read that the word means 'basin builder'. That's technically correct but historically wrong, as the building of basins was not a useful occupation in the Middle Ages when modern European family names came into being. Instead, 'Beckenbauer' referred to a man who had to hold down two jobs to make ends meet: he was a baker and a farmer. The German words for these trades are *Bäcker* and – and this is where the English word 'boor' comes form – *Bauer*.

In the years preceding Franz's birth in 1945, twenty families (or bachelors and widows) called Beckenbauer were resident in Munich. During the war, Munich had some 830,000 inhabitants and was the fourth largest German city, behind Berlin, Vienna (part of the German Reich after 1938) and Hamburg, ahead of Cologne and Leipzig. This would seem to indicate that the family name was not out of the ordinary. However, during those same years, not a single person by the name of Beckenbauer was listed in Berlin, which was then the fifth biggest city in the world. Hamburg, Cologne and Leipzig did not have any Beckenbauers either, while there was only one in Vienna, a carpenter called Josef.

This tells you that Beckenbauer is a thoroughly Bavarian name. The family branch we are interested in can be traced back to a hamlet called Walting some sixty miles north of Munich. Franz Beckenbauer's great-grandfather, a farmer also called Franz, was born here in 1795. He had two sons: the first was named Michael, the second – guess! – Franz. Michael was not cut out for rural life and went to Munich as a young man, where he got married and worked as a postman.

The Beckenbauers settled in Giesing, a poor working-class district some two miles south of the city centre. Michael's wife Katharina lost many children – some were stillborn, some died from diphtheria – but seven survived. The fourth saw the light of day in 1905, inevitably a boy called Franz. Three years later, Katharina gave birth to another son, whom his parents christened Alfons.

Franz trained to become a locksmith and the Munich address directories would list this as his occupation until well into the 1940s. However, he was not a healthy man, his back in particular causing him constant problems. Eventually, Franz followed his father's example and began to work for the Post Office, where he would ultimately become a chief secretary, a purely administrative role.

As often happens in families, Franz's younger brother Alfons must have been the total opposite. He found it hard to hold down a regular job and was unemployed for a long time. However, he was a gifted athlete and, in contrast to Franz, loved football. Alfons played for a club in Giesing called Sportfreunde 1912 (which indeed translates as 'friends of sports'). It wasn't a normal club, though. Sportfreunde was affiliated to the *Arbeiter-Turn- und Sportbund*, the Workers' Gymnastics and Sports Federation (ATSB), a German association that existed between 1893 and 1933, when it was smashed by the Nazis.

As the name suggests, the ATSB was a leftist organisation set up in direct opposition to sports associations such as the German FA (DFB), which it regarded as elitist, bourgeois and conservative. This may sound as if we're talking about a small and bizarre splinter group here, but nothing could be further from the truth. In 1930, the ATSB had about 1.2 million members, and more than 8,000 football teams fell under its umbrella. It ran a national football championship and also fielded a select XI, which played similar workers' organisations from other countries. While the ATSB stubbornly avoided the term 'national team' because it felt the expression smacked of jingoism and zealotry, the side was not undeserving of such a moniker. It was, after all, a representative team and the players were pretty good, as we shall soon see.

Alfons Beckenbauer, an inside left who was strong in the air and comfortable on the ball, was called up for five international matches in the build-up to the inaugural SASI European Championships in 1932, scoring eight goals. (SASI stood for *Sozialistische Arbeitersport Internationale*, Socialist Workers' Sport International.) However, only a few days before the tournament began on 25 September, he rendered himself ineligible by joining a much bigger and regular team. Alfons Beckenbauer had been on the dole for so long that he could not resist when this club offered to get him a job as a mechanic at the Dornier aircraft plant in Munich. It gives you an indication of how good Alfons was that his new team had just won the national championship of Germany, beating Eintracht Frankfurt 2–0 in the final. The name of the club was Bayern Munich.

More than three decades later, in the autumn of 1966, Germany's leading football magazine *Kicker* received a letter from a reader who had come across two Bayern line-ups from 1933 and stumbled over a familiar name: Beckenbauer. Was this mysterious player, the reader wanted to know, by any chance a relative of young Franz, who had just been voted his country's Footballer of the Year? Even *Kicker*, often referred to as the 'bible of the German game', did not know the answer, so they called Walter Fembeck, then Bayern's managing director (and the man who signed Gerd Müller).

'A Beckenbauer?' Fembeck wondered. 'A Beckenbauer in the 1930s? Well, we *should* certainly know about that.' Problem was, they didn't. And so Fembeck consulted Konrad 'Conny' Heidkamp, a member of the Bayern team that had been crowned champions in 1932. 'Yes,' Heidkamp said. 'There was a Beckenbauer, a skilful player. If I remember correctly, he had to retire early because of an illness. I can't remember his first name, though, and I don't know if he is related to Franz.' The *Kicker* reporter then called Franz's mother Antonie, who was able to shed light on the matter: 'Oh, that must have been Alfons!' she told the journalist. 'He is my husband's brother, Franz's uncle.'

The most puzzling aspect of the story as it appeared in *Kicker* a few weeks later was that Franz professed to have had no idea that his uncle used to play for Bayern Munich. At first, this seems scarcely believable. It was not as if Alfons had left the city, let alone the country. For the past thirty years, he had been living in a district of Munich known as Laim, four miles northwest of Giesing, and he often attended family meetings, as various photographs attest to. And yet there is a distinct possibility that he never told his nephew about his own playing days. As Heidkamp recalled, these ended very early – in 1933, to be precise, when Alfons was barely twenty-five. Franz's biographer Torsten Körner speculates that it was not just a combination of injuries, the sort of weak health that haunted many male members of the Beckenbauer family and a marriage to a wife who was not very keen on having a footballing husband that led Alfons to give up the game: 'The most important reason is apparently his antipathy to the politics of the National Socialists, who quickly "aryanised" Bayern Munich, discredited as a "Jews' club", and forced the Jewish president Kurt Landauer to step down.'

If this is true, it sounds quite plausible that Alfons was never greatly inclined to reminisce about those years, as he would have had to explain too many things, starting with his role in the ATSB. Also, is it too much to assume that he didn't like to talk at length about his own life in the first place? Munich's address directory of 1935 did list him as a 'mechanic', but three years later he had become a 'janitor' and, by the early 1950s, when he was still a comparatively young man, he was registered as a 'pensioner', probably on account of his health issues.

'We knew that Alfons had played football,' Franz's brother Walter says when I ask him about his uncle. 'What we really didn't know was that he had played for Bayern. My mother always told me that Alfons played for the 'workers' national team', but as a kid I had no idea what that was all about. He was a very nice man. We all liked him a lot and we saw him often, because his daughters, Erika and Helga, were great fun

17

to be around. But we really had no idea about this Bayern Munich connection.'

Even after his premature retirement, Alfons seemingly never lost his love for the game – and he must have been proud of his nephew. When *Kicker* arranged a photo shoot in November 1966, he travelled to Bayern's training camp in Grünwald, just outside of Munich. In the picture that was eventually published by the magazine, he has a smile on his face as he strolls next to Franz. The two men look almost like father and son, as there is a clear family resemblance, right down to the way they walk.

Actually, quite a few things would have been easier for Franz, the future Kaiser, if Alfons had indeed been his father. But it was Alfons's older brother Franz who met Antonie Hupfauf, a Giesing girl born just a five-minute walk away from the Beckenbauer family home. The two married in 1937 and, since money was very tight, they moved in with Franz's parents, Michael and Katharina, who lived in a street called St.-Bonifatius-Platz – which translates as Saint Boniface Square, even though it was not really a square. Many, many years later, this short lane was simply added to a neighbouring street, which is why people interested in footballing land-marks should not look for No. 2 St.-Bonifatius-Platz today but visit No. 6 Zugspitzstrasse instead.

Even though Munich suffered heavily during the war (seventy-four air raids destroyed half of all the buildings in town), the house in question still stands. Just fifteen years ago, it was run-down and dilapidated, covered in graffiti and nearly deserted. But even Giesing, once home to only the simplest of folks, has now been thoroughly gentrified. Today, No. 6 Zugspitzstrasse looks very nice indeed. In the now fully developed attic, and thus above the four-room flat where the Beckenbauers used to live, there resides somebody called, believe it or not, Kaiser.

It is a most peculiar building because, in the span of only three years, it produced not just one person who could rightfully be called the greatest German footballer of a generation, but, as illogical as it may sound, two. First, though, came Walter. In 1941, Antonie gave birth to a boy who would turn out to be a capable creative midfielder, good enough to play for Bayern Munich Schoolboys. People love a good myth and so there are those who stubbornly claim that Walter Beckenbauer had even more natural talent than his kid brother, an argument to which Walter has always replied the same thing: 'utter rubbish'.

This brother arrived four years later, on 11 September 1945. According to a family tradition that makes it unnecessarily hard for readers of biographies to follow events, he was christened Franz. As small and frail as he was, it was now getting rather crowded in the flat. Grandfather Michael had died prematurely, but there was not only his widow Katharina, Franz Sr and Antonie plus their two boys, there was also Franz Sr's youngest sister, Frieda, and her own two children. No surprise, then, that Walter and Franz would soon spend most of their time outside, on the street or on the football pitch that was literally in front of their doorstep. Recalling his formative years on the occasion of his seventy-fifth birthday in 2020, Franz said: 'Our greatest fortune was our neighbour. Munich SC 1906 was right across the street.' The club is now called Haidhausen 1906, but the facilities are still where they have always been. The field on which Walter and Franz kicked a ball about in the years after the war is now made of artificial grass, while the surrounding fence is no longer easy to scale. But, then as now, a football pitch is the first thing you see when you look out of the windows in what used to be the Beckenbauers' flat.

Of course, young Franz learned the game he would one day play better than almost anyone who ever lived from his older brother. But Walter was not his only teacher. There was also someone whose story remained virtually unknown until four years ago, when Bayern Munich's club museum appealed to the public to submit photos and documents relating to the history of women's football in the city. One person who replied was Brigitte Lettl, née Schmid.

Born in 1942, Brigitte lived on the floor just below the Beckenbauers with her mother and her older sister. (Her father had been taken prisoner of war and wouldn't return home until many years later.) Known as 'Gitta', she was perhaps even more of a born athlete than the Beckenbauer brothers. She could cycle faster than the boys, was a fine skier and skater, and played a lot of tennis in later life. Above all, though, she was a great footballer. 'Well, that's all we did – play football,' she says matter-of-factly six decades later from her home close to the Austrian border. 'Most of us were latchkey kids, very free. When we came back from school, we did our homework and then we went outside to play football until it was dark or dinner was ready.'

Most astonishingly, at least for the times, none of the boys ever objected to Gitta's presence, even though she was the only girl on the street team locally known as 'BoWaZu', after Bonifatius-Platz, Watzmannstrasse and Zugspitzstrasse. 'No, nobody ever said anything,' Gitta remembers. 'I suppose one reason is simply that I was quite good.' What sounds perky is actually an understatement. In 1955, when Gitta was thirteen, the DFB prohibited its member clubs from allowing women to play football, a ban that would only be lifted in 1970. But of course there were independent teams outside the DFB's reach. A former Bayern player by the name of Joseph Floritz even set up an unofficial national team that played around 150 internationals between 1958 and 1965.

Most of the players came from the western parts of West Germany, a stronghold of the women's game. Usually, the only international from the south of the country was Gitta Schmid. In the summer of 1957, more than 12,000 people came out to see her and her (much older) West German team-mates play England. Bert Trautmann performed the ceremonial kick-off and the game finished 1-1. The equaliser was one of forty-four goals Gitta would score in only forty internationals. In a different era, she would have been a star.

'Like I said, I was quite good,' Gitta continues. 'And Walter was also a really talented player. But Franz was always something else, an artist on the ball.' Another difference between the two brothers was their allegiance. Traditionally, Giesing is 1860 Munich country. The Blues, as they are known locally, were based just a fifteen-minute walk from the Beckenbauers' home, while Bayern Munich, the Reds, had their spiritual home in Schwabing, a borough in the northern part of the city. As the *New York Times* once put it, Schwabing was 'a traditional stomping ground of students, artists and assorted hangers-on. It has often been thought of as Munich's other half, artistic rather than bourgeois, cosmopolitan rather than Bavarian.' In other words, it was an alien place for a simple (and very Bavarian) working-class family like the Beckenbauers.

However, there was a twist. Even though West Germany would soon win the World Cup, German football was semi-professional at best. In fact, it was illegal to earn a living through the sport. While the players did receive money from their clubs, they had to prove they were holding down a regular job as well. Those clubs were not businesses but public, non-profit organisations that anyone could join, set up for the common good and serving a local community by offering sports facilities. One of the side-effects of this system was that only very few clubs actually owned the ground they played in, simply because you either had to have an awful lot of fee-paying members or some well-meaning wealthy patrons in order to finance a stadium. That is why Bayern Munich were nomads in their own city, renting a place here or there until they moved in with 1860 Munich in 1925 to share the ground at Grünwalder Strasse in Giesing. However, some people still regarded them as intruders.

'Bayern were from Schwabing, a place where none of us ever went,' Franz Beckenbauer once said in order to explain why he grew up as a fan of the Blues. His greatest hero was always Fritz Walter, the captain of the national team who came from Kaiserslautern, but locally he idolised two 1860 players: right-winger Ludwig Zausinger and inside-right Kurt Mondschein. Neither was ever capped, but young Franz dreamed of doing what they did – and to play for whom they played. Walter, on the other hand, had more than just a soft spot for the Reds, without ever being able to explain how this happened. Although Munich SC 1906 were his direct neighbours, he instead went to play for Bayern in 1952 when he was eleven.

According to one of the books bearing Franz Beckenbauer's name, Walter was also more of a rebel that his younger sibling. 'Basically, I did not long for the same things as my brother – smoking cigarettes, drinking beer or huddling in doorways with girls,' Franz wrote in 1975, adding that Walter would also often stand up to their father, a stern man who repeatedly told his sons that football was a terrible waste of time. In one of the key scenes of this autobiography, Franz describes how Walter once came home quite late, smelling of beer. It was the night that Franz, fearing the days of their BoWaZu team were nearing their end, decided to join a club himself: Munich SC 1906 on the other side of the street.

Like a great many things that Franz has either said or published under his name over the decades, this description has to be taken with a grain of salt and should be considered an apocryphal anecdote. That's because he walked across the street to join SC 1906 in late 1953 when he was eight, meaning Walter was just twelve and had only recently become a member of the Reds to play for Bayern Schoolboys. But the basic premise of the story is true. Franz possessed more dedication and determination than his brother. And, of course, more talent. 'With merely ten per cent of his natural ability,' Walter said as recently as 2020, 'I would have been a pretty strong amateur player.' Instead, he left Bayern as early as 1955 to follow Franz's example and join SC 1906, where all his friends were playing. Little did Walter know that his kid brother would fairly soon take the opposite route.

Less than a year after Franz had become an SC 1906 player, a true miracle happened. West Germany, captained by Franz's role model Fritz Walter, won the 1954 World Cup in Switzerland, beating Hungary 3-2 in the final. One of the greatest upsets football has ever seen entered the history books as 'the Miracle of Berne' and triggered a football frenzy in West Germany, a country still looking for an identity barely nine years after the end of the war. Overnight, the eleven simple men who had managed to defeat undeniably the best team on the planet were even more than just national heroes. They were instant living legends. That is, in the eyes of almost everyone.

'Tell me,' Franz Beckenbauer Sr said to his youngest son to begin a dialogue Franz Jr would never forget and often quote. 'What is this Fritz Walter, whom you adore so much, going to do with his life once he is too old to play? How will he earn a living, having done little more than kicking a ball about?'

'He is earning money now,' young Franz argued. 'And he will save some.'

'Footballers are too dumb to save money,' his father replied.

On 6 July 1954, two days after the final, Fritz Walter and the other dumb footballers who had represented West Germany at the World Cup arrived in Munich by train. They were supposed to travel from the main station to the town hall, which stood at the northern end of Marienplatz, Mary's Square, in open Mercedes limousines. Shops, offices and factories closed early and schoolkids were given the day off. Most accounts agree that at least 500,000 people – more than half the city's entire population – lined the streets to catch a glimpse of the World Cup winners. Almost needless to say, Franz Beckenbauer Sr volunteered to work; we can safely assume that he didn't even listen to the radio coverage of the event.

His wife Antonie, though, grabbed her sons by the hands and started the long walk towards the centre of town. (Upon recounting the story in 1991, the writer Hans Blickensdörfer noted that 'she saved the money for the tram, as was her wont', though all public transport must have been hopelessly overcrowded anyway on that day.) However, the three never even got close to Marienplatz. At one point, the throng became so overwhelming that Antonie feared she would lose the children if she pressed on.

A few years ago, Franz told a tabloid that he had 'only vague memories' of the day and that he wasn't even sure if he 'actually saw any of the players'. But when he had recounted the day for Blickensdörfer all those decades ago, he mentioned that a total stranger suddenly grabbed him around the waist, lifted him up and put him on one of the construction workers' shacks that lined the street. Walter even says he used to have a photo of Franz on that rickety hut until he gave the picture to someone and never saw it again. In any case, Franz suddenly had a clear view of the car parade. The only player he recognised was Fritz Walter. According to Blickensdörfer, he also felt that the Coupe Jules Rimet was a lot smaller than he had imagined.

Fritz Walter had become a double obsession for Franz Beckenbauer because of his coach at SC 1906. This was a 33-year-old man called Franz Neudecker, who had lost a leg in the war and was walking with two crutches. The story went that his disability didn't hinder him from sometimes training with SC's first team and that he possessed a very powerful shot. Put differently, he was the kind of man who leaves a deep impression on young boys, which is why Franz Beckenbauer never forgot the moment when Neudecker told him: 'If you don't lose your head, boy, you can become as good as Fritz Walter.' (When Franz asked his older brother what the first part of the sentence was supposed to mean, the in-the-know reply was: 'He is telling you that you mustn't allow girls to take your mind off the football.')

Neudecker was so protective of this precocious talent that he supposedly bought young Franz his first pair of proper football boots. Beckenbauer himself always liked to tell the story how, as a small boy, he took a heavy, ankle-high ski boot to a cobbler he knew and asked him to put cleats on it. This is very probably true, as contemporary address books reveal that a shoemaker by the name of Karl Winkler lived in the rear building of No. 2 St.-Bonifatius-Platz. However, this must have been before Franz joined SC 1906, as there are a couple of surviving team photos. The boys usually wear red shirts and white shorts, and their small feet are covered by normal football boots for the times.

Yet the story of the ski boots is still noteworthy, because Franz will have had a very good reason to ask the shoemaker for help, namely the weather conditions. It has become an integral part of the Beckenbauer myth that everything always came easy to him on the pitch, that he rarely headed the ball or tackled and that he disliked grafting. This has given rise to the idea that the physical side of the game was alien to him. (As we shall later see, the very first words a famous Bayern coach spoke to him were 'Have heard you're not a fighter'.) Of course, there is some truth to this, as Beckenbauer's playing style remains the benchmark for footballing elegance.

But as the Italy game in 1970, which left such an impression on J. L. Manning, attests, Franz was no shrinking violet. And how could he have been? He grew up in a part of town rougher and poorer than most of us can imagine. He almost always played against boys – and at least one girl – who were older and stronger than him. And he also had to learn how to cope with adverse conditions that kids from other parts of the country knew little about. In those days before global warming, the winters in Munich were fiercely cold and always snowy. Both Brigitte Lettl, the former Gitta Schmid, and Walter Beckenbauer remember how the children would pour water across the street and wait until it was frozen solid so that they could play ice hockey. Boots with cleats or studs were simply a necessity if you had to chase balls in the snow.

In fact, those conditions may have been a major reason why

young Franz joined a club in the first place. Nowadays, you would do so to either play at all (football in the streets being all but extinct) or play competitively. Children as young as seven can play in leagues and actually read the results and find the standings in Monday's local newspapers. But back in the early 1950s, organised football only started for eleven-year-olds (which is why Walter joined Bayern as late as 1952). It means that the younger Beckenbauer had to wait almost three years for real games. Yes, coach Neudecker fielded him in friendlies, but this cannot have been enough to get Franz's competitive juices flowing because he did take part in more or less serious games outside of the club.

First, there were the occasional matches with his church team. Munich's Catholic parishes had their own city championship, and the Heilig-Kreuz-Kirche in Giesing (the Holy Cross Church, where Franz had been christened) regularly won, not least because of Beckenbauer and two of his chums, who also played for SC 1906: Helmut Heigl and Wolfgang Steiner. Then there was school football. This is the part of any decent football biography where you will read how the future superstar, now rich and famous, hated school with a passion and that his teachers invariably told him he would never amount to anything. Not in this case, though. Franz Beckenbauer always used to say that his grades were average at best, yet most of his teachers remembered him as a quiet and inconspicuous pupil but a pretty good student. (By contrast, Walter, unsurprisingly, must have been a bit of a handful.) And Franz would also be remembered as a great athlete, of course, as he led his school team to triumphs not only in football but also in other sports.

So, somewhat unusually for an outstanding footballer of this generation, Franz enjoyed a thoroughly happy childhood, right? Not so fast. The living conditions for working-class families in Giesing were abysmal. The Beckenbauers' flat was not only cramped, but it also had no running water and no bathroom. The toilet was on the hallway, which was cold and unlit. Franz also told his biographer Torsten Körner that he refused to go to the coal cellar alone, because the basement scared the living daylights out of him – which probably tells us more about Franz's disposition than about the cellar, as Brigitte Lettl describes the same part of the building as 'smelling nicely, somehow homey'. Then there was the grumpy, unloving father. Franz Sr only rarely resorted to corporal punishment, but that was mainly due to his limited mobility on account of the bad back. While his mother would remain the most important person in Franz Jr's life, he almost never spoke about his dad. Körner is certainly right when he says that a great deal of what happened over the next thirty or even forty years can be explained by Franz's search for a father figure.

Such as Franz Neudecker. One of the attractions SC 1906 had held for Beckenbauer was surely the fact that the club had access to a proper gym, which meant he could now also play football during the harshest of winters. But having a real coach for the first time must have been an additional bonus. Two of the things Neudecker repeatedly drilled into young Franz were that he should always use his weaker foot and that he must never stop moving about on the field of play. There is a certain irony to this, considering that two hallmarks of Beckenbauer's future style would be nudging the ball with the outside of his right foot when he might as well have simply used the left one and possessing such a finely tuned spatial awareness that he always seemed to run less than anyone else. However, he must have listened attentively to his coach because at first Neudecker played him on the left flank. While Beckenbauer certainly had the physique of a winger – small, slender, lightweight – he grumbled a bit because Franz thought of himself as a centre-forward and a born goalscorer.

By early 1958, he had got his wish. Playing up front and scoring many goals, Beckenbauer should have been happy. But there were problems at SC 1906. Rumours were circulating that the club would not be able to offer Beckenbauer and his team-mates league football for the coming season. The problem may have been money, with one version of the story saying that the club scrapped its entire youth set-up. However, it's more likely that SC 1906 were simply lacking coaches or players. This was, and is, a common occurrence at small amateur clubs, where it can easily happen that you suddenly don't have enough players any more if two or three boys quit the game (for instance, because they allow girls to take their minds off the football). In any case, Franz and his friends were wondering what to do. And thus began the legendary and slightly mysterious story of the *Watschn* – Bavarian slang for a slap in the face – that altered the course of football history.

The first recorded retelling of the tale seems to originate with Franz Beckenbauer's first autobiography, which was ghosted by a noted columnist called Rolf Gonther and published in December 1966. 'My friends had decided to leave SC 1906 together with me and join 1860,' read the text next to a photo that showed Franz and his team-mates (dressed, incidentally, in red shirts, red shorts and red socks). 'But the moment when 1860's centre-half gave me a slap in the face during the final of a tournament in Neubiberg wreaked havoc with our plans. After this schoolboy game against 1860, which we lost 1-4, with me scoring our consolation goal from the penalty spot, we all went to Bayern instead.'

He confirmed this story two years later, first in March 1968 and then again in August, during a couple of interviews with *Kicker* magazine. By the time of the 1975 autobiography mentioned previously (and which was, amazingly, already the fourth book of this kind!), the anecdote had morphed into such a central part of the Beckenbauer myth that it was given plenty of room. In this version, told to yet another ghostwriter, Franz expanded on the tale. He mentioned that SC 1906's chairman, Karl Steiner, would watch him train and then exchange meaningful glances with Neudecker, adding that Steiner 'had a son who was playing for 1860's first team'. A few pages later, he said that 'if players from SC 1906 were looking for a career in football, they naturally joined 1860, like Karl Steiner's son had done'.

These asides must have been meant to underline how much of a foregone conclusion it should have been for Beckenbauer and his closest footballing friends to become Blues – until SC 1906 qualified for the final stages of an under-14 tournament alongside Bayern, 1860 and TSV Neubiberg. The semi-finals and the final were played in April 1958 in Neubiberg, a village just outside the city borders of Munich and right next to Unterhaching. SC 1906 had no problems in the semis, which set up the ill-fated meeting with 1860, during which Beckenbauer's marker lost his cool.

However, the story is not quite as straightforward as it seems. First of all, the identity of the culprit remained unknown for almost four decades. This in itself is certainly not strange, because who could predict how diehard 1860 supporters would react to someone who cost their club the greatest talent in history? But strange is what happened next.

In 1983, a man by the name of Günther Jahnke suddenly stepped forward and shouldered the blame. He certainly had links to the Blues, and even used to work as a press agent for Petar Radenković, the legendary former 1860 goalkeeper. 'Franz knocked me down and it really hurt,' he explained to the producers of a documentary. 'So I lunged out and gave him a clip round the ear. He instantly said to his pals: "We're not going with this lot, we'll join Bayern."' Unfortunately, there wasn't enough time to really look into Jahnke's story; he died as early as 1985, at only forty years of age. He was buried in Munich's Eastern Cemetery, which is worth a mention because this graveyard backs on to the street where Beckenbauer grew up.

When Franz celebrated his fiftieth birthday in 1995, ten years after Jahnke's death, he had a surprise in store: he could remember the name of the offender! It was not Jahnke, he said, but Bauernfeind. That sounded very plausible, because this was exactly the name Beckenbauer had mentioned in passing in June 1977, when he penned a piece about his first days in New York for *Stern* magazine. As it soon turned out, there had indeed been a player called Rudolf Bauernfeind on the 1860 team all those years ago. However, he was no longer alive and thus could not corroborate or deny the story.

With two suspects in the grave, a third man stepped forward. In 2010, Gerhard König, a former goalkeeper in 1860's youth system, met Franz for a television feature to unburden himself and apologise a tad belatedly. As König explained, he had to play in the outfield on that day in 1958 and found it hard to contain the lively Beckenbauer. In this version, he fouled Franz, not the other way round, which led to an exchange of expletives. 'Could be,' Beckenbauer chuckled when König told his story. 'I was a cheeky lad then.'

König, a renowned hothead himself, eventually saw red and slapped his opponent. 'It was only a lot later,' he added, 'that I learned this was the reason why Franz didn't join us.' König quit football a mere two years after the game in Neubiberg, when he happened to be late for training, was given a dressing-down and stormed off in a huff. And yes, his family name means 'king'.

The sudden surge of former 1860 players eager to make a clean breast of their darkest deed in youth football is not the only incongruous element of the story. There is also the fact that Karl Steiner's son Rudi was still playing for SC 1906 in April 1958. In fact, Rudi only joined the Blues in the summer of 1960, when Franz Beckenbauer was already the star of the Reds' under-19 side and playing alongside a certain Sepp Maier.

There was, however, a well-hidden family link between SC 1906 and Bayern Munich, which has only very recently come to light. Franz Neudecker, Beckenbauer's first coach, had an uncle by the name of Anton Ritter, who happened to be in charge of the Reds' schoolboy teams. In fact, when Bayern's official club magazine carried a photo of Beckenbauer for the very first time, the 66-year-old Ritter was standing right next to Franz, Helmut Heigl and Neudecker's own son. The close friends were three of the five players in total who had joined Bayern from SC 1906 after the Neubiberg final.

So, is it too far-fetched to speculate that Ritter and his nephew Neudecker had been pulling some strings behind the scenes in order to gently drag Beckenbauer and the other key members of SC 1906's team over to the red side of town? After all, SC 1906 had beaten none other than Bayern in the Neubiberg semi-finals, and quite convincingly so, which will have served as an extra incentive for the Reds to land the core of this side. Heigl, for one, now suspects that the historic decision had already been made before the 1860 game and that the famous slap in the face, if it ever happened, only served as a welcome excuse to eschew 1860.

In fact, there are more than a few observers who think that Franz, for all his unique talent, might have found it tougher to break through at 1860, who were just about to assemble a really strong senior side (one that would win the cup in 1964 and the league in 1966), a process that usually means a team can't have a lot of patience with homegrown players. 'Maybe Franz owes his great career to me,' Gerhard König, his voice weakened by an insidious disease, mused in 2020. 'He would have become a strong player at 1860, but he would not have been nurtured the way they did at Bayern.'

Whatever the truth – if, in fact, there is only one – it quickly became apparent that Franz had made the right choice. The team photo mentioned above graced the cover of the July 1959 issue of *Clubzeitung*, Bayern's club newspaper, because the under-15s had done exceptionally well. In Beckenbauer's first season as a Red, he played as a centre-forward again and scored more than a hundred goals. Unsurprisingly, given this tally, the team reached the final of the city championship. On 10 May 1959, Bayern met Wacker Munich in front of more than a thousand spectators and prevailed 3-1, with both Beckenbauer and his pal Heigl finding the target. It would not be the only title of the season; Bayern then also reached the final for the championship of Upper Bavaria. There they faced MTV Ingolstadt and won 12-2.

This all-conquering team was coached by an interesting man, one who is now widely regarded as perhaps the most important unsung hero of all at a club that has had more than its fair share of celebrated figures. Rudi Weiss, a law student, was only twenty-eight years old when Franz joined Bayern. His older brother, Werner, was also a youth coach, while his father, Anton, had been responsible for the club's entire youth set-up – some 500 boys and adolescents in all – since 1947. Rudi had been a talented player himself before being forced to quit the game prematurely after an opponent's reckless tackle ruined his knee. Even though he was so young, Weiss had already supplied Bayern's first team with one set of home-grown players (men like Ludwig Landerer and Erich Hahn) and was just about to do it all over again (with players like goalkeeper Fritz Kosar and Adolf Kunstwadl). However, the moment he laid eyes on Beckenbauer, he must have sensed that his – and the club's – first truly golden generation had just arrived.

Weiss, though not even sixteen years older than Beckenbauer, would turn out to be Franz's next father figure. To paraphrase the famous German poet, humourist and illustrator Wilhelm Busch, becoming a father is easy, being one is not. Over the next few years, Weiss would very often be delighted by the boy from Giesing. But he would also be driven to despair by him on more than one occasion. And that was even before Franz Beckenbauer, whom someone would someday compare to a Prussian officer, unintentionally found a scandalous way of dodging the draft.

LIFE I

Chapter Two

So, one last time: who gave Franz Beckenbauer the mythical slap in the face on that April day in 1958? Günther Jahnke? Rudolf Bauernfeind? Gerhard König? None of them? Maybe nobody at all? It's highly likely we will never find out. But I wouldn't be surprised if it eventually turns out that it was actually one of his own team-mates.

By all accounts – some of which were even printed in Bayern's *Clubzeitung* in the guise of match reports – the young Beckenbauer was a supremely annoying player. Oh, he was good. Of course he was good. Before he was sixteen years old, Rudi Weiss promoted him to Bayern's under-19 side, where Franz first met a sensational goalkeeper called Sepp Maier, more than eighteen months his senior. But this was probably as much due to Beckenbauer's performances as it was to Weiss's increasingly desperate attempts at disciplining him. The coach must have hoped that Franz would fall in line once he found himself surrounded by much older, almost equally talented and more experienced peers. Fat chance.

In his first autobiography, Beckenbauer admits that he

'used to complain about anything our youth coach said. I was always late, grumbled constantly and left early whenever he asked us to stay around after a game. I was a lout, what you would call a pubescent young man.' It was true, but it was also only half the story. Weiss was surrounded by adolescent boys who tended to be rebellious off the pitch. Knowing how to handle them was actually an important part of his job description. The problem with Beckenbauer was that he was also unruly on the field of play. Even half a century later, Weiss could rattle off the kid's numerous misdemeanours and character faults: 'He talked back to the referees. He retaliated if he was brought down. If someone's pass wasn't perfect, he refused to chase the ball and just made a dismissive gesture with his hand. He would tap his forehead and call his teammates twerps. It was unsociable behaviour.' It speaks volumes for Weiss that he did all he could to avoid the term that would soon haunt Beckenbauer (and the club he was playing for), but there are hardly two ways about it: on the pitch, Franz was infuriatingly arrogant.

Needless to say, he did have some reason to be. No matter which team Weiss put him in, Franz was usually the best player, and whenever someone botched a cross or a pass that he could have played blindfolded, he must have felt like Mozart sitting at the piano, listening to an orchestra making a mess of his latest composition. Beckenbauer, whom his father would forever call *Stumpen* (think 'stump', something small), also suddenly hit a growth spurt. While nobody would ever describe him as sturdy or robust, he now held his own not only technically but also physically, so that people watching from the sidelines could no longer immediately tell that he was playing above his age group – which, in a way, made his diva-like temper tantrums even less acceptable.

Although Beckenbauer would never really overcome this tendency to lose patience with lesser players and the habit of abruptly going ballistic (though almost exclusively in connection with football), he eventually learned to keep both traits in check. It was arguably Rudi Weiss's greatest achievement as a coach, although it's still debated in some corners what exactly led him to teach his most gifted charge an important lesson by suddenly demoting him. Some people say it was all about morale – team morale. Others claim it was about morals. Yes, Beckenbauer was definitely undermining the squad's discipline with his aloof antics and something needed to be done about it. But there was also the small matter of the one single piece of advice Beckenbauer had been given by a father figure he would forever find impossible to follow. What was it Franz Neudecker had told him about girls?

Funnily enough, the first serious furore Franz caused had to do with his attempt to be a good boy. Back in Beckenbauer's day, most kids left school – which in Germany starts at six years old – after eight years to begin an apprenticeship. His own brother Walter was already training to become a printer (a job he would hold down for the rest of his working life) and Franz's future team-mates were no different. Starting at age fourteen, Sepp Maier walked into a factory at 6.45 every morning to become a mechanical fitter, Gerd Müller learned how to operate a weaving machine, Franz Roth laboured on a farm. There would have been another option for Beckenbauer, though. His grades were fine and the teachers told his parents that he was qualified for upper secondary education. This was not a choice Giesing families normally had to make and many of those dismissed it out of hand, because boys who went to school cost money and didn't earn any.

Still, Franz Sr seems to have given the matter some thought.

Or maybe he just saw an opportunity to finally knock sense into his youngest son because, according to Torsten Körner, he told the younger Franz: 'It's either a proper education or football. You can't have both.' That settled the matter once and for all, though it's hard to imagine circumstances under which the son would have attended a secondary school, anyway. In Franz Jr's mind, there was no point at all in staring at blackboards, listening to teachers and taking notes. In a few years' time, Bayern Munich would offer him a semi-professional contract, pay him decent money and also make sure he would find an easy, pro forma job that gave him time to train and play.

The fourteen-year-old Beckenbauer found an apprentice-ship position at the Allianz insurance company – the exact same corporation that would later hold the naming rights to the arena which Bayern Munich opened in 2005. Franz earned ninety marks per month during the first year, 120 marks in the second. This would rise to 450 marks after his apprenticeship ended, when he had become a proper insur-ance clerk. To put this into perspective, according to DFB rules, a footballer's maximum wage – meaning a basic salary plus match bonuses – was not allowed to exceed 320 marks per month. Of course, the reality was often different, as star players received under-the-table payments or brought home wages from their other, purportedly regular jobs that stood in no relation to what they were actually doing there. But this just serves to show that Franz Sr's qualms with regard to football were not totally misplaced. The game certainly promised no great riches in late 1950s West Germany, when full professionalism was still a pipe dream.

Of course, Franz Beckenbauer never really worked as an insurance clerk for any long period of time. But that doesn't mean his years at Allianz had no lasting consequences. He was still sixteen when a co-worker called Ingrid, a beautiful brunette, caught his eye. She was a bit older than him, though not the 'three years' he would slip into his best-selling 1975 autobiography, perhaps to suggest a Giesing rube had been seduced. ('Rubes' are what Bayern fans to this day call 1860 supporters.) True, these were in general more innocent times, but despite his famed cherubic looks, Franz was no angel. Rudi Weiss once had to bench him for smoking cigarettes, and I bet you a pair of lederhosen that big brother Walter had long since taught him the difference between wheat beer and lager. It took Franz just four months to get Ingrid pregnant.

This was obviously not unheard of in those years before birth control pills. What was unheard of was Beckenbauer's reply when Ingrid told him: 'Now it's time to get married.' According to one of his own books, he simply replied: 'I wouldn't dream of getting married so young.' One page later, he adds: 'The boy was born, and we gave him the name Thomas.' Well, and that was that. Even Körner's 2005 biography, the only truly reliable Beckenbauer book we have, deals with the repercussions – real or assumed – of the pregnancy on Franz's football career in some detail, but devotes only a few lines to the perplexing fact that he never married the mother of his first child. Körner says the two got engaged (which must have pacified Franz Sr) and remained a couple until 1965, but then he simply adds that Beckenbauer 'inwardly resisted a steady relationship and marriage'.

Many decades later, when investigative reporters and the general public alike tried to make sense of what exactly Beckenbauer's role had been during Germany's complex, controversial 2006 World Cup bid, there was a theory that said he had been walking on the sunny side of life for so long that he thought – no, that he *knew* – he would always get away with anything. For nearly his entire adult life, the argument went, people had fallen over themselves to settle even the most uncomfortable matters in his name; not just managers or other club officials, but also politicians, powerful business-men – and especially Robert Schwan, the man who became Beckenbauer's personal agent after the 1966 World Cup.

Others said that Franz Beckenbauer may have danced with Mick Jagger, dined with Rudolf Nureyev and posed with Muhammad Ali, but was, deep down inside, just an ordinary man who happened to have been thrown into an extraordinary life. The people who followed this line of thinking, usually Beckenbauer fans, actually found the only explanation he ever really came up with to account for all those questionable cash flows rather plausible: 'I always signed anything blindly, even in blank. I wasn't only working for the World Cup, I also had other things to do. I was Bayern's club president.' In other words, a simple boy from Giesing had been out of his depth in the murky world of football politics.

Neither image of Beckenbauer can be complete, because how can they account for his (for the times) outrageous behaviour in 1963 and 1964? Long before he became a gen-uine star, before he was courted by the rich and potent, or before he had even met Robert Schwan, Beckenbauer seemed to consider himself above the petty morals and the customs of the day, even authorities like his parents or club representa-tives. It was almost as if he knew in his heart that he could get away with almost anything. And when Ingrid told him she was so ashamed of having a child at such an early age – not to mention one born out of wedlock – that she felt like throwing herself into the river Isar, he simply replied: 'Don't listen to what people say.' Four decades later, talking to Körner, she was still marvelling at Franz's complete disregard for public opinion: 'He always surprised me because, as young as he was, what with his career and the publicity, nothing ever really got to him.' She was wrong, though. One thing did get to young Franz – being put into the reserves.

On 28 October 1963, eight days after his son Thomas was born, Beckenbauer's name appeared, perhaps for the first time, in *Kicker*. The magazine published a short report about the semi-finals of the DFB's *Jugendländerpokal*, the youth states cup. This annual competition was contested by representative teams from the various regions of West Germany. The South was defeated 2–0 by the West (featuring Berti Vogts, then still playing for his hometown club Büttgen), which prompted *Kicker* to remark: 'Apart from centre-half Beckenbauer (Bayern Munich), the South's entire defence was weak.' Little did the magazine know that the player they had singled out for praise had been demoted at his own club.

Weiss always said that he did not send Beckenbauer from the under-19s first team to its reserves because the young player had fathered a child. While the coach was very aware of the scandal (in contrast to many of Beckenbauer's friends and team-mates, who were kept in the dark for quite some time), he insisted this never bothered him and that the degradation only had the disciplinary reasons mentioned above. Besides, Franz didn't have to stay in the doghouse for too long. He once remarked that Weiss soon changed his mind because the first team's goals were drying up, though it should be pointed out that the coach had already begun to use him in all kinds of roles on the pitch, not just up front (hence *Kicker*'s description of him as the South's 'centre-half'.) Weiss himself explained that Franz was allowed to come back once he had learned his lesson. But there could have been another reason.

It was not just *Kicker* magazine that had begun to notice the young Bavarian. The top brass of the West German game were also bandying his name about.

At the time, there was a prestigious annual competition known as the International Youth Tournament, which eventually would develop into the UEFA European Under-19 Championship. The 1964 edition would be staged in the Netherlands, between 26 March and 5 April, and the coach of West Germany's national under-19 team, a 38-year-old man called Dettmar Cramer, was thinking about calling up Beckenbauer. This is why he wanted to try out the youngster in an international against Switzerland in March. However, as Cramer quickly found out, there was a hurdle. That is why he phoned national coach Sepp Herberger, who was just a few months away from handing over his post to Helmut Schön.

'There is this very talented kid,' Cramer told Herberger. 'He is as good as Fritz Walter, maybe better. But he's done something really stupid. He has an illegitimate son. And now the guys on the youth football committee say he can't play for the national team because of that.'

Herberger attempted to resolve the matter by attending the next committee meeting and putting in a good word for Franz. But even that wasn't enough. It was only when Cramer promised to closely chaperon Beckenbauer – by not just sharing a room with him but actually a double bed – that the white-haired functionaries gave the green light. As Cramer later remembered, Beckenbauer and his diminutive coach slept 'under a down duvet' when the player was invited to a training camp in Duisburg in early February.

By that time, Beckenbauer had already made an international debut of sorts. While all biographies agree that he first played for West Germany's under-19s in that friendly against Switzerland, it's not entirely correct. On 11 January 1964, the squad Cramer envisioned for the tournament in the Netherlands played a semi-official preparation match against a select team from the southwest in a small town near Heidelberg. The game is noteworthy because Beckenbauer, playing in midfield, scored twice and was singled out for praise in a newspaper report. And also because the team was not only coached by Cramer, but also by Schön, the country's future national manager.

This performance earned Beckenbauer the invitation to Duisburg – where he shared the bed with his coach – and eventually also a nomination for the Switzerland game. Cramer again gave the young man a starting role in left-sided midfield, and Beckenbauer scored another brace as West Germany defeated the Swiss 2-1. Three days later, the DFB announced that he had made the squad for the International Youth Tournament.

Like many German football teams of the day did, Cramer's XI lined up in what was known as the W-M formation. Modern football fans are probably more comfortable with figures, so let's refer to the system as 3-2-2-3. The back-line was made up of the two centre-backs plus another defender. Germans sometimes called him the 'stopper', while the English stubbornly clung to the term 'centre-half', which dated back to the old pyramid formation, in which the centre-half had been the star of the show, a playmaker before the world knew this word. When he was pulled back into defence, his role changed completely, but the name stayed the same.

Even though some accounts claim that Beckenbauer was used as a centre-half in the Netherlands, this is not true. The Bavarian starlet played as a right-half at the International

Youth Tournament; using modern terminology, we could refer to him as a holding midfielder. The competition was comprised of twenty-three teams, playing in eight groups (the twenty-fourth team, the Soviet Union, had been denied visas at the last moment). Only the group winners went through to the quarter-finals, and at first things looked rosy for West Germany. In the opening game, Cramer's team defeated the favoured Swedes 2-1, with Beckenbauer scoring the first goal from the penalty spot after the Swedish centre-half had brought down striker Ulrich Kallius. In the second game, though, the Germans were overwhelmed by the hosts. The Dutch won 3-1, which meant that Cramer's charges finished last in their group, even though they were level on points with the other two teams. However, at least one German youngster had reason to be content. 'The best player on the team was the splendid wing-half Beckenbauer,' *Kicker* said, while the bi-weekly *Sport Magazin* noted that 'Beckenbauer was the focal point, constantly feeding the German attack'.

Reading all these accounts and glowing plaudits, one might wonder why Beckenbauer wasn't already playing for – or at the very least training with – Bayern's first team. Actually, that's exactly what the club's members had wanted to know as early as February during Bayern's general assembly. The first question was easy to answer. Under the rules of the regional Southern German Football Association, players could not see action in both youth and senior football during the same season, and since Franz (born in mid-September, six weeks after the cut-off date) had been registered with the under-19s, he couldn't be tried out, not even for a few minutes, in a senior match. This was a rule which not every regional association carried, a subtlety that would soon become important.

But what about training? The debate grew so heated that

Rudi Weiss had to step forward and deny rumours that he didn't want Franz to work out with the first team. The next man who had to explain himself was, obviously, that team's coach. He was a feisty, chubby Yugloslav by the name of Zlatko Čajkovski, who spoke German with a strong but lovable accent. Čajkovski all but launched into a laudatory speech, extolling Beckenbauer's virtues. He said the young man was so exceptionally versatile that he could be used in defence, midfield or attack, before explaining that he himself considered Beckenbauer a forward, adding that 'he can play centre-half later, when he is older'.

Čajkovski promised the members that he would soon be incorporating more youth-team players into the senior side, calculating that every homegrown footballer saved Bayern around 80,000 marks in the long term. However, although he talked a lot, he did not really explain why he still hadn't invited Beckenbauer to the odd session with the semi-pros. Finally, a club representative mentioned that Beckenbauer's father didn't want his son to train with the senior side because he was just coming back from an injury. It sounded somewhat half-baked, yet the members had no choice but swallow this version.

In his own memoirs, published only two years later, Čajkovski said he had been 'fighting' for Beckenbauer for a long time, though there are people who remember it differently. Among those was Franz himself, who once said that Čajkovski was initially 'reserved', which is a word you almost never read in connection with the hyperactive coach known to all and sundry as Čik (which is Serbo-Croat for cigarette stub). Beckenbauer suspected that his reputation was preceding him, meaning both his poor disciplinary and his remarkable reproductive record. He pointedly noted that

Čajkovski probably expected him to be 'the greatest sex fiend of all time'.

Others were less prudish than Čik and more pragmatic. Bayern's president since 1962 was the fifty-year-old building contractor Wilhelm Neudecker (no relation to Beckenbauer's old coach at SC 1906), a fiercely ambitious man, both privately and as a club boss. In the words of Gerd Müller's biographer Hans Woller, Neudecker 'had two simple principles: too many cooks spoil the broth and money makes the world go round'. He now followed the first of those wisdoms, though not exactly the second. Shortly after the annual meeting, he offered Beckenbauer a three-year contract worth 160 marks per month. Or rather, he offered that to Beckenbauer's father, who had to sign the paperwork because his son was too young (until 1974, the legal age in West Germany remained at 21). This was what Franz had hoped for back in 1958, when he joined the Reds. The problem was that things had drastically changed since 1958 – German football was no longer the same.

In 1958, Bayern Munich and 1860 Munich were both playing semi-professional football in the Oberliga Süd – the premier league south, one of five regional top divisions in the country. After the end of the regular league season, the very best teams from those five divisions competed for the national title through a play-off system that culminated in a grand final in May or June. To all intents and purposes, that's how it had always been in West Germany, the only truly major innovation being that the clubs had been allowed to pay their players some money back in 1949.

While many fans liked the Oberliga set-up – after all, it basically guaranteed hot-blooded derbies on any given weekend, while the later nationwide rounds were much-anticipated, spectacular affairs – it was beginning to become an economic problem. Technically, there were more than seventy top-level clubs and they all had to finance a squad of salaried players by and large through gate money alone, even though the smaller teams were not drawing huge crowds.

The bigger clubs, meanwhile, were having headaches of a different sort. More and more of them were losing good players to teams based in countries where footballers could earn real money. Italy was a popular destination, but even small countries like Switzerland looked attractive to a German semi-pro, such as Klaus Stürmer, a 24-year-old international who left Hamburg and joined Zürich FC in the summer of 1961. Only a few months earlier, Inter coach Helenio Herrera had personally travelled to Germany to offer Stürmer's more famous team-mate Uwe Seeler an annual salary of 155,000 marks after taxes (then the equivalent of £13,000). Seeler, whose wages and bonuses at the time came to just 6,000 marks – also per year, but before taxes – declined the offer, which helps explain why Beckenbauer would many years later say with some envy that Uwe was 'adored in a manner that was in equal parts gushing and matey'.

Still, something had to change and it eventually did. On 28 July 1962, following a drawn-out debate, the DFB delegates voted to set up a nationwide and professional football league in West Germany, the Bundesliga, scheduled to kick off almost exactly thirteen months later. The inaugural season would be contested by sixteen teams, but which ones? The DFB's selection process was complex, not to say arcane. All regions had to be represented, while past achievements were taken into account as well as current form. The governing body also felt that there shouldn't be two teams from the same city, though this was never officially cited as a criterion until it was too late. 'Too late' in this case means 6 May 1963, barely three months before the new season would begin. That was the day when the DFB at last announced that 1860 Munich would be admitted to the Bundesliga – at the expense of their local rivals Bayern.

The Reds were bitterly disappointed and rightfully so. The Munich-based but national newspaper *Süddeutsche Zeitung* declared that 'the case of Bayern seems particularly harsh. This Munich club can certainly point to tradition and quality. For the last four years, the club has been among the best teams in the south and has finished third twice in a row.' The newspaper also accused the governing body of 'arbitrariness' and quoted an 'important' but unnamed DFB official as having cynically said: 'We have kept numerous rankings in reserve for the selection of the Bundesliga clubs. We'll always find one that suits us.'

With hindsight, the DFB's controversial decision was quite possibly a blessing in disguise for the Reds. Dietrich Schulze-Marmeling, the author of numerous books about Bayern, went as far as arguing that 'it was a stroke of luck. If the club had been admitted to the new league, it would have been forced to radically change the face of the team. This would have put a substantial financial strain on the club and also sabotaged the coming-of-age of a young team which would soon make German and European football history.'

However, of course, the youngsters only made history because they stayed together. And they almost didn't. It was only some ten years ago that Beckenbauer, talking to Bayern's club magazine, disclosed that the Reds had nearly lost him to the Blues. 'There was a critical period in 1964, when I came close to joining 1860,' he recalled. 'We were still playing in the second division, but they were in the

Bundesliga and courting me.' Truth be told, it wasn't that much of a revelation, because anything else would have been shocking indeed. Of course 1860 must have made a move for Beckenbauer, the toast of the town, and of course he must have considered it, if only because of the money.

While German football had gone professional with the formation of the Bundesliga, it was not full, unfettered professionalism. As had been the case in England until 1961, there was a maximum-wage system in operation. It capped a player's total wage – the base salary plus bonuses or benefits – at 1,200 marks per month. (There were also restrictions as to the number of new signings a club could make per summer or how high the transfer sums should be.) Still, this was serious money in 1960s West Germany.

It goes without saying that this was not the kind of wage that Franz – an eighteen-year-old who still hadn't played against adults – could have expected from 1860. But there is also little doubt that the Blues will have dangled more than the modest 160 marks in front of him that Bayern boss Neudecker could offer – although Bayern also threw a very soft but well-paid job with a local clothing supplier into the bargain, meaning Franz wouldn't have to work for Allianz any more. In the end, though, Beckenbauer asked his father to sign the documents that bore Bayern's logo, perhaps because he was suddenly going places in the first team after all.

Čajkovski's team finished the 1963-64 season in second place in the southern branch of the multi-tiered second division, thus qualifying for the promotion rounds to the Bundesliga, where they would meet Borussia Neunkirchen, Tasmania Berlin and FC St Pauli. It was the latter club, based in Hamburg, that gave Neudecker an idea. Bayern's president asked the Southern German Football Association for special permission to field Beckenbauer in those promotion games, arguing that the Northern Association had no rule against the use of under-19 players and that Bayern would be at a disadvantage if they had to adhere to regional regulations. Then Neudecker and Beckenbauer walked over to the training pitch to inform Čajkovski that the president had made a decision about the broth without consulting other cooks first.

'Our president introduced me,' Beckenbauer later recalled, 'and Čajkovski said: "Have heard you're not a fighter."' It was an 'unpleasant reception', Franz felt, but once Čik actually had the teenager under his wing, he mellowed in record time. Only a few days after the special permit was granted, Bayern opened their promotion campaign away at St Pauli – and Beckenbauer was in the starting XI. He played as a left-winger in the 4-2-4 system Čajkovski had introduced at Bayern and even found the target in the convincing 4-0 win.

Four days later, when the Reds were held to a 1-1 draw at home by Tasmania, he was on the wing again. But only for an hour. Desperately needing an equaliser, the coach told stopper Rainer Ohlhauser – a trained striker – to move upfield. His place at the back was taken up by Beckenbauer, who did so well that he actually started the next game, against Neunkirchen, at centre-half. Bayern won 1-0 and *Sport Magazin* marvelled that 'as a stopper, the multi-talented Beckenbauer was the sensation of the game. Such calmness, such vision . . . at age 19!' (He was actually still only eighteen.)

However, that was as good as it got. With Beckenbauer as their central defender, Bayern lost the next two games. Although they finished the round-robin tournament on a high note – beating St Pauli 6-1 – the club fell one point short, as Neunkirchen surprisingly won promotion to the Bundesliga. This return game against St Pauli may have been ultimately meaningless, but it was still remarkable because it highlighted how complete Beckenbauer already was as a player. He started the game in midfield, but when Bayern's backline struggled to contain St Pauli's Togo-born striker Guy Acolatse (the first prominent black professional in Germany), he moved back into defence. Then, after the break, Beckenbauer switched roles with a veteran called Norbert Wodarzik, played in attack and scored Bayern's fourth goal. After the final whistle, St Pauli's coach Otto Westphal wondered why this Bayern team had failed to win promotion. Then he said: 'As far as I'm concerned, this young Bayern talent, Beckenbauer, is an outstanding class act.'

Well, a second-class act, more accurately, because Franz would now have to spend at least one more year outside the top flight. He was as unhappy about this as everyone else at the club. According to his (never-published) memoirs, president Neudecker was paying Čajkovski, a man of considerable reputation after leading Cologne to the national championship in 1962, a stunning 3,500 marks net per month. Even the vast majority of Bundesliga coaches could only dream of remuneration like that. But, of course, the idea had been that the Yugoslav would join this elite club by winning promotion.

During a quarterly meeting of the club's members in late July 1964, Neudecker launched into a tirade against the Munich press that left professional onlookers bewildered (and made sure the coverage wouldn't improve). Neudecker's rant about a pro-1860 bias, however irrational, wasn't hard to understand, though. The president was trying to deflect criticism from himself and his coach, while also venting his frustration. Once he had done that, and once everyone had calmed down, it was back to the boring business of running a club. And that included asking the 600 members in attendance to elect a new *Spielausschussvorsitzender*.

This unwieldy word – a good example for the endless compounds that garnered German a bad name among students of languages – roughly translates as chairman of the match committee. A better description would be general secretary. The man (and it was always a man) who held down this post at a club was responsible for everything to do with the nuts and bolts of actually getting the team into a ground and on to a pitch on time. Together with the president, his deputy and the treasurer, he was a key member of any club's board. And like everyone else not directly connected with the professional or semi-professional football division (coaches, players, physios), he was unsalaried.

All of this made it somewhat strange that the members elected a 43-year-old man called Robert Schwan. He was so unknown that one newspaper report about the assembly described him as 'a former Bayern player', which was actually quite funny if you knew that Schwan wasn't even particularly interested in – let alone knowledgeable about – football. But hardly anyone knew this. Schwan had only recently become a member of the club, and unless you bought your policies from the insurance company which he ran (no, not Allianz), chances were you had never even heard his name. Neudecker, however, had known Schwan since 1962 through business dealings. He considered him a financial genius and will have made sure that the members voted for the right candidate, *his* candidate.

But why did this financial genius agree to work for no money? Probably for the very same reasons that have led so many powerful and monied men to take up posts at German football clubs (which, remember, couldn't – and cannot – be bought or sold or owned): it brought publicity, it was good for the ego and it invariably led to useful business contacts. And maybe, just maybe, Schwan already sensed that Neudecker had plans for him. Some well-known clubs abroad had full-time employees who cut the big-money deals, from transfers to sponsorships. They were called technical directors or business managers, and now that the West German game had gone professional, however tentatively, it was only a question of time until you could no longer expect a *Spielausschussvorsitzender* to have the necessary expertise.

For the time being, though, Schwan was just that. In one of his autobiographies, Beckenbauer says he first met the man who would become his most trusted ally, adviser and friend during a training session in the summer of 1964. According to this account, Čajkovski told his players that they were expecting a man called Schwamm, which is German for sponge. (*Schwan*, of course, means swan, which is why some people would later refer to Bayern's brain as 'the great white bird', as if he were a Bavarian Voldemort whose real name must not be uttered.)

'I will keep it brief,' Schwan addressed the squad by way of an introduction, while Čajkovski and Neudecker were quietly listening. 'I cannot play football, that is your job. What I can do is take care of money, and that includes your money.'

We can safely assume that rarely before had a middle-aged club official caught the attention of a group of young football players so quickly and so thoroughly.

'I have been told that you always hear a nice speech when you've won a game,' Schwan continued. 'I don't like speeches, so let's do something else. When you win a game, you'll get 100 marks. When you draw a game, you'll get 50 marks.'

Beckenbauer says it was goalkeeper Sepp Maier who asked: 'You mean on top?'

'What else?' Schwan replied. 'We cannot and will not touch your fixed pay.'

Whether or not it's believable that the twenty-year-old Maier had never heard of match bonuses before, there is no doubt that Schwan had to part with a lot of money during the 1964–65 season. Bayern netted no fewer than 146 goals during the thirty-six league games of the regular season. Ohlhauser alone had forty-two of them to finish as the club's and the division's top scorer. It might have come out differently if Čajkovski had been a little less doubtful about a new signing, a young striker with massive thighs called Gerd Müller. 'I don't need a weightlifter,' the coach sneered when he first laid eyes on the shy teenager. Neudecker, the player's greatest fan, waited until October before he finally went to have a talk with Čajkovski. 'If you don't field the guy with the heavy legs,' the president said, 'I'm not going to watch another football game in my life.' Finally let loose, Müller finished the league season on thirty-three goals.

But for some, even this deluge wasn't enough. In late December 1964, *Kicker* magazine lauded Bayern's forward line, but noted 'the attack would be even more forceful with Beckenbauer as an inside forward'. But that's not what Franz was during those months. For most of the season, Čajkovski did the very thing he had dismissed back in February: he used the best footballer he found at his disposal as a centre-half, or stopper.

It seemed to run counter to every rule of coaching. How could you waste such a talent by asking him to man-mark some bull-necked centre-forward? Had anybody ever played Alfredo Di Stéfano at the back? Would anyone ever tell Pelé to marshal the defence? A year earlier, Beckenbauer's friend Helmut Heigl had gone to watch an under-19 game and was flabbergasted when he realised Franz was the centre-half.

'Why did you put him there?' he asked coach Rudi Weiss after the match. 'Franz is not a defender by any stretch of the imagination. In his entire life, he has never played anywhere but up front.'

'Whenever I put him up front,' Weiss sighed, 'he just stands there and complains about the passing. I have to keep him busy. He needs to have some responsibility.'

However, that's not why Čajkovski pulled Beckenbauer back. His high-flier no longer needed to be kept in check through some form of occupational therapy. It's rather that the Yugoslav, one of the last great romantics of the game and a man who would take a 6-5 win over a boring 2-0 every day of the week, had come to realise – in contrast to the nameless *Kicker* reporter quoted above – that a deep-lying Beckenbauer made his team nearly impossible to defend against, not less attacking but actually more so.

It is at this point that we have to veer into semantics for a moment – to quote Robert Schwan, I will keep it brief – because the centre-half, or stopper, should not be confused with a related but quite different position. During the 1950s, some teams had begun to tweak the W-M formation more than just a little bit by pulling yet another midfielder back so that he was effectively playing in front of the centre-half, who then dropped further back himself until he was positioned behind the centre-backs. Germans sometimes called this formation the double-stopper system, but that's misleading as the man who was now playing so deep that he could shake his goalkeeper's hand was no longer a stopper. He was not marking the centre-forward or any other opponent, which is why the Italians, who perfected this method, called him the free man, or *libero*. Germans, though, preferred a more hands-on expression. Since this player was primarily occupied with clearing those balls and stopping those attackers who had somehow slipped through the three defenders in front of him, he was called *Ausputzer*, almost literally: sweeper.

In 1964-65, Beckenbauer was not a sweeper. He was often playing in front of the central defenders, so although it was his main duty to man-mark the opposing centre-forward, we might go as far as characterising him, using modern football parlance, as a defensive midfielder. Many decades would pass before the emergence of Claude Makélélé and other holding-midfielders-as-playmakers made coaches rediscover what Čajkovski must have realised the moment he saw Beckenbauer in action: if the very same guy who stops an attack can also start one, you have struck gold.

The gung-ho style of this young Bayern team goes a long way towards explaining why the Reds were very popular during those years. There is a persistent myth that says people from Munich tend to support 1860, while Bayern fans usually come from the suburbs and surrounding areas (or even, once the club became a superpower in the 1970s, from remote parts of the country). But the Reds have always had their strongholds in the city, thus Bayern drew a very healthy 13,000 fans per home game during the regular season. This figure may at first seem modest when compared to 1860's attendances, which stood at 27,000 in the same year. However, the Blues were playing Bundesliga football against the likes of Cologne, Dortmund or Hamburg, while Bayern were hosting (and thrashing) teams like Ingolstadt, Pforzheim or Schweinfurt.

The club's true potential revealed itself during the promotion tournament, when the average home gate rose to nearly 36,000. After the last of these home games, a 5–0 win against Saarbrücken on 19 June 1965, a Bayern fan called Alois Eichhammer rounded up ten of his friends and formed the

FC Bayern Fanclub Steinsberg, one of the oldest supporters' clubs in Germany still in existence. (An 1860 fan club was formed four months later in Dingolfing, sixty miles north-west of Munich, but the vast majority of German supporters' clubs date from the 1970s.) One week later, several thousand fans then travelled the 380 miles to Berlin for the last match against Tennis Borussia. Even before the game had started, men wearing lederhosen darted aross the running track that circled the pitch, manically waving Bayern flags. At half-time, the Reds were up 3-0, but Čajkovski told the players in his artfully mangled German: 'We not stroll into Bundesliga. If possible, we deplume opponent.' It was possible. Bayern added another five goals after the break, and Beckenbauer – wearing the centre-half's number 5 that would one day become synonymous with his unique interpretation of the libero role – was at last a first-class act.

As such, as an established member of Bayern's first team and now a professional Bundesliga player, he began to make frequent visits to the Sportschule Grünwald. What translates as 'sports school' was actually a large complex of 113,000 square metres that had been built in 1950 by the Bavarian Football Association, together with the Bavarian Athletics Federation. There were no fewer than three football pitches, an indoor swimming pool, two gyms and other sporting facilities – for instance, for track and field. The main building housed conference rooms, a spacious dining hall and a restaurant, while five additional, smaller buildings offered almost 160 beds.

Schools and sports clubs from all over Bavaria used Sportschule Grünwald, a handful of miles south of Munich, for seminars, training courses or excursions. This was where Herberger had prepared the 'Heroes of Berne' for the 1954 World Cup and it was also a popular destination for Bayern and 1860 Munich, who often held brief training camps here if there were big games coming up or if the coaches felt there was something they wanted to work on without any distractions. This just goes to show that Neil Young was right when he noticed that the devil fools with the best laid plans, because sometimes distractions pop up where you least expect them . . .

Beckenbauer couldn't help but notice the blonde girl working as a secretary for the Sportschule because he saw her almost every time he walked past reception. Brigitte Schiller, née Wittmann, was almost exactly a year older than Franz and estranged from a husband she had married very young to get away from the province and move to Munich. Soon the two were taking walks during her lunch break. Then it was the cinema, then – a first for Franz – the theatre, as Brigitte was very interested in culture and the arts. You can guess the rest. Franz Beckenbauer, not yet of legal age, already had a son with a woman he had refused to marry. And now he was expecting another child with a woman who was married, although not to him.

As brazen as he was, Beckenbauer knew that this might be a bit much for the public to swallow, so he kept the relationship secret until Brigitte had been divorced. But, of course, he had to tell his parents, who were not happy at all, and his team-mates, who were less concerned about Beckenbauer's good name than about his good form. They needn't have worried. Not for the first and not for the last time did Franz prove beyond doubt that whatever happened off the pitch, stayed off the pitch. Despite even more turmoil in his private life, he was so good during his first season in the Bundesliga that when left-back and skipper Werner Olk was unavailable for a German FA Cup tie against title-holders Dortmund in early January 1966, Čajkovski gave Beckenbauer the captain's armband for the first time. On a heavy, muddy surface, the twenty-year-old marked the dangerous centre-forward Sigfried Held out of the game as Bayern won 2-0.

Yes, Franz was still the stopper, though this hadn't really been the plan. Ahead of the club's first Bundesliga season, Bayern signed a centre-half who couldn't have been any more different from Beckenbauer if he'd hailed from Mars: the tough-as-nails Dieter Danzberg from SV Meiderich (a club soon to be renamed MSV Duisburg). Danzberg duly played as the Reds' stopper in Bayern's very first game in the top flight, while Beckenbauer was the left-half, what Germans at the time sometimes called *Verbinder*, the link-up man.

Of all the opponents Bayern could have met in order to acclimatise themselves to the new league, the opening day of the 1965-66 season pitted them against none other than fierce rivals 1860 Munich. There were fisticuffs in the stands before a single ball had been kicked – the local newspaper *Münchner Merkur* said 'there were 40,000 honourable citizens in attendance, but also 5,000 hooligans' – and the match continued in this style. It was such an ugly affair that new national coach Helmut Schön left well before the final whistle, complaining to a reporter that he'd 'seen enough of that'. His premature exit meant that Schön missed the most important moment of the match. This was not the only goal of the afternoon, which was scored early on by 1860 striker Timo Konietzka, but a case of violent conduct.

The rugged, strong Danzberg was known for giving as good as he got – and he had it in for Konietzka ever since that first-minute goal, which was scored while Danzberg, knocked out by a Konietzka shot from close range, was lying on the ground. Bayern's new hard man was booked during a first half which, according to *Kicker*, 'had nothing in common with football', but that did nothing to cool his temper. A few minutes from time, he kicked the prostrate Konietzka and was given his marching orders. Even before the writers knew that Danzberg would be suspended for eight long weeks, the implications of his lack of self-control were obvious to all. Günther Wolfbauer, a veteran Munich writer, instantly typed: 'Now Čajkovski will be forced to pull the great midfield talent Beckenbauer back into the stopper position.' Čajkovski was and he did. The switch is why Danzberg, who died in 2019, would joke for the rest of his life: 'I discovered him. I discovered Beckenbauer, the libero.'

Led by centre-half Beckenbauer, Bayern Munich captured the public's imagination that season as the newly promoted team actually challenged for the league title. With only four games left, Bayern were level on points with 1860 and Dortmund. But then the Reds were beaten at home by Stuttgart, thanks to a controversial penalty for handball, and at last dropped out of the race. However, another title was still within their grasp.

The surprise win over Dortmund back in February had kick-started a cup run that took Bayern and Beckenbauer all the way to the final, played on 4 June in Frankfurt (until 1985, when it was moved to what was then West Berlin on a permanent basis, this annual showcase had no fixed location, as the concept of a 'national stadium' has never taken hold in Germany). The Reds' opponents were Danzberg's old team, Meiderich. Although Bayern were the favourites, thanks to their scintillating league campaign, it was a close, exciting game. Beckenbauer had such problems with Meiderich's young striker Rüdiger Mielke that he made only two of his trademark forays into the other half all game long. In fact, one newspaper would later refer to his role in this game as *Ausputzer*, that defensive sweeper, such was the pressure the Reds were under. Still, eight minutes from time, they held a narrow 3-2 lead, when Meiderich lost possession. Bayern forward Ohlhauser, helping out at the back, looked up to see a familiar, slender figure surge forward. The striker played a fine through ball, which Beckenbauer picked up a few yards beyond the halfway line. He ran all the way into the box and fired home a right-footed shot into the far corner to decide the final.

In the stands, thousands of delirious Bayern fans celebrated what was only the third proper trophy their club had ever won, after the 1932 championship and an unexpected cup triumph in 1957. One of those supporters brandished a very unusual item – a life-sized Beckenbauer cardboard cutout. This meant that he or she was not only a Bayern fan, but also a subscriber to *Kicker* magazine.

The publication had recently borrowed an idea from *Bravo*, the immensely popular German teen magazine. Since 1959, *Bravo* regularly published so-called 'star cuts', life-sized posters of celebrities (Brigitte Bardot was the first) that came in weekly instalments, meaning you had to buy every issue of the magazine so as not to miss a foot or an elbow. The first player to get his own *Kicker* star cut was Uwe Seeler, followed by 1860's cult hero Petar Radenković and Hans Tilkowski, West Germany's Footballer of the Year for 1965. In February 1966, the first part of a seventeen-piece Franz Beckenbauer star cut was unleashed on a not-so-unsuspecting public.

Seeler, Radenković (the Bundesliga's first pop star and a man we will have to come back to), Tilkowski: this was elite company for a twenty-year-old. But even while people were still calling for Tilkowski's head – to complete the poster,

I mean – *Kicker* received readers' letters that demanded the Bayern centre-half should be the subject of the next star cut. This proved beyond doubt that Beckenbauer was more than just a household name in Munich or Bavaria and an up-and-coming football talent. By February 1966, he was already a national sensation, if not a hero, thanks in no small part to the fact that he had had a most amazing international debut.

LIFE I

Chapter Three

Helmut Schön found himself in a bit of a spot. Following Sepp Herberger was always going to be a tough act, but the new national coach did not help his case in the public relations department when the team dropped precious points in his very first game in charge, a World Cup qualifier against Sweden in Berlin. The annoying 1-1 draw in November 1964 brought everyone down to earth in a hurry, because now West Germany had to win the return game in Solna, near Stockholm, against one of their bogey teams.

This do-or-die match in September 1965, a classic nail-biter, has taken on mythical proportions in German football lore and became a key element of the Beckenbauer legend, because Schön trusted him so much that he gave him his debut when all the chips were well and truly down. However, although Franz won his first cap on this day, it was not the first game he played for the national team. That was a match on 16 February 1965 against – quick, guess! – Chelsea FC. Yes, it was an unofficial preparation game, but it was by no means a low-key affair. More than 30,000 people came out to see the match in Duisburg, and it made the cover of the nationwide *Sport Magazin* two days later.

It cannot have been a particularly pleasant experience for the youngster, who was still a second-division player then, the only one in the squad. On a very cold evening, the only goal of the game was scored by Barry Bridges with a powerful shot from some twenty yards. The crowd started booing the home team even before an hour was up. And to add insult to injury, the influential columnist Hans Körfer put a poison pen to paper and quipped: 'Čajkovski has repeatedly called Beckenbauer the greatest talent in all of Europe. The Munich player seems to believe that himself, because he carried himself with an arrogance as if this had been his seventy-fifth international.'

However, there were mitigating factors. Schön was not only missing key players like Helmut Haller and Karl-Heinz Schnellinger, who were not released by their Italian clubs, there were also so many injuries that the national coach admitted that, 'thirty hours before the game, I had no team'. Second, Schön was trying out a new formation for the first time, the 4-2-4 system he would mix with 4-3-3 at the World Cup in England the following year. Finally, not all observers agreed with Körfer. Or maybe they just differentiated between how Franz carried himself and how he performed. Hans Fiederer, a former international and now a writer just as respected as Körfer, declared that 'the find of this floodlit evening was Beckenbauer'.

When *Kicker* magazine asked Schön how he had viewed the kid – was Franz 'presumptuous' or 'supremely talented' – the coach replied: 'Presumptuous? Don't make me laugh! Perhaps his style of play looks arrogant. But as far as I'm concerned, he was, if anything, too restrained and too reserved today.' Schön added: 'For me, he is the player of the future. Maybe not even in midfield, perhaps up front. Unfortunately, all this comes one year too early for him.'

Something must have happened over the next weeks and months that made Schön rethink the last sentence. In March, he gave Beckenbauer a game in the reserves (West Germany having fielded a so-called 'B' team between 1951 and 1986). In mid-August, Franz played in yet another high-profile but unofficial friendly against Chelsea, this time in Essen in front of 40,000. The Germans won this one 3-2 and Beckenbauer was so good that Fiederer elevated him to the status of 'first-choice' player in print. Then, on 1 September, there was another game involving the 'B' team, a match against the Soviet Union's reserve side. This encounter – won 3-0 by West Germany – has unjustly been by-passed by most history books. On paper, Schön was just giving his second-stringers a run-out. In truth, though, he was playing no fewer than six men who would three weeks later start the most important game of his young reign. This was not a 'B' game, it was a crucial test. One of the players who passed it with flying colours was Beckenbauer.

Much has been made of the fact that Schön gave Beckenbauer his first full cap only a few weeks after the player had turned twenty, in an away game against a strong team which the Germans had to win to qualify for the World Cup. Torsten Körner describes how the national coach was so unsure whether or not Franz would be able to cope with the pressure that he asked Uwe Seeler for his opinion; Seeler replied, 'You're the boss. Play him.' However, in devoting four pages to this game in his first autobiography, and then nine in his second, Schön only mentions Beckenbauer in passing. The player Schön was really concerned about was centre-forward Seeler, who had torn his Achilles tendon seven months earlier and was still looking to regain match fitness. Actually, Schön decided to start Seeler even though the player himself had misgivings. Beckenbauer? Yes, that was a bit of a risk. But the future was here and now.

Among those much more anxious about the young man's inclusion in the starting XI were the six people who, on the day of the game, were huddled in front of the television set in the flat where Franz Sr and Antonie Beckenbauer were now living. This was no longer in Giesing, as the married couple had moved to Schwabing a few years earlier. It had nothing to do with their offspring's footballing success, though. Rather, the Post Office had found a nice home in a modern co-operative tenement house for their deserving, long-standing employee, Franz Sr. The living quarters were not luxurious – fifth floor, no elevator – but both parents would reside here for the rest of their lives, even though their son could have easily bought them a house in the suburbs.

By coincidence, No. 29 Stauffenbergstrasse, the Beckenbauers' new address, was only a short walk away from the area that would one day become Munich's Olympic Park. In the 1970s, when Bayern played their home games at the Olympic Stadium, Franz Jr would almost always pay his mother a visit before or after a match, not least because of her famed meatloaf. (According to writer Hans Blickensdörfer, who hung out with Franz at the Stauffenbergstrasse address on more than one occasion, 'she did that better than any chef'.)

On 26 September 1965, the flat was quite busy. Antonie's brother had dropped by with his wife, and a few other relatives were there as well to see the baby of the family represent his country. That we know all this is first and foremost a testament to how popular Antonie's son already was, because a press photographer had been dispatched to the apartment to capture the commotion. One family member was conspicuous by his absence in the resulting image. 'My dad was taking a walk in Luitpoldpark,' Franz Jr later wrote about the photo, referring to an adjacent recreation area. However, this was not another instance of the father giving the son's choice of career the cold shoulder. Quite the contrary. No. 29 Stauffenbergstrasse was now the official address for Beckenbauer's fan mail, and his parents marvelled at the amount of letters and postcards that were arriving each day. Antonie patiently and politely replied to a lot of the correspondence, while Franz Sr will have been extra proud about this connection between his son's occupation and his own.

If Franz Jr's remark implied that the father was too excited to watch the World Cup qualifier, his old man certainly had reason to be. Shortly before the break, Tilkowski terribly misjudged a free-kick and the hosts took the lead. Now the Germans found themselves in a deep hole. Schön hung his head in desperation and was just about to walk into the tunnel that led to the dressing rooms when Meiderich's Werner Krämer scored the equaliser in first-half stoppage time. Nine minutes after the break, the 1860 Munich midfielder Peter Grosser stormed down the right flank, the Swedish goalkeeper couldn't hold on to his cross, and who was there to poke home the loose ball? Seeler, of course.

There was still a lot of football to be played, which is why Tilkowski walked over to a certain defensive midfielder who was notoriously fond of joining in the attack. 'You stay at the back now,' the goalkeeper yelled at Beckenbauer, 'or I will kick your butt!' For once, Franz knew better than to talk back. When the final whistle rang, he was not only a full-blown, proper international, but a national hero who could look forward to playing in the 1966 World Cup. A few months down the line, he would even win a major title, the cup. You could say the only thing that he was missing now as an athlete was a decent nickname.

In the mid-1960s, Franz Beckenbauer was still quite a few years away from well and truly becoming the 'Kaiser', an epithet that was not widely in use until 1970, probably 1971, and whose origins are, as we shall later see, a matter of some controversy. However, I think the seeds were sown as early as 1965-66 – and, of all places, in the blue part of town. Because despite Bayern's promotion and their cup win. despite Beckenbauer's heroics for West Germany, this was really 1860 Munich's year, especially that of their charismatic Belgrade-born goalkeeper Petar 'Radi' Radenković.

The Yugoslav was known in Munich as 'the King', which is why the record he released in the spring of 1965 was called 'Bin i Radi – bin i König' ('I'm Radi, I'm King'). It sold more than 400,000 copies in West Germany, rose to number five and stayed in the charts for fourteen weeks. Yes, this singing footballer did outsell the Beatles, at least for a while. (Music ran in the family. Radi's father used to be a folk crooner and his younger brother was having some success in the United States as a wild garage rocker using the moniker Milan the Leather Boy.) Thanks to the record, the nickname took hold all over the country, not least because Radenković followed his success in the world of pop music by leading the Blues to the 1966 Bundesliga title.

Needless to say, Radenković was not the first king in shorts. Pelé was already known as O Rei, while German football fans had once bowed before Dresden striker Richard Hofmann, known across the country as König Richard. So we can confidently assume that there were Bayern fans who not only chafed at the fact that an 1860 player was considered Munich royalty, but who also wondered if there wasn't something less mundane than a mere king. Add to this Beckenbauer's regal style of play (although Hans Körfer might have chosen a different adjective here) and 'Kaiser' was a fairly obvious tag, especially considering that neighbours Austria were still going on about their legendary Kaiser Franz Joseph all the time. Put differently, there must have been a few Bayern fans in 1966 who were privately calling Beckenbauer the Kaiser. And soon, someone would put it into print for the first time.

For now, though, Beckenbauer was still simply 'Franzl', and as such he was about to travel to England with the national team for the World Cup, by far the youngest player in the squad (the second youngest was Frankfurt forward Jürgen Grabowski, more than fourteen months older than Franz). However, it wasn't Beckenbauer's tender age that concerned the coaching staff, but his new price tag. Even before the World Cup had begun, Beckenbauer was making headlines again.

It all started in early June 1966, when Bayern president Neudecker received a phone call from Italy. The caller identified himself as Hans Benini, a Milan-based journalist who spoke German.

'I'm calling on behalf of AC Milan,' Benini explained. 'We would like to invite you to come to Milan.'

'Why? What is this all about?' Neudecker asked.

'It's about one of your players.'

'Well, if that's the case, then I suggest you come to Munich instead,' Neudecker replied.

On 8 June, not even five weeks before the World Cup, the Italians did just that. Bruno Passalacqua, Milan's general secretary, met Neudecker and Schwan at a hotel near Munich Central Station and offered Bayern a cool 2 million marks for Beckenbauer's contract. At the time, the Italian FA had imposed a ban on the signing of foreign players, valid until the end of the 1966–67 season. Milan must have been very confident the restrictions would not be extended beyond this date, because two weeks after travelling to Munich, they also entered into negotiations with Manchester United over an option on Denis Law's contract.

Ten days after the meeting, the *Rossoneri* confirmed their serious interest in Beckenbauer in writing, even suggesting a medical after the World Cup. Neudecker composed a reply letter which pointed out that Bayern 'had not agreed to an option on Franz Beckenbauer', adding Milan were free to renew their interest 'at a later point in time', always provided the player 'expresses the wish to relocate to Italy'.

More than half a century later, Beckenbauer would say that the one thing he regretted about his stellar career was never having played in Italy. In an interview with *Sport Bild*, a German weekly, he said: 'Inter [sic!] were after me in 1966. I went to Italy a few times with Rolf Gonther, a newspaper columnist. It was sensational, San Siro alone! A stadium for 100,000 people, with the sort of atmosphere that just didn't exist in Germany. I was so fascinated, it was a move I certainly wanted to make.'

But first, there was the World Cup. If thoughts of Milan, San Siro and bags of Italian *lire* were buzzing around in Beckenbauer's head, he never let on. In fact, one suspects ice water must have been running through his veins, as his casual elegance in his first-ever game on the biggest stage of them all – against Switzerland at Hillsborough – was mind-boggling. Suffice it to say that the young man scored two goals, the first of which was such a classic that FIFA TV analysed it in 2018 for its 'Anatomy of a Goal' series.

When the move began, with Tilkowski throwing the ball to right-back Horst-Dieter Höttges, Beckenbauer was still deep in his own half, playing in midfield again, because West Germany's stopper was Hamburg's Willi Schulz (who would acquire the inevitable nickname 'World Cup Willi' during those weeks in England). As Höttges played a long pass to right-winger Helmut Haller, Franz picked up pace. When he received the ball from Haller, he was in a central position, some twenty yards in front of goal. Evading a tackle and dashing forward, Beckenbauer played the sort of one-two with Seeler he would soon perfect with Gerd Müller. Franz picked up Seeler's return pass just inside the box, weaved through the two centre-backs and gently pushed the ball past the onrushing goalkeeper with his left foot. On the following day, the *Daily Mail* declared that 'Beckenbauer – the fabulous Franz – is tall, dark, good-looking and only 20 years old. He is destined to become a big star at this World Cup.' (Fabulous Franz – now there was a nickname to rival World Cup Willi!)

While Franz would, by and large, preserve his excellent form, his team could not, as the rest of the road to the final was pretty bumpy for the Germans, starting with an ugly scoreless draw against Argentina. In his 1975 book (and it will become apparent soon why I hesitate to use the word 'autobiography' here), Beckenbauer prepares the reader for the nastiness of this match by recounting in great detail (seven pages!) a trip to South America with Bayern before the World Cup. After playing Racing Club in Buenos Aires, the two teams travelled to Chile on the same airplane, and Beckenbauer chatted with Racing's defender Roberto Perfumo.

'Señor Francesco,' Beckenbauer quotes Perfumo, 'you and me will play in the final in England. It will be the greatest game in world football. You will score and I will score, there will be extra time and many people will collapse with broken hearts. But then we will win. I will score another goal, and Argentina will lift the World Cup for the first time.'

A few days later, Beckenbauer says, the draw was made, and it put Argentina and West Germany into the same group, thus somewhat reducing the chances of a final between the two sides. But an undaunted Perfumo reassured Franz: 'We'll come first in the group, you will finish second. Then we'll both win every game and meet again in the final, Don Francesco.'

Beckenbauer, even though he had just been elevated to the status of a 'Don', must have mixed up more than just a couple of things here. The draw for the World Cup was made on 6 January 1966, four days after Franz captained Bayern for the first time and two days before the Reds stunned Bundesliga leaders 1860 Munich, winning the derby 3-0. What's more, the South American tour Beckenbauer recalls so vividly in his book actually took place in December 1966, five months *after* the World Cup. Plus, Perfumo didn't even play in Racing Club's 3-2 over the visiting Bavarians – although he might have been in the squad, of course.

So we must yet again have a grain of salt at the ready when Fab Franz remembers that the man he calls 'my friend Perfumo' suddenly refused to shake his hand before the group game in England. (Of course he did, Franz. He had never met you before!) Or that 'some Argentinians had a watery, grey foam around their lips', making Beckenbauer wonder if they were on drugs. In a way, all this fits into what most of us have been taught about this World Cup, namely that the South Americans were undisciplined rowdies (to avoid the term 'animals', which England manager Alf Ramsey so unwisely used). But, of course, this is the European point of view. Others exist, and West Germany's quarter-final against Uruguay may serve as an illustration.

Schön's team had reached the knockout rounds after the draw with Argentina and a tense 2-1 win over Spain. Against Uruguay, there was bad blood from the word go. Horacio Troche was sent off for kicking Lothar Emmerich, though the latter's agony had a touch of melodrama about it. ('That was Emmerich's best moment in the match,' a West German journalist noted sarcastically.) Then Héctor Silva kicked Helmut Haller for what must have been the fifth time and was also dismissed. All those theatrics and antics, however, have made us forget that the South Americans were the better team for much of the first half and that they should have taken an early lead after five minutes, when Karl-Heinz Schnellinger blatantly handled the ball on the line. That the English referee Jim Finney did not punish the West German's unsporting save will have rattled the nerves of the Uruguayans, who were smelling a conspiracy anyway – without even knowing that a German referee was, at the very same time, losing control over the game between England and Argentina. When the hostilities ended, West Germany had won 4-0. Oh, and Don Francesco had scored his third goal of the tournament.

He added another one in the semis against the Soviet Union, who – not at all unlike Uruguay – found themselves effectively reduced to nine men very early on. First, play-maker Yozhef Sabo twisted his ankle in the opening stages, which turned him into a limping, forlorn figure. Then Igor Chislenko was sent off before the break for kicking Sigfried Held's left foot from behind. (Held surely made the most of the foul, rolling around four times while, for unknown reasons, clutching his right knee.) Haller scored West Germany's first, then Beckenbauer beat the great Lev Yashin with a left-footed strike which the legendary goalkeeper underestimated, thinking it would go wide.

Almost twenty years later, Beckenbauer would travel behind the Iron Curtain to meet Yashin for a magazine story, published in the illustrated weekly *Stern*, about players he admired and opponents he considered friends. 'Remember the goal you scored against me at the World Cup?' Yashin asked over a glass of vodka (or two) in his modest Moscow flat. 'It was a bitter day for us.' Yashin had lost a leg to thrombosis two years earlier and would not live to see Beckenbauer win the 1990 World Cup, but the photos taken on that day leave no doubt that Franz deeply, truly admired the Russian, hanging on his every word. Beckenbauer was almost embarrassed when Yashin raised his walking stick just above his head. 'The ball was this high,' he said. 'I just didn't see it coming.'

The shot he didn't see coming put the game out of the Soviet Union's reach and sent West Germany into the final. However, it wasn't entirely clear whether or not Beckenbauer would be able to play in it. He had been booked in the Argentina game and then again in the semi-final. Back then, however, suspensions were not automatic, as FIFA's disciplinary committee reviewed every sending-off and caution to confirm the decision – or not. In Beckenbauer's case, they chose not to. *The Times* quoted the DFB's press officer Hermann Joch as saying that 'it is a relief that this decision has been made. We were worried because it was the second time Beckenbauer had been cautioned, and must have been an error. Possibly, the referee confused Overath with Beckenbauer, who did not protest because we do not encourage our players to do so.'

So Beckenbauer was free to play – and yet you could say he

didn't, because the national coach famously, and against the advice of his assistant Dettmar Cramer, asked the youngster to closely mark Bobby Charlton. With the benefit of hindsight, Schön's decision is now widely regarded as a key factor in the outcome of the game, as it supposedly robbed the Germans of their most creative force. However, saying that Schön blundered is harsh indeed. In the immediate aftermath of the game, the jury was out. A neutral observer, the Austrian reporter Franz Pilsl, thought 'the Germans made a tactical error when they pitted Beckenbauer against Charlton'. But there were others who argued differently. *Kicker* correspondent Robert Becker even reported that 'the plan of having Beckenbauer mark Charlton worked a treat. England's great idol played only a modest role.'

Perhaps it would be more correct to say that Schön's idea, as controversial as it was, had no real effect on the game at all. In the words of the British historian David Downing, it made both Charlton and Beckenbauer 'largely peripheral figures', almost like extras in a drama. And what a drama England's 4-2 victory turned out to be! Schön's players, whom the British bookmakers had considered 14-1 outsiders to claim the trophy three weeks before, snatched a last-minute equaliser and forced an additional thirty minutes.

Actually, they would have forced a replay as well, if it hadn't been for two illegal goals – one where the ball didn't cross the line and one with spectators on the pitch. No coach can prepare for that. Let's just say there was extra time and many people collapsed with broken hearts, and leave it at that – except maybe to very briefly mention that there had been a remarkable game at this World Cup which didn't concern West Germany in any way at all and would yet have unforeseen consequences for Beckenbauer.

Actually, you could even say that the Wednesday before the World Cup final turned out to be a lot more important for Beckenbauer's future than the 120 minutes of football at Wembley. On 27 July 1966, Bayern Munich held their bi-annual assembly and the members voted to make a few changes. The most crucial one was that Robert Schwan left the club's board. He had to, because under German club law this body consisted of honorary officials only. Schwan, however, was no longer that. From 1 August on, he would be a full-time employee with a monthly salary of 5,000 marks. His title was 'technical director'.

Every longer article you'll ever read about the man says that this made him the first business manager in the Bundesliga; even the *Munzinger-Archiv* − an encyclopaedia considered scripture by German journalists − says this. It's still wrong. A man by the name of Georg Knöpfle had beaten Schwan to it by a couple of months, having been signed by Hamburg as technical director in June. Also, you could argue that Cologne's new coach Willi Multhaup was fulfilling pretty much the same function, without carrying the title. This explains why the *Süddeutsche Zeitung* said about the Reds' assembly that 'Bayern have taken the same step as Hamburg and Cologne before them'.

Yet Schwan could indeed lay claim to being the first manager in German football. Personal manager, that is. The *Daily Mail* had been spot on: Beckenbauer did become a big star at the World Cup, and it was beginning to cause problems. As his girlfriend Brigitte told Torsten Körner many decades later, 'everything was raining down on us, and we had to cope with the situation. The press, the games with the national team, the calls, the contracts. Suddenly we had to deal with all these foxes, big foxes. We didn't know what to decide, we were no match for these people. So we said: where can we find a manager, an agent?' Their first idea was to ask Dettmar Cramer. He was certainly a fox, but not with regard to business matters. Schwan was the obvious solution, as he had just taken on a similar post at Bayern.

It is not entirely clear when exactly Schwan became Beckenbauer's agent. Usually you read that his first official act as the player's representative was to cancel a deal with the German equivalent of Brylcreem, a product called Brisk. The company was paying every international 1,000 marks for the rights to use his image. Since Schwan got out of his contract on the grounds that Franz was not yet of legal age, this must have happened before September 1966. (Schwan easily found Beckenbauer a much more lucrative deal, as Knorr were willing to part with 12,000 marks to have the footballer promote their instant soups. Some twenty years later, the soon-to-be legendary television spots with young Franz would lead to a German international being sent home from a World Cup . . .)

In any case, Schwan's first recorded instance of publicly acting as Beckenbauer's personal adviser was on Bayern's trip to Milan for a friendly on 7 September. The *Süddeutsche Zeitung* reported that 'Beckenbauer's interests are being represented by technical director Robert Schwan', because there was no doubt in anyone's mind that the sole reason for this game was the player's imminent move to Italy. After the match, which Bayern lost 4-2, president Neudecker announced that Milan were 'still seriously interested in Beckenbauer. We have negotiated in earnest, and they are willing to accept our conditions, when Italy will lift the ban on foreign players.'

A few weeks earlier, Čajkovski and Beckenbauer had posed

for the press, with the coach draping a banner over the player's shoulder that read 'Not for sale'. But, of course, Neudecker and Schwan would have personally carried him over the Alps for 2 million marks (plus a signing-on bonus for Franz and his new agent that was rumoured to be in the region of 500,000 marks). With a heavy heart, the Munich newspaper informed its readers that 'it will be difficult, if not impossible, to hold on to Beckenbauer' after the end of the 1966–67 season.

Pak Doo-ik to the rescue! Just eight days into the World Cup, this corporal in the North Korean army scored one of the most famous goals in the competition's long history, knocking overwhelming favourites Italy out of the tournament. It was a disaster not only for the national team, but also for the big Serie A clubs. The shock defeat meant that public opinion now swung against lifting the restrictions on foreigners, as the influx of stars from abroad was supposedly hurting the development of homegrown talent. On 15 September, the Italian FA voted to extend the ban until June 1971. *Arriverderci, Milano!*

But still the most eventful year in Beckenbauer's life – certainly up until this point, arguably ever – was not over. On his twenty-first birthday, 11 September, Franz drove to the airport to pick up Dettmar Cramer. His coach and fatherly friend had not travelled to Munich on footballing duties, though. This was a very private matter, or so everybody hoped. Brigitte, meanwhile, went to the cinema, sneaked out through a side entrance and jumped, spy film-like, into a waiting car chauffeured by Robert Schwan's son-in-law. Both cars then headed for Wörthsee, a scenic town twenty miles west of Munich, where everybody bundled into a third limo that took them all to the register office. The ploy worked well, as only friends and family members were present when

Franz Beckenbauer, with Cramer as his best man, married the recently divorced and visibly pregnant Brigitte Schiller.

Four weeks after he tied the knot, Franz was voted Germany's Footballer of the Year by a landslide. He received the trophy, coincidentally but fittingly, right before the Munich derby, which the Reds won most convincingly, 3–0 again. (The writers particularly lauded an eighteen-year-old defender by the name of Georg Schwarzenbeck, making only his second Bundesliga appearance.) Six days after this game, Brigitte gave birth to Franz's second son, whom his parents named Michael. Parental leave, though, was never an option for Beckenbauer, whose life was becoming increasingly hectic. On the day after Michael had come into this world, his father played football for Bayern in Cologne. And on the day after that, he recorded his debut single for Polydor Records.

It was not a commercial success. The A–side sank without trace, while the B–side barely dented the charts. ('A global hit,' the amateur crooner told a film crew on the occasion of his seventy-fifth birthday. 'Number seven in the international hit parade, the Beatles were at eight.' Maybe he was serious. Maybe he was having them on. These days you never know with Beckenbauer.) The record was also not an artistic triumph, as both songs fell into that dreaded category of European pop music known as German *Schlager*.

'Ah, the songs were okay,' says Walter Beckenbauer. 'Our mother adored them.' As the designated rebel of the family, surely he would have preferred something more rocking? 'No, not really,' he admits. 'I liked the French chanson, Jacques Brel or Charles Aznavour. Rock music wasn't my cup of tea.' Those Beckenbauers just didn't cut it as purveyors of cool, because Franz actually liked the sappy stuff. He was a big fan of the Austrian singer Freddy Quinn, whose surname stemmed from an Irish-born father and who was most famous for melancholic songs about sailors and the sea.

In the same month that Beckenbauer became a Polydor recording artist, Quinn released the song 'Wir', meaning 'We', sometimes referred to as the most controversial *Schlager* of all time. It was a scathing attack on the peace movement, hippies (or 'bums', as the lyrics have it) and the counter culture in general. It triggered a heated debate that would have been even stormier if more people had listened to the other side of the single, which defended the United States' involvement in the Vietnam War. Quinn later apologised for the release, saying it was 'an attack on young people because they have long hair. It was idiotic.'

A mere three years later, Beckenbauer would find himself at the centre of a very similar debate and was pigeonholed as a conservative, if not reactionary, if not worse. In late 1966, though, he probably didn't even notice the furore suddenly surrounding his favourite singer because everything had become a bit of a blur. Shortly after filming the Knorr TV commercial in his own living room (in only three takes), Franz boarded a plane to travel to South America with Bayern. When the team touched down in Rio de Janeiro, plenty of Brazilian reporters were waiting for the club that had been in the second division only 540 days earlier and was now a sensation, thanks to one man only. 'They were chiefly there because of Franz Beckenbauer,' Schwan told German newspapers. 'But the brouhaha really started once we were in Buenos Aires. He and Čajkovski were dragged from one interview to the next.' Sadly, Schwan neglected to say whether or not he had seen Beckenbauer deep in conversation with Roberto Perfumo.

The journey to the other side of the world lasted only

eight days, because the players wanted to spend Christmas with their families. Since Schwan was in charge of the trip, everything went according to plan. The team was back in Munich at five minutes past two in the afternoon on 24 December. We don't exactly know what Beckenbauer found under the Christmas tree, but it doesn't take a lot of imagination to claim that a few copies of a book entitled *Dirigent im Mittelfeld* – which translated to 'conductor in midfield' – will have been lying around the house. It was his first autobiography, fresh off the press and written by the reporter who had shown him around Milan, Rolf Gonther. (Gonther's name was not to be found anywhere in the slim volume, which set a precedent for Beckenbauer books over the next 50 years.)

And then it was finally over – 1966. A year that had brought so many changes to Franz Beckenbauer's life – all to the better, as he saw it – that '6' would from now on be his lucky number. Not the '4' he'd worn in England, nor the '5' he would make famous. When Beckenbauer, by his own admission a superstitious man, travelled to the 1990 World Cup in Italy as the national manager of West Germany, he made sure that all his bags, suitcases and clothes were marked with the number 66. Two are better than one, you know.

In 1967, the *libero* was the latest rage in Germany. Talking about him, that is. The year began with Dettmar Cramer touring the country and holding a lecture in front of DFB coaches called 'Tactical Developments in International Football', which dealt in large parts with the 'free man' and his role in the Italian system. (He may have been unable to stop Pak Doo-ik, but Inter and Milan had won three of the four most recent European Cups, hence everybody's fascination with the game on the peninsula.) In February, the grandmaster of *catenaccio*, Helenio Herrera, was given three pages in *Kicker* to explain modern football. He talked in great detail about the *libero*, but regarded him exclusively as a safeguard: 'Since the *libero* holds the fort in the penalty area, any of the other defenders can join in the attack. Of course he has to retreat immediately if the threat of a counter attack arises, but the *libero* has since taken up his position and won't leave it until the defender has recovered from returning back into defence.' (The bit about recovering from tracking back makes you wonder if Herrera was indeed such a stickler for fitness as we've been led to believe.)

For Herrera's Inter, this extra attacker was usually full-back Giacinto Facchetti, who scored almost sixty goals during his club career, a stunning figure for any defender, especially for one plying his trade in Serie A. Beckenbauer would later often explain that watching Facchetti had given him the idea for his own interpretation of the *libero*. 'Facchetti, as a left-back, could only move forward or to his right. But since I was playing in a central role, I could also move to my left. I was free to roam.' Well, not entirely free, because he still needed his team-mates. Some of them had to cover his back (this would become the role that made Schwarzenbeck an unsung hero of German football), others were needed to link up with him.

One month after Herrera pontificated on the pages of *Kicker*, former national coach Sepp Herberger granted the magazine his own analysis of the state of the game – and was amazingly abreast of the times for a seventy-year-old pensioner: 'When Beckenbauer surges forward,' he explained, 'he needs "walls" for the ball to rebound to him once he has "given and gone".' Gerd Müller, today mainly remembered as a finisher, had already become so adept at being a wall player he could actually read Beckenbauer's feet. 'If he played a soft pass, I was meant to give it back,' the striker once explained. 'If the pass was sharp, I was supposed to do something with it.'

Although the expression *libero* was steadily taking hold, it was only rarely applied to Beckenbauer during those early years, probably because it was quite obvious that he was doing something very different from his colleagues in this position; he was neither sweeper nor stopper. So what was he? Maybe this confusion was behind the first backlash. It began in January 1967, when West Germany played an unofficial friendly against Luxembourg in Aachen. The hosts won 2-0, but the 30,000 in attendance had expected a goalfest. At one point, they started booing Beckenbauer, who had wasted two good chances. 'Eventually there were catcalls every time he touched the ball,' *Kicker* writer Robert Becker reported, before trying to find an explanation for this. 'Everything comes so easily to Beckenbauer that he sometimes appears nonchalant. When he gets stuck in, nobody notices, because he isn't grimacing. This is, let's say, unfamiliar. For people who confuse playing football with working a blast furnace, it is almost a provocation. But I'm willing to bet that all those people who call Beckenbauer arrogant have never spoken to him.'

However, it wasn't just the people in the stands. A few days after the game, the veteran writer Georg H. Meurer said in his regular column for the *Hamburger Abendblatt* that 'Beckenbauer is too young to understand that a blasé attitude and arrogance do not make a good role model for the youth. They don't befit the people's game.' When Bayern were beaten 1-0 in the quarter-finals of the Cup Winners' Cup away to Rapid Vienna in February, Austria's former national coach Karl Decker said: 'You cannot compare this Beckenbauer to the Beckenbauer from the World Cup. Munich's most famous player shied every from every challenge, he was a parlour player against Rapid.' Soon the notorious tabloid *Bild* got in on the act, gleefully publishing readers' letters that said things like 'Beckenbauer may be a first-class footballer, but as a human being he is second-class. His arrogance cannot be surpassed.'

It needs pointing out that Beckenbauer, although he was constantly in the press, had not yet given what we today would regard as an in-depth interview. He had appeared on a popular late-night sports TV show as early as September 1965, and a few months later there was also a short film profile that has become famous because a rosy-cheeked Franz looks at the camera and says: 'I don't want to have anything to do with football in later life, and a coaching job is probably no option for me.' But none of this was (yet) in any way contro-versial. It seems he just rubbed people up the wrong way due to the way he played the game.

Others, though, admired this way. On 6 May, Bayern played another derby against 1860, this time in the semi-finals of the DFB-Pokal, the German FA Cup. Even though they were missing Müller, who had broken his arm playing for the national team a few days earlier, the Reds scored three goals in a twelve-minute spell in the second half and won con-vincingly against their local rivals. This led the 27-year-old Nuremberg-born reporter Peter Ramsauer to write: 'Turmoil in Munich. "King Radi" had to yield his empire to ... Kaiser Franz.' His piece appeared in the issue of *Kicker* dated 8 May 1967. It is the oldest reference to the now ubiquitous nickname that I have been able to find. However, for reasons outlined above, I wouldn't credit Ramsauer with having invented it – nor even with popularising this regal sobriquet.

Having trawled newspaper archives for much longer than seems reasonable, I have no doubt that the one person who really could lay claim to its popularisation was an old friend of Franz's and a colourful figure in Bayern's history, even if the vast majority of fans will be totally unfamiliar with his name: Hans Schiefele. When Schiefele died in 2005, his Bayern Munich membership card bore the number 1, as he had joined the club in 1928, a few weeks before his ninth birthday. (This number is always assigned to the oldest living club member, currently one Heiner Jüngling, who was registered as a Red by his father shortly after his birth in 1939.) Schiefele later made a few appearances for Bayern's senior side and was reportedly even considered for the national team, until senseless slaughter intervened. After the war, Schiefele found a job working in the archives of a Munich newspaper, from where he climbed the career ladder until becoming the chief football writer for the *Süddeutsche Zeitung*, while also editing Bayern's club magazine on the side.

It was in the self-same *Süddeutsche Zeitung* that Schiefele referred to Beckenbauer as 'Kaiser Franz' ten months after Ramsauer had done, on 25 March 1968. Schiefele must have liked the sound of it because he used the term again on 1 April. In early June, he travelled to Hanover, to report on what would turn out to be a historic friendly between West Germany and World Cup holders England, as the hosts won 1-0. Many years later, Beckenbauer would say about this match: 'It was the first time in history we beat the English. Guess who scored the goal? Yes, I did. It was a real piledriver. No, come to think of it, it was a crappy deflected shot with my left foot.' Schiefele's article, published on 4 June 1968, included yet another 'Kaiser Franz', the third such mention in fewer than three months. I rest my case – albeit knowing full well it will have to be reopened soon.

Schiefele did more for Bayern than just make a Kaiser out of Franzl. In May 1963, he urged the club's president to approach a well-known coach who happened to be between jobs. 'Mr Neudecker,' Schiefele said, 'if Čik Čajkovski is available, you have to make him an offer.' Neudecker followed Schiefele's advice, which would directly lead to the greatest day (up until this point) in Bayern's history. This was 31 May 1967, the day of the Cup Winners' Cup final. Bayern had managed to turn things around against Rapid in the return game, before making short shrift of Standard Liège in the semis, to become the third Bundesliga team in a row to play for this piece of European silverware – and the third to face a British team in the final, after 1860 Munich had lost to West Ham United in 1965 and Borussia Dortmund overcame Liverpool in 1966. This team were Rangers. 'They were the overwhelming favourites,' Franz Roth, who had joined Bayern the previous summer, says about the Scottish giants. 'They had been playing in Europe for years and years, whereas it was all new for us.'

The final, staged just 100 miles north of Munich, in Nuremberg, was broadcast into twenty-four countries. Photos taken that night in the streets of Munich remind you of scenes from post-apocalyptic movies: the city was totally deserted, as not just the inhabitants of No. 29 Stauffenbergstrasse were sitting at home, glued to their television sets and watching what *The Times* called 'an exhilarating game of attack and counter-attack'. After a few early exciting solo runs, Beckenbauer was soon forced back, leading the German television commentator to remark that he was 'condemned to playing as a no-frills stopper today'. Rangers were indeed dangerous, though as *The Times* added: 'Bayern were experts at covering each other in defence, and in Beckenbauer, of recent World Cup memory, they had a player who was mightier even than the best in Rangers' defence.'

'It was only ever a question of who would score first,' Beckenbauer said after the game. 'If it had been Rangers, I reckon they would have won.' But they didn't. Instead, the man who made the difference on the night was the Bull. The reader may recall that this was one of the nicknames Beckenbauer jealously listed in his 1975 book to illustrate who was a man of the people and who wasn't. Franz Roth, who grew up on a farm, certainly was. Beckenbauer first met him after his, and Sepp Maier's, special leave in the wake of the World Cup, when Čajkovski introduced them to Bayern's summer signings. 'And this is Roth, has strength like moo-moo,' the coach had said. Maier interjected: 'No, no, Čik. We don't say someone has the strength of a cow. We say he is strong like a bull.'

Now, fewer than ten months later, Roth's goal after 109 minutes won Čajkovski the most important trophy of his career. And although Beckenbauer and Maier would go on to win more important ones, they were well and truly swept away by this triumph. Almost literally, because as soon as the final whistle rang, there was a full-blown pitch invasion. The police had to mark off space for the trophy presentation with a cordon, while Čajkovski gave each and every one of his players a bear hug, tears streaming down his rotund face.

The following day, more than 100,000 people lined the streets of Munich to cheer the team. The four men who led the parade, driving the trophy around in a Porsche 911 Cabriolet – red, of course! – were Čajkovski, Neudecker, Schwan and captain Werner Olk. They would have to get used to this; barely a week later, the Reds defended the German FA Cup, beating Hamburg in Stuttgart. It meant that Bayern had not been knocked out of a domestic or European cup competition since December 1964, an amazing run that the club would extend until May 1968. But, in a way, it was this very success that sowed the seeds for Čajkovski's downfall.

In their first two Bundesliga seasons, Bayern had finished third and then a rather disappointing sixth. But when the Reds found themselves in the number eight spot a quarter of the way into Čajkovski's fifth season in charge, Neudecker and Schwan began to ask themselves questions. Why was the team with the Bundesliga's best goalkeeper and the best centre-half – or whatever you called Beckenbauer these days – shipping so many goals, no fewer than fifty-eight in 1967-68? Was Čajkovski's gung-ho style perfectly suited to knockout rounds under floodlights, but the wrong approach for a drawn-out league season? Even before the winter break, the club's head honchos decided not to extend Čajkovski's contract. They instead went to look for someone who was the exact opposite of the immensely popular, lenient, gregarious, attack-minded Yugoslav. They found him in February 1968.

The Zagreb-born Branko Zebec had played alongside Čajkovski for Yugoslavia at the 1954 World Cup, where they lost to West Germany in the quarter-finals, but nationality and chosen profession were the only things the two men had in common. Zebec was the greatest tactical genius to coach Bayern until Pep Guardiola came along, the sternest disciplinarian until Felix Magath showed up and the greatest pragmatist until ... well, we're still waiting. 'I instantly knew that we wouldn't have half the fun we'd had under Čik,' Beckenbauer later said about Zebec's arrival. 'He never

In 1978, Franz Beckenbauer – then with the Cosmos – paid pre-gentrification Giesing a visit to show a photographer the house he grew up in.

This undated private photo was taken either in 1962 or early 1963. If it was the latter, then Beckenbauer had just fathered a child even though he wasn't yet allowed to drive the Lloyd 600 in the background.

Beckenbauer played in his first full international, a crucial World Cup qualifier, shortly after his nineteenth birthday in September 1965.

The 1966 World Cup established the Kaiser on the international stage, though it's still debated whether or not it was a good idea to have him man-mark Bobby Charlton in the final.

After the 1966 World Cup, the young footballer received up
to a thousand letters or postcards – every day.

In 1966, Beckenbauer celebrated St Nicholas's Day with his wife
Brigitte and his second son Michael. And, obviously, with the press.

The media was also present shortly after Stephan Beckenbauer came into the world in December 1968. His brothers Michael and Thomas (who had been legally adopted nine months earlier) showed some interest but kept their distance.

In the 1969 cup final against Schalke, the crowd began to boo whenever Beckenbauer touched the ball. He responded by playing keepy-uppy while the match was in progress.

The men who created a dynasty: goalkeeper Sepp Maier (*left*), striker Gerd Müller and *libero* Beckenbauer in 1969, when Bayern lifted their first Bundesliga title.

The Beckenbauers at the dawn of the 1970s. True glamour was still a few years – and a move to New York – away.

In late 1970, Beckenbauer triggered 'the beard war' – but sporting facial hair clearly wasn't his only daring fashion statement.

In the summer of 1973, Beckenbauer and his wife starred as themselves in a film that, according to one critic, 'hurled football into the intellectual poorhouse'.

'Johan was the better player, though I'm the one who won the World Cup.' Beckenbauer and national coach Helmut Schön celebrate the 1974 triumph.

Beckenbauer's foul on Allan Clarke in the 1975 European Cup final went unpunished, which was one reason why the Leeds fans rioted after the match.

Beckenbauer was awarded the Ballon d'Or for the second time in 1976, only months before he went to America. He is still the only primarily defensive player to win this trophy more than once.

On 24 May 1977, Beckenbauer's parents accompanied him to the airport before he left for New York. His father, Franz Sr, was already suffering from the disease that would kill him six months later.

A few weeks into his second life, Beckenbauer walked the streets of New York with his friend, agent, adviser and perhaps svengali Robert Schwan. It's surely only a coincidence that Schwan bore an uncanny resemblance to Beckenbauer's father.

talked with any of us face to face. Sometimes he said nothing at all for days on end. He was holed up in his room and
would only come out for the training sessions. Then all we
would hear were his orders.' But he also added that 'Zebec
demanded a lot. After Čik's soft methods, that was exactly
what we needed.'

Interestingly, the one thing the stern, defence-minded
Zebec never even considered was to curb Beckenbauer's
pleasure trips across the halfway line. The new coach simply
adopted the system devised by Čajkovski and the player, no
questions asked. 'Oh, of course he did that!' exclaims Franz
Roth, in his mid-seventies but still powerful like a moo-moo.
'Branko had been a fine player himself. He knew the game –
which means he knew that you must never rob a player of
Franz's calibre of his greatest asset. When Franz moved forward, one of the defensive midfielders dropped back to defend
against counter attacks. It was never hara-kiri. We knew what
we were doing.'

Zebec's slave-driver methods yielded results almost immediately. In the 1968-69 season, the Reds won the league for
the first time in the club's history (the 1932 national championship having predated the Bundesliga era), and quite
convincingly so. Suddenly they had the best defence in the
country, conceding only thirty-one goals. Of course, there
may have been other reasons for this sudden turnaround.
Before the season began, Beckenbauer had asked Neudecker
and Schwan for a new kit. 'We need different shirts, otherwise it's never going to work,' he told them. They humoured
him, probably because Schwan was no less superstitious than
his client. When Bayern played away at Cologne in late 1965,
he went shopping in the city and, despite his proverbial stin-
giness, treated himself to an expensive lambskin coat. 'Then

we lost the game 6-1, and that coat never left the wardrobe again,' Beckenbauer later revealed.

With the new kit – featuring vertical stripes, red and white or red and blue – came success, but that success also seemed to foster a growing indignation. It's hard to pinpoint when exactly people began viewing Bayern as evil incarnate, but that first season under Zebec is as good a starting point as any, as football teams have this inexplicable tendency to assume their manager's style and character. Čik's boisterous, fun-loving kids, who thought nothing of conceding three if they scored four, had become cold calculators. This was a combination widely considered unpopular, as Beckenbauer found out on 14 June 1969.

That was the day of the cup final between Bayern and Schalke in Frankfurt, which the Reds won 2-1 to claim their first double. It was an interesting, even fascinating game, though not as historic as people have been led to believe by Torsten Körner's (otherwise excellent) 2005 Beckenbauer biography. Körner claimed this final marked the origin of the 'Kaiser' nickname, because two journalists used it in their match reports to describe the same moment in the game. One was the 27-year-old Bernd Hildebrandt, the younger brother of a very famous satirist. His article in the then recently launched Munich tabloid *Tz* said: 'Losing his footing, Munich's "libero" held on to Libuda's shorts. "Kaiser" Franz, who was now booed whenever he touched the ball, reacted calmly. Following Sepp Maier's throw-out, he provocatively juggled the ball for numerous seconds.' The other writer was, almost needless to say, Hans Schiefele. His piece about the final included these lines: 'At one point, Schalke's fans discharged their anger, because "Kaiser Franz" grabbed the "King of Westphalia". It inspired Munich's football royalty to a Rastelli-like stunt.'

So, what happened? With twenty-five minutes gone and the score 1-1, Schalke's tricky right-winger Reinhard Libuda ran into Bayern's box, but Beckenbauer cleared the situation by kicking the ball into touch before being knocked down by Libuda. The crowd expected a throw-in, but when they realised the referee had awarded Bayern a free-kick, they began to boo, accusing Beckenbauer of having made the most of the slight contact with the delicate Libuda. Only two minutes later, Libuda found himself in a one-on-one with Bayern's stopper again, fifteen yards into the opposition's half. Beckenbauer attempted a rare tackle, but Libuda went past him, whereupon Franz grabbed him – by the leg rather than by his shorts, the footage seems to suggest. Now there were shrill catcalls whenever Franz was anywhere near the ball and a section of the crowd loudly chanted: 'Beckenbauer out!'

On thirty-one minutes, Maier rolled the ball out to Beckenbauer, who was standing to his goalkeeper's right, just outside the penalty area. As the whistling became louder, Beckenbauer began to play keepy-uppy. A colourful account of the following moments from a Berlin newspaper has over the years been quoted to death in Germany – although it is so patently absurd that we must conclude the man who penned it (Ulfert Schröder, a writer we'll meet again) never saw the actual game. Beckenbauer didn't juggle the ball 'for forty seconds', only for seven. He didn't use 'his head and then the foot again', just his feet. The Schalke players did not keep their distance because they 'were transfixed to the spot'; it's simply that there wasn't much they could do under the rules of the day, because if they had made a run at Beckenbauer, he could have simply nudged the ball back to Maier. Finally, the vast stadium wasn't 'suddenly completely quiet'. Quite the contrary, the booing grew more intense with every one of Beckenbauer's eight touches.

As showboating goes, it wasn't really reminiscent of Enrico Rastelli, the legendary Italian acrobat and juggler. It was also not, as Körner believed, 'the initial impetus for the "Kaiser" metaphor'. Schiefele had used this expression on many occasions before, not to mention Ramsauer, and to suggest that it had any connection to the fact that Libuda was sometimes called the 'King of Westphalia' is far-fetched indeed. (Libuda was known to all and sundry as 'Stan', for his version of the Matthews move, while some writers referred to him as the 'Garrincha from Schalke'. The King moniker was only rarely used.)

Yet the juggling act was a memorable moment nonetheless. 'This unrepentant defiance was new for a German audience, which loved its heroes but demanded humility from them,' Körner argued. 'Beckenbauer didn't care about this tacit agreement; instead, he claimed total authority. By freezing the match and subjugating the ball to his will, he not only underlined that he felt freed from the crowd's demands, he also demonstrated quite casually that it was him who controlled the game and that he would not let anyone challenge his claim of sovereignty on the field of play.' There is some truth to this, though thankfully Körner immediately added that none of this was actually on Beckenbauer's mind. Instead, the player was actually in a state of shock himself.

'The booing was so loud that I wished the ground would open and swallow me up,' he later described the minutes before his keep-ups. 'I was startled. What had I done wrong? A foul, like thousands of players had committed before me and thousands would after me. But offence was taken only when I was involved – Beckenbauer.' Little did he know that those vociferous catcalls and boos were nothing compared to the trouble he was heading for, let alone that it all had to do with the 1969 West German federal election, held three months after the Schalke game.

LIFE I

Chapter Four

In the autumn of 1969, Schwan and Beckenbauer made their first serious mistake. It is entirely unclear why Schwan made it, because the deal he agreed to netted his priceless charge the sort of money he normally wouldn't even get out of bed for. Why Beckenbauer made this mistake ... well, we can guess.

In March 1968, he and his wife had officially adopted Thomas, his first son, born out of wedlock. Six months later, he became a father for the third time, when Brigitte gave birth to his son Stephan. There must have been occasions when he succumbed to the sort of temptation only rock stars and famous footballers can really consider commonplace. (When the German monthly *11Freunde* quizzed Werner Olk in 2011 about Beckenbauer's legendary effect on the fair sex, Bayern's long-time captain smiled and replied that there were training sessions 'when us mere mortals were warming up while Franz was loosening his limbs somewhere'.)

Still, all accounts agree that he did love his young wife dearly. And Brigitte, in turn, inspired him. Mrs Beckenbauer was very much interested in the arts, in literature, in dance and theatre, even in the opera. Gradually, she opened up a new world for her husband, one which he found increasingly interesting. Finally, there was his new home in a well-to-do southern suburb called Solln, an eight-room house invariably described as a 'villa' in the 1960s, though the reader is advised to lower their expectations here.

It would have been only natural for a regular Giesing boy if Beckenbauer had felt the urge to show off. He had arrived, he had made it, he had done everything his father said he couldn't do with football. Actually, he had managed to have it both ways – a most unusual professional career and at the same time a traditional, respectable family life. It was even a bit boring, but in all likelihood that only added to Beckenbauer's satisfaction. This is why he said 'Yes' when ZDF, one of West Germany's two public-service television broadcasters, offered him a paltry 5,000 marks for a thirty-minute behind-the-scenes feature about his life. After all, there was no risk involved at all. Schwan cannot have been happy about the money, but at least he was professional enough to make sure that he and Beckenbauer would have approval of the final cut.

And so the filmmaker and investigative journalist Reinhart Hoffmeister followed Beckenbauer around. 'We'll be close on his heels for a whole month,' Hoffmeister said in September 1969, 'no matter whether he is on the pitch or in his house in Munich Solln.' These were highly politicised weeks and months in West Germany. For the past three years, the country had been governed by a grand coalition of the two major political parties of the times, the Christian and Social Democrats (think, very broadly, Tories and Labour). Disillusionment with this monolithic structure and political impasse eventually led to the emergence of the West German student movement and the loose organisation known as *Ausserparlamentarische Opposition*, or extra-parliamentary opposition. When the Social Democratic Party won the 1969 election and Willy Brandt became chancellor, many people breathed a sigh of relief, as Brandt – immensely popular not just with members of the New Left – seemed to represent reform, change and progress.

Hoffmeister's film – entitled *For Example: Franz Beckenbauer* – was aired on 13 January 1970. Its protagonist quickly realised that while he and his agent had seen the actual footage and given it the green light, they had never heard the voice-over. Hoffmeister described the supposedly glamorous star player as a bland petit bourgeois controlled by his svengali agent (who, unbeknown to the director, pocketed 20 per cent of every fee he negotiated for his client). Then Hoffmeister mentioned almost in passing 'Franz Beckenbauer's belief that Willy Brandt is a national diasaster for Germany and Franz Beckenbauer's admiration of Franz Josef Strauss'.

Some sympathy for Strauss, the autocratic, right-wing leader of the Bavarian government, was to be expected, but the line about Brandt was somewhat heavy. Schwan immediately denied that Beckenbauer had said anything like this, whereupon Hoffmeister not only named two witnesses who had overheard the off-camera remark, but also claimed that Beckenbauer's following lines had been: 'I predict we will all be dispossessed and lose our homes if the Social Democrats remain in power. Then we won't be Bayern Munich any more but Red Star Munich.' Even though Hoffmeister's film also said that Beckenbauer 'hasn't done a lot of thinking about politics and hardly finds the time to read', his flippant quote was taken very seriously. Bayern members threatened to quit the club, while the newspapers had a field day.

Those newspapers had recently become a real problem, particularly in Munich. For many decades, there had been only one tabloid in town: the *Abendzeitung* – the evening newspaper. But in 1968, the *Tz* (which stood for *Tageszeitung* – the daily paper) entered the fray, the publication in which Bernd Hildebrandt had referred to Beckenbauer as 'Kaiser'. Only one year later, the notoriously sensationalist, nationwide *Bild* opened offices in Munich. Faced with the dilemma of being a public figure and one of the biggest celebrities in a city that now swarmed with nosy hacks and paparazzi, Beckenbauer had two options: keep the press at arm's length or jump in bed with them. He chose the latter, not least because it promised to be more lucrative. Beckenbauer was already on good terms with the *Abendzeitung* columnist Rolf Gonther, who had ghosted his first autobiography. (The paper's editor-in-chief, Edgar Fuchs, would write the fifth one in 1992.) He soon also maintained excellent relationships with the other tabloids, especially *Bild*. This strategy meant that Schwan and Beckenbauer could exert some sort of control over what was printed and what wasn't. But pacts with the devil come at a price, in this case perpetual publicity. When three-year-old Michael contracted a very dangerous form of meningitis in February 1970 and had to stay in a children's hospital for more than three weeks, snappers were there to photograph Beckenbauer at his sickbed.

Such was his visibility that even a small fashion statement caused an uproar that became known as the *Bartkrieg* – the beard war – towards the end of the year. The farce began in October, when West Germany played a European Championship qualifier against Turkey in Cologne. On the plane back to Munich, Beckenbauer abruptly announced he was going to grow a moustache. It's tempting to say that his opponents had inspired him, but only a few of the Turkish players had facial hair, so maybe his role model was indeed Omar Sharif in *Doctor Zhivago*, as the tabloids speculated. In any case, Gerd Müller instantly said: 'I'm going to do the same.'

Within only five days, the duo sported such visible peach fuzz that they made the cover of *Bild*. The newspaper announced that president Neudecker 'had declared war' on his two star players, his argument being that 'the neck and the face of a German footballer have to remain free'. The affair quickly took on such preposterous proportions that *Kicker* marvelled that 'the German game must be in a very good shape, if some people think that the most pressing problem is whether or not Beckenbauer and Müller should let the hair between their upper lip and their nose grow'. Still, the public pressure became so strong that Müller reached for the razor as early as November.

Beckenbauer, though, held out. He later recounted that he received hate mail, including a letter in which his moustache was termed 'a subhuman look', adding: 'My defiance awakened. I reasoned that even the employee of a football club has some basic rights after all.' But a man's pride can be a cumbersome thing. When Beckenbauer noticed the odd speck of ginger hair in his moustache, he felt forced to regularly dye his beard. In the end, Franz found a smart way to save face but not facial hair. In late February 1971, he got a shave live on television and for a good cause, namely the lottery that helped finance the 1972 Summer Olympics in Munich. If anything, the silly episode showed that he was not his agent's puppet and couldn't be bossed around by his president. He was certainly no revolutionary, but maybe Beckenbauer was a tiny bit more of a free-thinker than Hoffmeister had given him credit for.

Then again, Hoffmeister was in no way the only observer who found Beckenbauer wanting in some regards. Although the football got better and better, especially with regard to the national team, Beckenbauer's press in the quality media (as opposed to his tabloid cronies) got worse and worse in the early 1970s. In October 1971, for instance, the respected author Horst Vetten, once described by a colleague of his as 'the Beckenbauer of the writers', was so appalled by Franz's recently published third autobiography that he sat down to write a profile for *Stern* magazine entitled 'The Fearful Hero'.

First, Vetten became the next in a long line of observers trying to dissect the very strange relationship between the country's best footballer and the country's football fans. 'His sight alone drives tens of thousands of Hannover fans crazy, a few days later miners from Schalke demand his head,' he wrote. 'Whenever Franz Beckenbauer enters a ground, the stadium becomes a pillory.' Why was he booed like nobody else, why did 'the football nation love to hate him'? Vetten started with the obvious, his style of play. Exhibit A was an international in June against Norway during which Beckenbauer had taken a free-kick by lobbing the ball over the wall from a standing position. 'A set-piece which players normally turn into a pompous ritual,' Vetten wrote without ever having seen Cristiano Ronaldo, 'became a circus act. A circus act involving a star and his support cast. Beckenbauer is the star, the others are clowns.'

But there was more to it. Beckenbauer's latest auto-biography (I'll spare you the name of yet another German ghostwriter), Vetten said, 'is testament to the manipulated behaviour of a man trained to perform who considers himself "boring and uninteresting". The book is one single cliché. Beckenbauer agreed to it because he was paid money. Clichés and money determine his non-sporting life, he is remote-controlled.' The writer concluded: 'Franz Beckenbauer is severely hurt when people call him arrogant, in reality he is rather fearful, suspicious and reserved. Primarily, though, he is mentally lazy and taciturn. This combination creates the impression of arrogance.'

Barely two months before this diatribe was published, Bayern travelled to Vienna to play one of those countless friendlies Schwan was constantly arranging to finance the expensive Bayern squad. On the day after their 4–0 win over Austria, the players were invited on to a tour of the Hofburg, the imperial palace in the centre of Vienna. Whether by intent or an on impulse, Beckenbauer stopped next to a tall bust of Franz Joseph I. He looked up at the famous Kaiser of Austria almost longingly. At that very moment, the 44-year-old photographer Herbert Sündhofer released the shutter. The photo appeared in *Kicker* on 16 August and, from that moment on, Beckenbauer was the Kaiser for good, even outside of Munich.

This is why a motion picture that premiered in West German cinemas a few days before Christmas 1973 used the tagline: 'Kaiser Franz – how millions admire him but only few really know him.' Yes, despite his experiences with the Hoffmeister film, Beckenbauer had agreed to star in another movie. It's unlikely he did so just because of the money. (Torsten Körner claims he was paid 15,000 marks, which must be a typo. Contemporary reports say Franz's fee came to 250,000 marks, plus a 7 per cent share of the profits.) Rather, it just sounded all really good. First, it was not going to be a straight documentary but a narrative film interspersed with real-life scenes. This way, the flick could present Beckenbauer the way he actually was and at the same time paint an entertaining, colourful portrait of the football business. Also, the screenwriter was a best-selling author, the cinematographer had worked with some well-known directors before, and a whole slew of capable, seasoned actors would co-star in the film.

The only unknown quantity was the young director Wigbert Wicker. The whole project was his idea, as he had approached Schwan in the first place. But when filming began in June of 1973, Wicker didn't have a lot of experience, let alone with a production of this magnitude (while Beckenbauer admitted to a journalist that he 'hadn't been to the cinema in a long time'). Over the summer, the director shot almost 200,000 feet of film, but ended up using only 8,200 of it for a motion picture that ultimately ran for fewer than eighty minutes.

This alone tells you that Wicker struggled to combine the documentary scenes with a storyline that tackled too many topics. There was a player's constant fear of career-ending injuries: a fictitious team-mate breaks his leg, which makes Beckenbauer contemplate the fleeting nature of his job, a sub-plot probably inspired by the real-life case of former Bayern striker Wolfgang Sühnholz, who had suffered an injury in April 1972 and who never played for the Reds again. There was the fickleness of the fans and the tricks of the tabloids. There were also the machinations of the money people looking to profit from football's popularity (an equally fictitious entrepreneur is trying to have Franz endorse his products).

The movie has gone down in history as an unmitigated disaster and possibly one of the worst sports films of all time, which must be, to paraphrase Jonathan Wilson, a field almost as contested as that of loathsome football politicians. It's true, the movie was considered a box-office bomb and you don't have to look hard to find scathing reviews. The *Frankfurter Allgemeine Zeitung* said the film 'has hurled football into the intellectual poorhouse', while the weekly *Die Zeit* considered the plot 'shambolic, unrealistic and in parts downright embarrassing'. The *Süddeutsche Zeitung* found Wicker's imagery 'clueless and often unintentionally funny'.

But the longest and perhaps most stinging attack came a few weeks after the film had died a sudden death in cinemas across the country. In early 1974, four months before the World Cup in West Germany, Ulfert Schröder published the first serious book about Beckenbauer that wasn't an autobiography penned by an unnamed journalist. (An earlier attempt, dating from 1969, was little more than a gushing hagiography.) Schröder devoted four pages to the film, which he described as 'total nonsense', and concluded that 'Kaiser Franz stumbles politely and a little bit naïvely through this dilettantish hokum'. Wicker was hit hard by the negative reception, but Beckenbauer – no stranger to boos and malice – took it in his stride and seems to have retained a soft spot for the silver screen's version of himself.

And, indeed, history should have been less harsh on Wicker's debut. The football scenes are gorgeous and brilliantly shot, while Beckenbauer, whose acting is nothing to be too ashamed about, comes across as artless, humble and congenial. The same goes for his family, as Brigitte and the three boys enjoy plenty of screen time. The encyclopaedia *Fussball im Film* – a 1,100-page volume that has to be seen to be believed – says: 'That Beckenbauer supposedly tried to buy up every existing copy of the film years later to have them destroyed could be one of the countless rumours and legends that have grown around this film. It would have been unnecessary, because the movie isn't much worse than the average West German feature film of the time.' The reference book argues that 'Beckenbauer was too much of a controversial figure at the time for the film to be judged irrespectively of his star persona'. In other words, Wicker's movie was doomed from the start because too many cinemagoers – not to mention reviewers – were critical of Beckenbauer. The title of the film? Why, *Libero*.

There is a moment in *Libero* where Franz Beckenbauer tells a (fictitious) friend that he is going to quit the game. 'I'm fed up,' he says. 'I can't do this any more, and I don't want to.' This threat was primarily the filmmaker's flight of fancy, of course, but it wasn't completely unfounded in reality. Attentive observers will have heard echoes of a famous statement Beckenbauer had made five years earlier, in late 1968, when he confided in journalists: 'Sometimes I think I should chuck in football altogether.' What he really meant was that he contemplated retiring from international duty at an early age, all because of his role on the field of play.

Things really came to a head in December 1968 when West Germany were touring Central and South America. In the build-up to the high-profile game against Brazil in Rio de Janeiro, national coach Helmut Schön decided to have the tenacious 'World Cup Willi' Schulz man-mark Pelé. This meant someone else had to play stopper. Enter the man who was already doing this every weekend in a Bayern shirt.

Despite wearing the number 4 shirt, it was the first time that Beckenbauer played as a centre-half for his country, and he didn't do a bad job. Brazil took a 2–0 lead before the break, but the first goal came from a direct free-kick and the second was the result of a rare Maier blunder, the goalkeeper unable to hold on to a long-range Gerson strike, allowing Edu to bury the rebound. But the visitors came back strongly after the restart. Sigfried Held scored with a header and Klaus Gerwien, a man who won only six caps during his career, tied the game with a stunning, Brazilesque bicycle kick. True, there was an embarrassing moment when Pelé nutmegged Beckenbauer, only to then put the ball wide from ten yards. But Franz played well and even found time for his advances, once forcing a save from the Brazilian goalkeeper with the wonderful name of Picasso.

It wasn't the game that made headlines though, but Beckenbauer's reaction to it. He told the reporters travelling with the team that he was sick of being shuffled around and felt it was hurting his performance: 'I'm the libero at my club, but I have to play in midfield for Germany.' Then it got personal. 'From now on, I want to play only libero for the national team,' he declared. 'What Willi Schulz is doing is not modern football. Even the free man must be ready to help his team's offence.'

Eight days later, in a scoreless draw with Mexico, Beckenbauer played sweeper again, but decided to keep his forays at a minimum, prompting Schulz to hit back: 'So, was that this modern libero?' These astonishingly frank verbal spats were not a spur-of-the-moment thing, as became clear upon Beckenbauer's return. On Boxing Day, he ran into Hans Schiefele and explained his defensive role against Mexico. 'I joined in the attack a few times, but I couldn't risk too much at 0-0. Also, Willi Schulz would have had a feeling of schadenfreude if something had gone wrong, and I couldn't allow that.'

Amazingly, this was a fight which Beckenbauer would not win until twenty-eight months later. The national coach continued to use the reliable workhorse Schulz at the heart of the defence, and when the international career of 'World Cup Willi', who was seven years older than the Kaiser, slowly wound down during the 1970 World Cup, Schön decided to make left-back Karl-Heinz Schnellinger the new sweeper (he was a more attack-minded player than Schulz, but certainly no Beckenbauer). Looking back on it half a century later, the dispute seems bizarre, because the Kaiser has entered the pantheon of the greatest of greats as the very prototype of the libero, almost the definition of the position. And yet many people at the time felt that Schön had excellent reasons for being so stubbornly reluctant to give in to Beckenbauer's demands.

First, like a lot of observers, the national coach was afraid that his best player was somewhat wasted at the back. Schön is today often seen as the man who didn't give Günter Netzer the international career the player deserved because he considered the Gladbach maverick too unpredictable. But deep down inside, the national coach was an incurable romantic who dreamed of a super-cultured German midfield consisting of Beckenbauer, Netzer and Wolfgang Overath. This, however, was always destined to remain a pipe dream, football's equivalent of asking Stanley Kubrick, Federico Fellini and Francis Ford Coppola to direct the same movie.

And here was also the big difference to Bayern Munich. During the club's first golden era, from the mid-1960s to the mid-1970s, the Reds never had one of those out-and-out playmakers who were such a hallmark of the entire era, save maybe for the one really good season – 1968-69 – that the Austrian August Starek enjoyed in Munich. Due to Beckenbauer's very peculiar interpretation of the stopper role, they didn't need one – and maybe they couldn't even afford one. Imagine any classic number 10 having to leave his natural habitat in the hole behind the strikers all the time, just because this defender with the shirt number 5 had decided to come striding through central midfield yet again. Schön, on the other hand, had plenty of those playmakers at his disposal, Netzer and Overath being only the most marvellous ones. How to use them if Beckenbauer played at the back and stuck to his adventurous style? And if you told the Kaiser to please stay back and just sweep up ... well, what was the point of that?

But there was another thing at work here, which you could define as the underlying theme of this stage of Beckenbauer's career, namely an indeterminate distrust towards the man combined with a common misunderstanding of his style. Schröder, his first proper biographer (as opposed to ghostwriter), referred to it as a 'dysfunctional relationship between the football fan and his – statistically speaking – favourite player'. Putting it bluntly, many people suspected that Beckenbauer's vociferous demands to be 'the last man', as the sweeper position was sometimes called, simply sprang from his innate laziness.

Accusing Beckenbauer of, to use Schröder's expression again, 'retiring from working life' at twenty-three years of age sounds absurd, but you have to remember that only the Munich writers (and fans) had seen him interpret the libero role as a box-to-box position every weekend. By his standards, he had been very cautious against Brazil and Mexico, not only because he hated the idea of a gloating Schulz, but also because he knew there was no Bayern defender in the national team who would immediately and quietly slip into the place on the pitch he'd just vacated. It was simply very difficult for a contemporary football fan or writer to imagine that one could play as a centre-half and run just as much, if not more, as a midfielder.

Even a former footballer like Hamburg's Gerhard Krug, now turned journalist, argued in print that 'Beckenbauer has grown out of his *Sturm und Drang* phase sooner than most talents. He has bid farewell to unconditional commitment; even five-figure sums are no longer enough to bring him out of his shell and make him take unreasonable risks.' When Schön, in 1971, at long last gave in and let the Kaiser have his way, his weary explanation was telling indeed. 'Beckenbauer in midfield was always my greatest wish for the national team. I have come to realise that this dream will remain unfulfilled, because Franz just doesn't have the kind of fighting spirit you need in this position.'

In late 1968, however, Schön had not yet resigned himself to the fact that the Giesing chap would never locate his inner grafter. And so Beckenbauer reluctantly had to shuffle back into midfield, mumbling curses to himself. There was never any real danger he would carry out his threat of prematurely retiring from the national team, not least because one of his most important business partners would have been very unhappy about that. Actually, it was more than just a partner. Over the years, Beckenbauer's business ties with Adidas had evolved into an intimate relationship. One day, this entanglement of friendship and finances would play a role in spoiling his reputation, but for now the alliance was mutually lucrative. The endorsement deal paid well, while it's not taking things too far to say that Beckenbauer was instrumental in the company's rise from a shoe manufacturer to a sportswear giant. After all, the tracksuit model 'Franz Beckenbauer', issued in 1967, was the very first item of apparel Adidas ever marketed.

The company, based just north of Nuremberg, was also practically synonymous with the West German national team, although the story behind this symbiotic relationship is to this day shrouded in controversy and mystery. In 1948, brothers and business partners Adolf and Rudolf Dassler had a massive falling-out, maybe over a woman, maybe over politics, maybe over recognition or the lack thereof, maybe just because their joint company had become too small for their egos. In any case, each set up his own firm. Adi Dassler formed Adidas, while his brother launched Puma. Since they had been producing sports shoes for more than twenty years together, they both knew Sepp Herberger well, and of course both of them were interested in supplying the national team.

There are many theories as to why and how Adi beat Rudi to it, but the story told by former Puma employee Georg Hetzler in 2007 seems to be the most plausible. 'In 1950, Herberger came to us and made some steep demands on Rudolf, our boss,' Hetzler told writer Michael Ashelm. 'He wanted money on top of the Puma equipment he got for free. When our employer refused, Herberger left the house and walked over to Adidas.' (It was literally a walk, as only a river separated Adidas's headquarters from Puma's.) Hetzler added that even in the run-up to the 1954 World Cup, often seen as the one single event that sent Adidas into the stratosphere, half of Herberger's players were still wearing Puma shoes. 'Adidas then bought them, one by one,' Hetzler surmised. 'That's the only explanation I have for why they suddenly all changed suppliers.'

Some sixteen years later, when West Germany were travelling to Mexico for another World Cup, the ties between company and team had become so strong that every player was wearing Adidas boots and tracksuits, though they were not yet obliged to do so. (The kit supplier was still a company called Erima, which was eventually acquired by Adidas in

1976.) This didn't constitute a problem for Beckenbauer, of course, but quite a few members of the squad were unhappy, either because they were playing in Puma shoes at their clubs or because they wanted some compensation for endorsing Adidas live on television – or both. When the rumour made the rounds that Puma were offering players 10,000 marks per head to defect from their rivals, the tabloids reported a 'boot war' – and Schön put his foot down. 'Anyone who demands to play in a certain boot can take the first plane back home,' he said. 'An Adidas boot is as much a part of our outfit as the black shorts and the white shirt. That's how it has always been.'

It's highly doubtful whether the West Germans would have done any better in Mexico with a few Puma boots thrown in for good measure (and booty). After all, they came agonisingly close to reaching the World Cup final yet again, and for the second time in as many major tournaments they could tell themselves they had not been beaten by the opposition, only by fishy refereeing.

Under normal circumstances, the one match involving West Germany everyone would remember from this tournament should have been another clash with England, this time as early as the quarter-finals. 'Franz,' Schön told Beckenbauer before the game, 'you'll take care of Bobby Charlton again.' Before the player could protest, the national coach added: 'But you won't be marking him. Play your game, move upfield, make him follow *you*.' As Schön would later recall, he was very optimistic before the game. For one, he felt that his team's 1-0 victory over England in Hanover (through Beckenbauer's 'piledriver') had lifted a mental blockade.

Also, Schön's biggest headache before the tournament had not been the Kaiser's threat to abdicate – but Gerd Müller's.

Yes, the man they unfortunately called the Bomber had caused the biggest pre-World Cup ruckus by telling the tabloids in February that 'I don't have to go to the World Cup, you know? I might as well stay home.' The bone of contention was Schön's loyalty to the ageing Uwe Seeler. Müller felt he should be the target man, not the Hamburg striker. Ultimately, Schön found no other solution but to simply play both centre-forwards, Müller up front and Seeler in a deeplying role. Then the national coach closed his eyes and hoped against hope the two alpha males would somehow stay out of each other's way. West Germany promptly scored ten goals at the group stage. Seeler had two of them, Müller seven. Schön looked like a genius.

Until the England game, that is, because somehow he forgot to tell his team to show up. After an hour, the World Cup holders held a 2-0 lead in the stifling Mexican heat (the game kicked off at noon, when the temperature was well above forty degrees, though merciful clouds started to appear during the second half) and could have conceded a third after sixty-five minutes, when Beckenbauer gave the ball away trying to play one of his delicate passes with the outside of the foot, inviting a dangerous counter-attack. Up until this point, West Germany had mustered little more than a few half-hearted distance shots from Beckenbauer who, instead of luring Charlton out of position, had his hands full stopping England's 32-year-old midfield maestro. *Kicker* would later lament that 'Beckenbauer once more failed to win the duel with Charlton'. Yes, indeed. On one occasion, he lost possession so stupidly to the Englishman that he glanced skywards in a mixture of disappointment and shame. And yet Gladbach's coach Hennes Weisweiler, when asked for comment after the final whistle, would say that 'Beckenbauer was outstanding'.

That's because he scored West Germany's crucial first goal with a strike from just outside the box that beat the man between England's sticks, Peter Bonetti. It was one of the two moments that turned the game and the reason why almost everyone – fans and reporters – later argued England would have won if Gordon Banks had been available. (A 'foolish argument', David Downing wrote. 'Of course Banks would have saved such a shot nine out of ten times, but the same was true of Bonetti.') The second moment came barely a minute later, when Charlton was taken off. Looking back on the game years later, Alan Mullery said: 'As soon as Bobby went off, Beckenbauer was released into a more positive role.'

A famous Seeler back-header took the game to extra time, where inevitably Müller put West Germany ahead. But then Beckenbauer and his team-mates began to sit back, making the same mistake England had made after taking what looked like a commanding lead. With 'six minutes and forty-five seconds left on the clock', as the West German television commentator Wolfgang Schneider told his viewers back home, all of them presumably on the edge of their seats, Schön's side were momentarily disorganised, because Seeler was writhing on the ground (certainly in pain, but also trying to waste precious time). Play had not been halted, though, and suddenly a Norman Hunter cross from the left flank found Colin Bell near the penalty spot. The Manchester City midfielder turned defender Berti Vogts with a very sweet first touch and was about to go past Beckenbauer with his second when the Kaiser attempted a tackle that was as desperate as it was late. He missed the ball but not Bell's legs. Miraculously, the Argentinian referee did not point to the spot and West Germany had their revenge for 1966.

This quarter-final may have been a bona-fide classic, but

it was quickly overshadowed by West Germany's semi-final against Italy, which J. L. Manning called 'the most remarkable game I have seen anywhere in 40 years', before going on to make that comparison of the Bavarian Beckenbauer, who had avoided the draft by bringing a child into this world before he was eighteen, with a Prussian officer. Italy took an early lead, then the Germans scored their traditional last-minute goal – through sweeper Schnellinger, no less. For the second time in just three days, Schön's team had to go the full distance of 120 minutes, and it was simply too much. There were five more goals in extra time, three for Italy and only two for the fading Germans.

However, many observers felt that it was not a question of stamina. 'The turning point was unquestionably the foul on Beckenbauer,' Brian Glanville opined. 'He had been brutally chopped down, not for the first time in the game, while in full, spectacular flight towards the Italian goal, accelerating with that sudden, irresistible power and grace which are so much his own.' This happened on sixty-five minutes, only moments after Overath's strike from thirteen yards had clipped the crossbar. Beckenbauer was fouled by Pierluigi Cera, who was standing on the line of the box, which is probably how he knew it wasn't going to be a penalty. The Kaiser – remember, the man who lacked the fighting spirit to be a real midfielder – dislocated his shoulder but played on.

Still, according to most German players, officials and reporters, the team was not beaten because the players were tired or because a key member was handicapped. During the break before extra time, Müller walked over to Beckenbauer and simply said: 'We are being robbed.' At that point, all German players were convinced they should have had three penalties, including Cera's cynical foul on the Kaiser because it was very difficult to spot that it happened outside the box. The other two claims were valid, though. After seventeen minutes, a trademark Beckenbauer solo run that began just a few yards into the opposition's half ended in the Italian penalty area, where Giacinto Facchetti, of all people, tripped him.

With twenty minutes of the regular ninety to go, substitute Sigfried Held saw his shot from an angle blocked just in front of the goal line by Facchetti. As Seeler lunged for the rebound, Mario Bertini brought him down. 'That's a penalty,' ITV's Hugh Johns exclaimed. 'That must be a penalty!' But again referee Arturo Yamasaki waved play on. 'If that isn't a penalty, then I've never seen one,' Johns huffed, and he had plenty of company. The next day, the front page of *Kicker*, certainly one of the least sensationalist magazines in the world of football, screamed: 'The referee screwed our team!' (Yamasaki, of Japanese descent, was born in Peru but represented Mexico at the time of the tournament.)

The drama in Mexico City meant that the last three tournaments had resulted in heartbreak (twice) and infamy (once) for the West Germans. The latter befell the team in October of 1967, when a scoreless draw in Albania – which has entered the country's history books as the *Schmach von Tirana*, the disgrace of Tirana – knocked Schön's side out of the inaugural European Championship at the qualifying stage. Beckenbauer had missed this game due to a dodgy ankle, while Maier and Müller were rested. It was an early indication how much the national team needed the Munich players in order to have success, a development that would be accelerated in the months following the 1970 World Cup, when Schön not only added another three Reds to his squad, but also adopted the system Bayern used. In a way, it all went back to a conversation between Schwan and Beckenbauer in November 1969.

That was the month when Branko Zebec told the club's board that he would not extend his contract, due to expire at the end of the season. (Some say Zebec didn't get along with Neudecker, others claim he resented Schwan's presence on the bench almost as much as the business manager's reluctance to spend money in the transfer market.) As Bayern's technical director, it was Schwan's task to find a new coach, which is why he asked someone for advice who not only knew more about football than he did, but who would also have to work under this coach: his own client. And what did Beckenbauer reply after giving the matter a few minutes of thought? 'Well, what about Udo Lattek?'

It was a baffling suggestion. Lattek was not yet thirty-five years old. He had never played professional football; in fact, he'd worked as a PE teacher in two small towns near Cologne before accepting an offer to join the DFB. Now he was coaching the national youth teams – and, crucially, serving as an assistant to national manager Schön. That's why Beckenbauer knew and rated him. All the players liked Lattek, who was the total opposite of Zebec. Before November was over, Bayern sent Beckenbauer to Cologne to have a word with him. 'I'm speaking on behalf of the board of Bayern Munich,' the player explained. 'They want to know if you'd be interested in coaching the team.'

Stunned, Lattek hesitated for a moment. He had been Schön's assistant coach since April 1965 and, according to the unwritten rules under which the DFB operated, this meant he was being groomed for the main job and was set to become national coach as soon as Schön retired, either in four or eight years' time. Still, Beckenbauer's offer was the chance of a lifetime. The highly ambitious Lattek knew he had to grab it with both hands, even if that meant jumping in at the deep end. He told Beckenbauer that, yes, he would be interested in succeeding Zebec.

It wasn't the last time the Kaiser found a coach for his club, but this one came with a bonus. Or rather with two of them. Not long after the chat with Beckenbauer, Lattek packed his bags and travelled to a small town south of Hanover, where his national under-19 team would be playing Denmark. On a frozen pitch, West Germany went ahead after thirteen minutes. The goalscorer represented TSG Ulm and his name was Uli Hoeness. In the second half, Lattek brought on a player from Freilassing, very close to the Austrian border, called Paul Breitner. (Also, playing in midfield was a lad called Rainer Bonhof, who until recently had held Dutch citizenship.) The game ended 1-1.

After the match, Lattek approached Hoeness and pleaded with him to not sign a pre-contract with any of the umpteen Bundesliga clubs who were courting him. 'Wait just a little bit longer before you commit yourself,' Lattek said, and Hoeness promised he would. Fewer than three weeks later, Robert Schwan parked his car in front of the Hoeness family's butcher's shop in Ulm to make the young player an offer. Hoeness would later say that he liked Schwan's no-nonsense manner. And, of course, the fact that the business manager told him Lattek would be the Reds' new coach.

In January, Hoeness announced he would become a Bayern player. His close friend Breitner soon followed suit. Thus Beckenbauer's inspired idea decisively changed the face of both his club and the national team, as Hoeness and Breitner would not only quickly break into Bayern's first team, but also win their first international caps in the run-up to Euro 1972. These were not just good players; they were also welcome allies in the Kaiser's fight for his libero throne. Even more important was a third Bayern player. He was also arguably the most unlikely German international ever.

In the spring of 1971, the Beckenbauer debate was still in full flight, along the tired old lines. But it wasn't taking place just on coaches' benches and editorial pages. *Kicker* could have devoted a whole section to readers' letters that addressed this matter of national interest. Not untypical was a tirade from one Gustav Schalensyk in Ludwigsburg, who ranted that Beckenbauer 'is no midfielder and no defender – because he is yellow. Whenever the going gets tough, he ducks out. Into the libero role!' Gerhard Stelzer, a resident of Köndringen near Freiburg, felt the same: 'The reason Beckenbauer wants to be the libero is his complacency. He has admitted that it's annoying to being closely man-marked in midfield.' Bernd Möhlenbruch from Hennef was less critical of the Kaiser's mettle, but argued that 'any manager who has a world-class libero like Schnellinger at his disposal will choose to play Beckenbauer in midfield'.

Helmut Schön even asked Bayern coach Lattek to move the player into midfield so that he wouldn't have to juggle roles all the time (Lattek politely but firmly rebuffed this meddling in the club's affairs). Finally, in March 1971, Schön travelled to Munich to watch Bayern play Liverpool in the Fairs Cup. After the game, he spent the evening in the Kaiser's imperial home in Munich Solln. While watching highlights from the European Cup game between Celtic and Ajax, the two men talked football. Neither of them ever disclosed what exactly was spoken, but later comments leave little doubt that the following arguments were exchanged.

'Franz,' Schön said, 'you became an international star in 1966. As a midfielder.'

'You have four potential sweepers,' Beckenbauer replied. 'Schulz, Schnellinger, Gladbach's Klaus Sieloff and me. I'm by far the youngest, time is on my side.'

This point was a thinly veiled reference to the fact that West Germany had been awarded the 1974 World Cup. Schulz would be almost thirty-six then, Schnellinger thirty-five, Sieloff thirty-two. Schön had a little over three years left to build a team for the tournament on home soil. When would he start?

There was no public statement after this one-on-one, but the events of the following months seem to suggest that Schön decided to grant Beckenbauer a trial period, while thinking about ways to tweak the team according to his needs. When the West Germans lined up for a Euro qualifier in Turkey four weeks after this late-night conversation, Beckenbauer was the sweeper. The next international, in June, was another qualifier, this time against Albania. Beckenbauer was the libero again, while Sieloff was used as the *Vorstopper*.

Only few languages have a proper equivalent for this idiosyncratic German word, mainly because it describes an idiosyncratic position, peculiar to the old sweeper system. It translates as 'pre-stopper' and essentially refers to the centre-back in front of the libero – the stopper before the stopper, if you will. His main job was to closely guard the other team's centre-forward, but under certain circumstances he had to do more. Those circumstances arose if and when the sweeper had ants in his pants and felt the sudden urge to go on an exploration trip. Then the *Vorstopper* had to plug the gaps and holes. Ideally, he had mastered telepathic communication with his sweeper.

Now, against Albania, Schön gave a debut to a 23-year-old player who was born in Munich and had gone to school 300 yards away from Bayern's training ground. However, that didn't mean that Georg Schwarzenbeck was born to be a footballer. He was tall and heavy and had to work hard on his technique. He was not very fast and not a gifted dribbler. Everybody who first saw him described him as 'angular'. In fact, the renegade author Wolf Wondratschek wrote a poem about him that included the lines: 'How strange that someone/Square like an empty box of sweets/Can hit something that is round.'

Put differently, he was the exact opposite of Beckenbauer in most every regard, the beast to his beauty. And yet he became, in the words of writer Christoph Bausenwein, 'the Kaiser's life insurance', not least because his appearance was deceptive. Even renegade authors don't write poems about talentless klutzes. Schwarzenbeck could play, he could read a game – and he could even score, as he would famously prove on the night when Bayern's rise to global stardom was nearly nipped in the bud.

First of all, though, he became the Kaiser's most trusted foot soldier, not only in Bayern Munich's red and white, but also in West Germany's black and white. As early as June 1971, after an international in Sweden, journalist Hans Fiederer predicted that 'the days are not far away when people will demand that if Beckenbauer is the libero, Schwarzenbeck must be the stopper'. In other words, Dieter Danzberg may have discovered Beckenbauer, the libero, but Schwarzenbeck certainly crowned him. Which makes it all the more intriguing that, in what history insists was their greatest game, this perfectly attuned duo became a trio.

*

'This was so long ago, I have forgotten most of the details,' Günter Netzer says from his home in Switzerland. It's true, half a century has passed. But once he starts talking about it, the memories come back. 'I remember saying to Franz: "We can consider ourselves lucky if we don't concede five goals today." That was right before the game. See, the preconditions were anything but perfect. We were missing many injured players.'

The game in question was, of course, the first leg of the Euro 1972 quarter-finals against England at Wembley. Ten years ago, the German weekly *Sport Bild*, which bills itself as the biggest sports magazine in Europe, voted this the greatest match ever involving a German national team (ahead of, gasp, the Miracle of Berne!). But Netzer is right, hardly anything indicated a magic night. Things were so bad that Schön had little choice but to go with two inexperienced youngsters, Hoeness and Breitner. Wolfgang Overath, Berti Vogts and Wolfgang Weber were all sidelined, while Netzer himself was still feeling the effects of a pulled muscle but had to grit his teeth and play.

In the team's training camp, Netzer approached Beckenbauer and suggested they try something new. 'I had perfected this interplay with Hans-Jürgen Wittkamp at Gladbach,' he says. 'I would often be man-marked in midfield, so I dropped deep, luring my marker out of position, and then Wittkamp would use this space and move upfield.' Netzer now wanted to try the same with Beckenbauer, who was, after all, a trained midfielder and attacker (just like Wittkamp, who had joined Gladbach in the summer of 1971).

The relationship between the footballers Beckenbauer and Netzer, who liked each other as people, within the national team could at times be very complicated. The reader may recall the Kaiser's extremely nonchalant free-kick against Norway, which writer Horst Vetten compared to a circus act. Well, this was actually a set-piece that Netzer was supposed to take. The Gladbach playmaker tended to celebrate such occasions (turning them into what Vetten called a 'pompous ritual') and he was also taking his time in Oslo when suddenly Beckenbauer, standing next to Netzer, chipped the ball over the wall and into the back of the net. Netzer would later say that this was akin to 'throwing down the gauntlet' to him, but ten months later, in the build-up to the England game, this impudence was forgiven, though not forgotten.

Beckenbauer agreed to Netzer's plan, while Schön supposedly just said: 'Just do what you think is right, I don't mind.' It seems hard to believe that the national manager would cede control of what happened on the pitch so casually, but, Netzer says, 'as a coach, Schön was a genius. He always knew what he had to do. And sometimes all he had to do was keep us in good spirits.' The interplay between Beckenbauer and Netzer which Schön so quickly rubber-stamped came to be known in Germany as *Ramba Zamba*, a colloquial expression meaning hurly-burly. On the pitch, it meant that it was not Beckenbauer's trusted deputy Schwarzenbeck who would slot into the libero position once the Kaiser had decided to survey the premises but Netzer, a man normally so averse to tracking back that his Gladbach team-mate Herbert Wimmer was known as his personal 'water carrier'. But desperate times call for desperate measures.

The ninety minutes that followed have taken on such huge mythic proportions – in Germany, where the country's first-ever win on English soil is still the stuff of legend, but also in England, where people watching on television marvelled at, in the words of Jon Spurling, 'Netzer's and Beckenbauer's creative, blue-sky thinking' – that we often forget how close the game actually was. The score still stood at 1-1 going into the eighty-fourth minute when the visitors won a penalty, which Banks almost saved. The third goal came only two minutes from time. Still, there was no doubt that the much better team had prevailed. In his book about the history of English-German football encounters, David Downing says that 'the Germans had won 3-1, a score line which flattered their second-half performance but which hardly did justice to the gulf in quality which had marked the first half'.

Covering the match for *The Times*, Geoffrey Green admiringly said about Schön's players that 'they have an infinite variety to their game as they stroke the ball around in a flood of angles on the ground and in the air. It is like light being fed through a prism.' And that was the great legacy of the rainy Wembley night, that the Germans had found ways to beat you that went way beyond their traditional never-say-die attitude and opportunism. They could now outplay anyone who came their way. Netzer was one symbol of this, the other was that Red who was so yellow he always ducked out. Ron Greenwood had been right all along when he said that 'a libero should lead from the back and that is why it is a specialist's job – a job that wouldn't be wasted on the best player in the side. Franz Beckenbauer was the first and the finest.'

The return game in Berlin was as forgettable as the first leg had been memorable, an ill-natured 0-0. Still, it earned West Germany a trip to the four-team finals for the trophy in Belgium, these being the days before European Championships became nearly as bloated as World Cups, not to mention the monstrosity known by the misnomer Champions League. Having knocked out England, Schön's team entered the mini-tournament as overwhelming favourites, because the other three teams were not Italy, Sweden or the up-and-coming Dutch, but Belgium, Hungary and the Soviet Union, who the Germans had just expertly dissected in the official opening game of the Olympic Stadium in Munich, winning 4-1.

In fact, during the press conference before the finals, Beckenbauer was asked if West Germany were now the best team in the whole world. 'I don't know about that,' the Kaiser replied diplomatically. 'All I can say is that this is the best Germany side since I joined the team in 1965.' (In those days, the West German players and reporters always referred to the team as 'Germany', just as if East Germany didn't exist – which, technically, it didn't for them, because the Federal Republic never officially recognised the Democratic Republic on the other side of the Wall.)

Everything went wrong on the way to Antwerp the day before the semi-final against the hosts. An unannounced NATO military air exercise meant that the team had to sit and wait on their plane for ninety minutes before they could take off from Frankfurt and fly to Brussels. In the Belgian capital, the team coach got stuck in rush-hour traffic, then got lost. When the team at long last arrived in Antwerp, all roads to the ground were blocked by broadcasting vans. The players then walked over to the stadium, where they found the dressing rooms locked because they were so late.

The football, though, was never really going to be a problem. 'Our team played together like a club side,' Beckenbauer says in the official UEFA documentary, and of course it almost was – not just for him, because there were no fewer than five other Bayern players (Maier, Müller, Breitner, Hoeness and Schwarzenbeck), but for once also for Netzer, because just as many of his Gladbach team-mates were in the squad (Vogts, Bonhof, Wimmer, striker Jupp Heynckes and reserve goalkeeper Wolfgang Kleff).

In the semis, Belgium were tenacious and physical opponents, and Maier was forced into a couple of fine saves. Most reports simply say that the much more talented team deservedly won this game, which is probably true, but the 2-1 scoreline does reflect how close the game suddenly became in the closing stages. With seconds left on the clock, Erwin Vandendaele's header from a corner went wide of the left-hand post. 'We weren't necessarily the better team on the night,' Beckenbauer told UEFA's film crew, looking back. 'We just had more luck.'

The final, by comparison, was one-sided, and not only on the pitch. 'We came out and the entire stadium was full of German flags,' the Ukrainian midfielder Volodymyr Troshkin recalled. There was also the memory of the crushing defeat in Munich only three weeks earlier, which is why Troshkin added that he 'didn't have any confidence we could win, except through some sort of luck'. But before an hour had been played, West Germany were 3-0 up. Soon, hundreds or maybe thousands of delirious German fans began to circle the pitch, standing so close to the touchline that throw-ins became impossible. 'It felt as if the whole of Germany was in that stadium,' Troshkin said. When the final whistle rang, the pitch invasion was jubilant but peaceful. All the supporters wanted to do was celebrate their team's second major trophy – and of course the wonderful football, which even an East German match report had to describe as 'modern and attractive'.

The stupenduous 1972 side is most closely associated with Netzer, mainly because it would be his one moment of international glory, as injuries and squabbles with Schön hampered the remainder of his West Germany career. Yes, Netzer was the soul and the heart, but Beckenbauer was the brain – and also the captain. He had first been given the iconic armband in April 1971, when Overath was unavailable (the Cologne midfielder having taken over the captaincy from the retired Seeler). But after the European Championship, the Kaiser would always lead the national team out on to the pitch.

What he didn't know was that he would soon be asked to lead the side in other ways as well. Because the next big tournament, a mere two years after the free-flowing and fun-filled Euro 1972, would be very, very different. It would be full of rancour, tension and in-fighting, and would teeter on the brink of the abyss – until the libero felt he had no choice but to take over the team.

LIFE I

Chapter Five

When Udo Lattek lured Paul Breitner and Uli Hoeness to Munich, Bayern became a different club. That was partly because of the two players' characters, as they were brash, smart and fuelled by the arrogance of youth, and partly because Beckenbauer had unwittingly tilted the balance of power ever so slightly when he suggested this new coach. It was only natural that Lattek would have a special relationship with the two youngsters he had nurtured and then, for all practical purposes, signed.

Beckenbauer may not have written his best-selling 1975 memoir by himself, but most of the sentiments expressed in the book were certainly his. 'Lattek should have been grateful to me – and for a few years he was,' the Kaiser complained. 'I even called him Udo. But later Lattek told me: "It would be better if you'd call me Mr Lattek again." He wanted more. Encouraged by Paul Breitner, who like himself resented the fact that Gerd Müller, Sepp Maier and I were the centre of attention, Lattek prepared a mutiny – against business manager Robert Schwan and myself.'

This may sound like paranoia creeping in, but it wasn't. Many years later, in 1979, Breitner would describe the Bayern Munich of the early 1970s as one never-ending internal strife. 'It was group against group, everyone against everyone,' he told *Kicker*. 'The only reason it worked was because we had success.' Whatever happened to the family atmosphere Čik Čajkovski had so carefully cultivated? Some of Breitner's lines still send shivers down the reader's spine: 'If Sepp had not been making his jokes all the time, this whole conglomeration would have been unable to bear. There was no room for any feelings.' Without any detectable sense of irony, he then described his friendship with Hoeness as 'an oasis in the desert', as if he and his chum had been innocents abroad instead of fast learners in the art of intrigue.

Of course, it wasn't just the arrival of Lattek, Hoeness and Breitner that caused all those rifts; it was also the curse of success and the trappings of fame. 'Beckenbauer and Schwan were sacrosanct, invulnerable, inaccessible,' Breitner continued in his description of the club he joined. 'They did just as they pleased. Franz enjoyed many privileges.' That he still found all this venom inside him almost a decade after the fact tells you something about the man – but primarily gives you an idea of how jealous he and Hoeness must have been. And probably with good reason. Even Müller, who by general consensus worshipped the ground on which the Kaiser walked, sometimes felt marginalised, which was one reason he regularly toyed with the idea of a move. As early as September 1971, he told *Bild*: 'I will always be in Beckenbauer's shadow. At some other club, I would have the chance to be the number one. Financially as well.'

Ah, the money. The players wanted more, rightfully so, but where was it going to come from? In those days before television deals and merchandising, a club had only two sources of income. One was membership fees. Bayern had made the occasional concerted effort to increase their number, reaching 8,000 in 1967, which translated into fees of 400,000 marks. (One of the newly recruited members that year was Franz Josef Strauss, the politician whom Beckenbauer admired so much.) The other source was gate money. Bayern easily played around ninety games per season, sometimes more, because Schwan arranged countless friendlies. He thought nothing of jetting off to Brussels or Barcelona in between two Bundesliga games to pocket cash. The players didn't really mind this hectic schedule; they understood very well the money would go into their coffers, not the club's, as Bayern made almost no profit at all during these years with everything being reinvested back into the team. Still, the financial rewards didn't make all that travelling less draining.

By the way, the term 'pocketing cash' is not a metaphor, as Müller's biographer Hans Woller explained. 'The amount of income from the friendlies at home and abroad remained a well-kept secret. Contemporary witnesses cited large sums of marks and dollars, which Robert Schwan always collected in cash and never properly entered into the accounting books. After an extensive tour through South America with many games, he wrote a profit of only 5,000 marks into the books. The lion's share of these illegal revenues directly went to the players.' One day, Schwan's tendency to take liberties with the tax laws would come back to haunt him and his most prominent client.

For the time being, though, this client made good money and spent it, although not always wisely. In November 1970, Beckenbauer acquired a new nickname, one much less admiring than 'Kaiser'. A Hamburg newspaper printed a photo that showed him wearing a stylish and expensive midi coat with high leather boots (plus that controversial moustache we've already mentioned). The caption quoted an unnamed member of 1860 Munich as saying: 'He looks like the Cockalorum from Giesing.' People called him this – *der Gockel von Giesing* – not only behind his back but also in print, and the mockery would only increase over the years, as Beckenbauer began to move in circles that were considered alien to footballers and developed an interest in activities not normally associated with athletes.

The Beckenbauers had become good friends with the actor Joachim Fuchsberger and the opera singer Karl Helm. The couple took dancing and piano lessons together. As the *Bild* tabloid marvelled, 'Franz Beckenbauer is now a gentleman from tip to toe. He has taken up horseback riding. He has left his humble beginnings far behind him. He is reading books by Erich Maria Remarque and Heinrich Böll. *The Godfather* is almost too trivial for him.'

Helmut Schön, the son of an art dealer, often made a point of taking the national team to the theatre, but he always picked the light fare, usually boulevard comedies, so as not to irritate his players. Mr and Mrs Beckenbauer, though, had already progressed beyond the playhouse. They went to the tradition-laden ballet festival week in Munich and soon they would even be seen at the pinnacle of German high art, the Richard Wagner Festival in Bayreuth. However, their most public societal appearance came in March 1973, when the two accepted an invitation to the Vienna Opera Ball. It was a high-profile social event always covered live on Austrian and Bavarian television.

During the broadcast, Brigitte and Franz were interviewed separately. Asked about their marriage, Brigitte said her husband was still the same man she'd met all those years ago, poignantly adding that it was 'a pity that so few people realise this'. She also said she always attended the football games and would often go to the terraces in disguise rather than to the VIP area because 'it's interesting to hear what the regular people there have to say'. When she was asked if it was true that she was the driving force behind the couple's cultural activities, Brigitte replied: 'Well, I think an interest in the arts had always been lying dormant in him. I may have kindled it.'

Her husband, meanwhile, resplendent in full evening dress, was sweating profusely during the interview, but not because he was nervous in this setting, rather because he had just been dancing in the insufficiently ventilated opera house. The Kaiser said that he had already been to four balls in Munich this season, though of course these couldn't be compared to the famous Vienna Opera Ball. The interviewer, a distinguished Austrian called Heinz Fischer-Karwin, who had cultivated an air of subliminal snootiness, could have been expected to be condescending towards Beckenbauer. After all, this was the early 1970s – footballers were still not supposed to mingle with aristocrats and artists. (Hoeness and Breitner, both A-level students who would have gone to university had there been win bonuses and endorsement deals for academics, were just beginning to break the mould.) But Fischer-Karwin seemed genuinely interested in Beckenbauer. He even asked questions about football. 'What is your pre-diction for the game between Ajax and Bayern?' he wanted to know. 'For me, Ajax are the best club side in Europe,' Beckenbauer replied. 'We have to make sure we don't lose the first leg in Amsterdam by too big a margin.'

Five days later, Beckenbauer met Johan Cruyff for the first time. It was 0-0 at half-time, but then the roof fell in.

Ajax won 4-0, practically knocking the reigning Bundesliga champions out of the European Cup even before their home leg. A few hours later, Sepp Maier opened the window of his hotel room in Amsterdam and threw his entire kit – shorts, shirt and, most forcefully, his gloves – into the canal below. The goalkeeper, convinced he should have saved at least three of the goals, then told a few reporter friends he would give up the game and go looking for a proper job. A furniture dealer promptly took Maier up on this offer, but either the 3,000 marks per month the man could tender were not enough or the goalkeeper had managed to calm down, because he continued between the sticks.

This was a wise decision. On the first Saturday in May 1973, Bayern Munich defended their league title with four games to spare, earning themselves another shot at the European Cup. It turned out to be a campaign that set a lot of precedents. For a much larger part of the 1970s than people think, Bayern would struggle in the league, usually ceding the title to their new rivals Gladbach, while finishing as absurdly low as tenth in 1975, seventh in 1977 or even twelfth in 1978. It was an entirely different story when the real fleshpots were at stake, though – meaning Europe, where the Reds became all but unbeatable. Truth be told, though, it wasn't always beautiful, let alone deserved, and it didn't win them many friends.

In the second round of the 1973-74 European Cup, Bayern were drawn against Dynamo Dresden. Since the end of the war and the division of the country, there had never been a competitive game between club sides representing West Germany and the communist East Germany (GDR), even though both countries had sent teams to the various continental cup competitions for almost twenty years. For

Neudecker, this delicate and politically charged pairing was a dream come true. Bayern's new home was the vast Olympic Stadium, an aesthetically pleasing but not very homely ground. It had been built with the Summer Olympics in mind, meaning it offered very little shelter from rain, sleet and snow. But surely everyone would come to watch this game, so the club announced that the cheapest seat on the roofless East Stand would cost 25 marks, or five times what members normally had to pay (non-members usually paid 10 marks). In his weekly column for *Kicker* magazine, editor Karl-Heinz Heimann noted: 'The two games will be the matches of the year. What a pity that Bayern are determined to turn it into the business deal of the year as well.'

Then there was the matter of the away leg. Breitner and Hoeness had represented West Germany at the 1969 UEFA Youth Tournament, held in various East German cities. Hoeness now informed his president that some Western teams had suffered from diarrhoea and that there were rumours their food had been tampered with. So the president cancelled his team's stay at a hotel in Dresden at very short notice; instead, the night before the game was spent in Hof, a Bavarian town close to the border. 'Dresden is situated 116 metres above sea level,' Neudecker told the press. 'Munich is 567 metres above sea level. This difference might turn out to be detrimental to our performance and two days in Dresden do not suffice to acclimatise ourselves.' Nobody informed the East German fans who were waiting in front of the hotel to catch a glimpse of their idols from the West. There were at least 500 of them; some reports speak of as many as 1,000.

Bayern were not winning any popularity contests, but at least they won the tie, though the aggregate score of 7-6 was nothing the well-paid capitalists could be proud of. Still, six months later they found themselves in the final against Atlético Madrid in Brussels. The game would be fairly emblematic of the team's entire European campaign, because once again Bayern were the younger and better side, but puzzlingly failed to perform. (In the first round, they had even needed a penalty shoot-out to squeeze past Swedish part-timers Atvidabergs FF.)

With less than a minute of extra time remaining and Atlético defending a 1-0 lead, Beckenbauer was in possession, ten yards inside the Spanish half. His team-mate Jupp Kapellmann signalled for him to hoof the ball upfield, but of course the Kaiser would never stoop so low. However, what he did instead was curious. Beckenbauer didn't try to find Müller or Hoeness. He passed the ball to Schwarzenbeck, who was walking – yes, *walking* – through midfield. The defender collected the ball and accelerated. Then he looked up to see where the goal was. Legend has it that he heard two distinct but very different shouts. 'No!' a panicking Müller yelled. 'Don't shoot!' But Beckenbauer screamed: 'Just shoot!' In any case, Schwarzenbeck had already made up his mind. He struck from almost thirty yards. The next thing he knew was that Beckenbauer jumped into his arms. There are people who say it was the most important goal in Bayern Munich's history. Two days later, the team won the replay in great style, 4-0.

In early 1975, the long-simmering conflict between Beckenbauer and the Lattek-Breitner-Hoeness triumvirate escalated into open tabloid warfare. Udo Lattek had just been fired by Bayern, fewer than eight months after becoming the first coach to win the European Cup with a German club. His successor was Beckenbauer's old friend and best man,

Dettmar Cramer. You didn't have to be a genius to put one and one together, at least that's how Paul Breitner saw it, who was now playing for Real Madrid (not even two years after famously being photographed studying the *Beijing Review* under a portrait of Chairman Mao).

While being interviewed in Spain, Breitner accused Beckenbauer of having been the driving force behind the sacking of Lattek and the recruitment of Cramer. While he was at it, he also claimed that the Kaiser had thrown Hoeness out of the national team during the World Cup and was jealous of him, Breitner. Oh, and he said in so many words that Beckenbauer was his wife's puppet.

The Kaiser immediately hit back, telling *Bild* that 'Breitner is spreading insults, plain lies. If he doesn't stop, I'll put my lawyers onto him.' Warming to the subject, he added that 'character has never been one of Breitner's strengths. I suppose it has never been said this directly, but my team-mates and I breathed a sigh of relief when we learned that he had been sold to Madrid.'

Now it was Breitner's turn again. Talking to the illustrated weekly *Quick*, he retorted: 'Only my friends or people who know me really well can make a point about my character. And Franz doesn't know me well enough. Actually, I came to realise I have never known him at all.' Despite this new-found insight, he went on to share his own character analysis with the magazine. 'I consider Beckenbauer the phlegmatic type. He wants to be left in peace because he has his hands full with his fame.'

It's unlikely this sentence earned him a cease and desist letter from Beckenbauer's lawyers, because the Kaiser would have been the first to admit there was a lot of truth to it. In fact, during long talks with the award-winning political journalist Hermann Schreiber, trying to explain why his friend and agent Schwan was making all business decisions for him, Beckenbauer had described himself as 'unstable' just a few months earlier. The resulting profile appeared in *Der Spiegel* in June 1974 and was headlined 'A rather displaced hero'. Schreiber had encountered 'an impeded romantic searching for himself', a man who deep down inside indeed only wanted to be left in peace.

The great irony of it all was that just as *Der Spiegel* was being delivered to the nation's newsstands, Beckenbauer had not for the first time become the leopard who changed his spots, because if need be, he could morph into this other Beckenbauer. Not the romantic but the realist. Not the phlegmatic type but the go-getter. Not the man who wanted to be left in peace but the leader who made the decisions. And Breitner should have known this better than anyone, because he was there on one of the two most famous occasions this alternative Kaiser came forth – not to mention that it might have saved Breitner's hide.

The place was another Sportschule, this one in Malente, some sixty miles north of Hamburg. That's where West Germany set up their training camp for the first half of the 1974 World Cup on home soil. It felt more like a prison camp, though. Following the terrorist attack during the 1972 Olympics that had cost nine Israeli athletes, coaches and officials their lives, and in view of the danger posed by the Red Army Faction terrorist group, the police had intensified their security precautions. They patrolled the premises at Malente with guard dogs, and there were sharp-shooters and helicopters everywhere.

However, that wasn't the main reason why the mood among the twenty-three-man squad was bad, very bad, on

8 June, just five days before the opening game of the tournament. The reason was money. The DFB had offered the players 30,000 marks each for winning the trophy, which sounded fine – until you read in the papers that the Italians stood to make four times as much. The players debated the matter, decided they wanted at least 75,000 marks and told their captain to conduct the negotiations.

It was probably not what an 'unstable' man (not in the sense of mentally unstable, of course, but double-minded) like Beckenbauer cherished, but at 9.30 p.m., he began to bargain with the head of the delegation, the 63-year-old Hans Deckert. It was the beginning of the first of two evenings known as the 'Nights of Malente' that would see Beckenbauer in a central role – and decide the outcome of the World Cup.

Things dragged on because no real progress had been made after more than three hours of haggling. Deckert had offered 50,000 marks, the Kaiser countered with 60,000 marks, without consulting the rest of the team first. Deckert declined. Stalemate.

The national manager, meanwhile, was becoming more and more disgusted by the minute. 'All I ever hear from you is money, money, money,' Schön eventually hissed. 'That is bad form!' Then he stormed off. Upstairs, he heard Breitner bickering loudly. On the spur of the moment, Schön opened the door and told the player: 'Cut it out right now! You are undermining everything!' Then he went to his room and reportedly tried to figure out what he would have to do in order to send the entire squad home and play the tournament with the reserve side. Breitner, meanwhile, started to furiously pack his suitcase, convinced that Schön had singled him out as the ringleader of this revolution (Chairman Mao, remember?) and would throw him off the team.

While everybody was feeling the pressure, Beckenbauer was on the phone to DFB president Hermann Neuberger, bypassing Deckert. The two men settled on a bonus of 60,000 marks. Then the Kaiser informed the team of this new offer. A vote was held that resulted in a draw: eleven for, eleven against. Now all eyes were on the phlegmatic type who only wanted to be left in peace. 'We should regard this as a good-will gesture from the DFB,' Beckenbauer said. Then he voted to accept the offer. It was 1.30 a.m. The World Cup was on.

Or was it? Barely a week into the tournament, Neuberger could confidently assume he would not have to pay this lot anything, not 30,000 marks, let alone 60,000. Yes, they had won their first two group games, but the team's form was appalling. Beckenbauer, meanwhile, had to sit down to face the press and make an apology about his personal conduct. 'I'm really sorry that I have allowed myself to be provoked into this gaffe,' he said contritely. 'I can only hope people won't stop supporting us now.'

Beckenbauer's 'gaffe' had come during West Germany's lacklustre group game against Australia when he had spat in the direction of the stands after being booed for giving the ball away. The media compared his loss of temper to the day in December 1968 when he had made 'an obscene gesture' towards the crowd in Hanover and was fined 1,000 marks by the DFB. (The gesture, in case you wonder, was pretend-ing to urinate.) 'I was called a "Bayern pig" and just went ballistic,' Beckenbauer explained. 'I regret this. However, my reaction was only directed at those ten or fifteen people. I'm sorry that the other spectators felt offended.' He finished his statement by saying he was hoping to make up with the home crowd by playing well in the final group game two days later. Little did he know that this match would turn out to be one of the greatest debacles in the history of the team.

There is a conspiracy theory that says – after beating Chile 1-0 and Australia 3-0 – West Germany lost their final group game intentionally to avoid meeting the Netherlands, Brazil and Argentina in the second stage of the tournament. However, Group Three (with the Netherlands and Sweden) and Group Four (with Italy and Argentina) both completed their schedule on 23 June, which meant that their final standings weren't known when West Germany took to the pitch in Hamburg on 22 June. And even if they had known that the Dutch would top their group while the Italians would prematurely wave bye-bye to those 120,000 marks, it wouldn't have made any difference, as this was one game they could not afford to lose. The opponents were also Germans, only from the enemy half of the country.

Helmut Schön was born in Dresden, but left what he always referred to as his 'beloved home' in 1950 like a thief in the night, when he realised there would be no place for him in the Soviet-controlled GDR. We can only imagine what he felt (or perhaps we can't) when Magdeburg striker Jürgen Sparwasser scored the only goal of the only game that was ever played between West and East Germany with thirteen minutes left on the clock. While the 61,000 fans in the stands stared in stunned, shocked silence (save for the 2,000 East Germans who were allowed to leave their country because they had been handpicked by the party), Beckenbauer was the only player in white who did not lose his head. In fact, *Kicker* would even later praise his 'great game'.

A few weeks earlier, he had told Hermann Schreiber 'I'm not a German, I'm a Bavarian', but this didn't mean he wasn't aware that West Germany could not lose this game. After his team fell behind, he practically became a central offensive midfielder, tirelessly spreading the ball around. Two minutes into stoppage time, he even ran past three opponents and into the box, socks very uncharacteristically rolled down to his ankles, until a tackle stopped him. He hurried over to the sideline to take the throw-in, before angrily yelling at the ball boy who had given the ball to some other player, as if the Kaiser knew everyone was under shock but him. Eighty seconds later came the final whistle. It was 9.19 p.m.

On his way to the dressing rooms, Beckenbauer was approached by the GDR's midfielder Harald Irmscher, who offered him his shirt. The East Germans had been discouraged from swapping shirts with the class enemies, but as far as Irmscher was concerned, this only applied to an exchange on the pitch, where the whole world would witness such an outrageous act of fraternisation. Irmscher was very disappointed when Beckenbauer replied he first had to undergo the drug test, thinking his chance had passed. But later there was a knock on the door of the East German dressing room, and the Kaiser himself walked in. Irmscher has the shirt to this day.

The mood in the other dressing room was, of course, very different. Schön icily announced 'We'll have to talk about this', before walking out to give what he always called the most difficult press conference of his career. Later, back in Malente, he took Beckenbauer aside. 'Franz, you are my captain. Now you must act like one.' Then he went to his room, an ashen-faced ghost of a man, while the Kaiser joined the rest of the squad in the basement bar.

It has often been said that Beckenbauer took over the national team during the second 'Night of Malente', which is only wrong if one takes it to mean that Schön was reduced to a peripheral figure. Of course, he still called the shots. But from now on, Beckenbauer sat next to him during the press conferences and did most of the talking, while Schön would finish many of his own statements by saying something like 'Franz feels the same way'. The German coaching legend Rudi Gutendorf closely watched this double act and concluded that 'Beckenbauer is now Schön's equal'.

Schön and/or Beckenbauer made four changes for the next game, benching Hoeness among others, hence Breitner's accusation a few months later. More important than the new line-up, though, was the new attitude. It was now a different World Cup for the West Germans, although you could say they still needed help from the heavens to reach the final against the Netherlands, because after wins over Yugoslavia and Sweden, they beat Poland in a match that should never have been played. A rainstorm of biblical proportions had hit Frankfurt shortly before kick-off and the drainage just couldn't cope with the deluge. On an absurdly waterlogged pitch, the Poles' dangerous wingers literally got stuck in the mud and could do nothing but watch as Kaiser Franz booked another date with King Johan.

Few games have undergone, and maybe still do, so many changes in evaluation as the final between 'Beckenbauer's West Germany and Cruyff's Holland' (as the game is invariably billed, as if only the captains mattered). In the days directly after the hosts' 2-1 win in Munich, the jury was still largely undecided, not least because both first-half penalties seemed unclear. Was Cruyff brought down in the box by Hoeness after only fifty-three seconds – or just outside? Referee Jack Taylor was in a perfect position to judge this and he never had any doubt. (Taylor later recalled with indignation that Beckenbauer came over to him and said 'You're an Englishman', suggesting anti-German bias.) And did Wim Jansen really bring down Bernd Hölzenbein after twenty-four minutes, or was the cunning German gratefully accepting a clumsy invitation to dive? 'It was a trip or attempted trip – and that's a penalty,' Taylor always replied to this question. Müller's winning goal two minutes before the break was undisputed, which cannot be said of who deserved to win this World Cup.

After the game, the *Daily Mail* argued that 'neutrals have no doubt that the better team has lost', while the *Daily Express* said 'the Dutch were too arrogant'. Gradually, a combination thereof became the most widely held theory: the men in orange had grown too confident after taking an early lead, they allowed the Germans back into the game and were then unlucky during a dominant second half. However, a solid case can be made that the hosts were the unluckier of the two sides after the restart. On fifty-eight minutes, Müller scored a goal that Taylor disallowed, although the striker had beaten the notorious Dutch offside trap by a full yard. Even more controversial was Taylor's decision five minutes from time, when Jansen brought down Hölzenbein in the box yet again. This time it was the clearest penalty since Beckenbauer's late tackle on Colin Bell in Mexico, but Taylor waved play on.

Perhaps Scott Murray put it best when he wrote for *The Guardian* in 2008 that 'West Germany deservedly won the World Cup, though the Netherlands grabbed arguably the more precious prize, the title of People's Champions. But while it's a shame that Cruyff and Neeskens didn't get their hands on the World Cup – nobody's saying they weren't a great team – the alternative would have been far worse: no World Cup winner's medals to show for the careers of Beckenbauer, the ridiculously good Müller, Breitner, Vogts or Maier.'

Although the 1974 final would trigger a simmering resentment in the Netherlands and was the starting point for one of the fiercest rivalries in world football, the men who led the two teams not only respected each other (before and after that fateful day) but actually became friends. When Cruyff died in March 2016, Beckenbauer had withdrawn from the public eye due to the allegations surrounding Germany's World Cup bid, health issues and a personal tragedy. It meant he couldn't be reached to comment on the passing of a man he admired so much that he always used to say that 'Johan was the better player, though I'm the one who won the World Cup'. However, Beckenbauer did tweet his respects. 'I am shocked. Johan Cruyff is dead. He was not only a very good friend but also a brother to me.'

'Brother' seems a far-fetched word here, but it doesn't sound so incongruous any more when you look at the countless similarities in the lives of the two men, starting with the three European Cups they won on the trot, being filmed for a cinematic documentary in the same year (though *Nummer 14 Johan Cruijff* by Maarten de Vos was not as vilified as *Libero*) or missing the 1978 World Cup despite being still active and in good shape.

They also both left Europe for the United States before finishing their careers, bizarrely, with their hometown club's rivals – Cruyff at Feyenoord, Beckenbauer at Hamburg. They even went into management within just a few months of each other, in 1984–85, though neither had bothered to acquire the necessary coaching badges before, which is why new job titles had to be invented for them. Plus, as Cruyff once said to explain their friendship: 'We both know that life at the top is lonely.'

On the occasion of Beckenbauer's seventieth birthday in

2015, the Dutch genius spoke of him to the German magazine *11Freunde*. 'I can't say exactly when we became friends. But even when we were still playing, we instinctively had a great respect for each other and that organically grew into a friendship. We often saw each other, because I always went skiing in Kitzbühel, where Franz was living. We did sport together and then, in the evenings, sat together. Over the years, the connection became stronger and stronger.'

So, exactly when did they become friends? We can assume it did not happen as early as 1974-75. The two men may have shared a word or two during the post-final banquet at Munich's Hilton Hotel, but that legendary evening soon descended into chaos, so Beckenbauer at least will have been too distracted to rub shoulders with Cruyff. The sorry mess began when Hans Deckert asked Susi Hoeness to leave because the players' wives were not invited. An almighty quarrel ensued that saw first Müller, then Overath, plus Grabowski and finally Breitner retire from international duty. (Müller, for one, did not act on the spur of the moment. He had intended all along to step down after the World Cup because he was angry at the DFB for blocking his move to Barcelona in July 1973.)

Also, Beckenbauer was irritated by Cruyff later in 1974, though this was not the Dutchman's fault. On the penultimate day of the year, Cruyff won his third Ballon d'Or, narrowly ahead of Beckenbauer, who told the reporters: 'Well, second place isn't bad.' As if! Secretly, the Kaiser must have wondered how a player who had won both the European Cup and the World Cup in the same year could fail to be awarded the trophy. He found an answer of sorts.

In July 1975, Beckenbauer granted a Dutch weekly an interview during which he uttered a remark about Cruyff's agent (and father-in-law) Cor Coster that made it sound as if the latter had bribed the journalists who were casting votes for the Ballon d'Or. Coster went through the roof and threatened a lawsuit, which Schwan called 'ludicrous'. In the end, it turned out that Beckenbauer had phrased his lines much more carefully, saying little more than that Coster had been in touch with the writers entitled to vote. Still, Coster sent Schwan a copy of the audio tapes and asked for an apology.

At this point, Beckenbauer had one Ballon d'Or (won in 1972) to his name. Perhaps this tally was not totally in line with his class, his status, his success and his stellar reputation among his peers. After all, his team-mate Gerd Müller had lifted two. On the other hand, the Kaiser was the only defensive player since Lev Yashin in 1963 who had been awarded the trophy at all – and would remain the only one until 1996 when another German libero won it, Matthias Sammer. It was and is very difficult for a player who does not make or score goals to be properly recognised. Philipp Lahm, the best German player of his generation, couldn't even win Germany's Footballer of the Year award until he had retired and the writers suddenly noticed their oversight. So there were no two ways about it: Beckenbauer would have to win some more European Cups before they would give him the Golden Ball again.

The first of these wins became nearly as notorious in England as the 1974 World Cup final did in the Netherlands. But after knocking out another GDR side, Magdeburg, Bayern Munich first had to overcome the excellent AS Saint-Étienne in the semis. The away leg in France finished scoreless. The return match was barely sixty seconds old when Beckenbauer remembered that it was and is very difficult for a player who does not make or score goals to be properly recognised. So he did something stupendous.

In the inside-right position, the Kaiser received the ball from Hoeness, who was playing a corner short. He should have crossed into the box, but his first touch failed him (no, really, it did!), which wasted precious time. Suddenly Beckenbauer found himself surrounded by green shirts. There was no passing lane. The Kaiser turned around as if he was about to play a back pass, then he quickly turned again and darted into the box. Resembling an NFL quarterback who runs the ball because it can't be thrown, he left four defenders in his wake and then fired the ball home from a tight angle.

Five weeks later, Beckenbauer and Bayern travelled to France again for the final against Leeds United, who had eliminated Cruyff's Barcelona in the other semi-final. The game has entered the annals as the 'Shame of Paris', because Leeds fans rioted before, during and after the match ('Blood-lusting bullies crucify the name of sport,' ran the *Yorkshire Evening Post*'s headline). It has also gone down in British football lore as the night Leeds were robbed. While it's true that the team were given ample reason to feel hard done by, it must also be noted that Leeds should have been reduced to ten men after all of three minutes and fifteen seconds, when Terry Yorath brutally broke Björn Andersson's leg.

It was only the first of a great many controversial incidents. On thirty-seven minutes, Allan Clarke went past Beckenbauer in the box and the sweeper missed the ball with his tackle, instead hitting the striker's right leg. It was an obvious penalty, but the French referee Michel Kitabdjian gave a corner. In the second half, Peter Lorimer fired home a volley from twelve yards. He raised his arms and raced away to celebrate, while the Bayern players hung their heads and Maier quietly picked the ball out of the net. Then

Beckenbauer noticed something. The linesman was waving his flag. Calmly, the Kaiser raised his right arm to indicate an opponent had been offside. It was another very dubious decision, provoking enraged English fans to throw ripped-out plastic seats and bottles on to the running track and into Maier's penalty box.

Amid all this tumult and nastiness, an Englishman found the time and the composure to wax lyrical about Bayern's libero. 'Beckenbauer, always calm at the height of a crisis, smoothed the ball around the pitch like a connoisseur,' Geoffrey Green noted for *The Times*. The two Bayern players who eventually found the target, though, were those who always scored in Europe: Franz Roth and Gerd Müller. When the final whistle rang, Bayern's new coach at first seemed strangely unmoved. Dettmar Cramer just made a strange gesture, touching the side of his nose with his index finger. It was only later that he revealed this had been a secret signal for one particular person on the pitch: 'Franz responded by doing the same,' Cramer explained. 'It's something we picked up from the movie *The Sting*. It means that something has gone according to plan.'

Not quite. Not even his second consecutive European Cup could earn Beckenbauer another Ballon d'Or, as the 1975 edition of the trophy went to Oleg Blokhin. The Kaiser was again the runner-up, this time a rather distant second behind the Dynamo Kyiv forward. It seemed the German libero could not win this coveted award again for love nor money – both, by the way, obviously now handled by Schwan for his client.

Of course, the money had always been Robert Schwan's forte, and it was indeed rolling in. As early as 1971, Beckenbauer had sold that house in Solln and bought a villa in Grünwald – this time a proper one: fourteen rooms plus an outdoor swimming pool – for 1 million marks. Still, there was nothing Schwan could do about the fact he was so good at his job that Beckenbauer had long since fallen into the maximum tax bracket. 'If I remember correctly, it was fifty-six per cent at the time,' the Kaiser wrote in his fifth autobiography, published in 1992. 'But my additional income, since it went through our own company, was subject to a 73 per cent tax. Of every mark I earned with my non-footballing activities, there were only twenty-seven pfennigs left. That hurts.' It hurt so much that Schwan began to look for ways around this problem.

In the same book, Beckenbauer says a meeting was held between Schwan, himself and three politicians, among them the Bavarian minister of finance. When Schwan only half-jokingly declared that 'we might have to leave the country and go someplace where they have humane tax rates', the politicians advised them to move their company to Switzerland to save money. This is how the Kaiser described the set-up: 'The footballer Beckenbauer paid all taxes on his wages in Germany. But the business person Beckenbauer had a company in Switzerland together with Schwan that made out invoices in his name, collected the money and then sent a part of it to Munich, where it was taxed. Another part, however, remained in Swiss bank accounts, as a pension plan.'

It's just about believable that Beckenbauer honestly considered this to be legitimate. He remembered that the minister told him: 'Franz, if there ever happens to be a problem, just call me.' It sounds exactly like the sort of thing Bayern Munich officials and players would constantly hear from Bavarian party people. (Hans Woller's award-winning biography of Gerd Müller is in large parts a cold-hearted look at the long-time collusion between the club and the ruling Christian Social Union, or CSU. For instance, Woller says of Schwan that 'he entered the annals of German football – and German criminal history, though his exact place in the white-collar crime sector still remains to be determined'.) But are we really supposed to swallow that Beckenbauer's agent, too, thought this Swiss model was legal? It beggars belief. He must have known it could all blow up in their faces. He just didn't know when.

A fairly recent development, meanwhile, was Schwan's important role for Beckenbauer in matters of the heart. In July 1975, Schwan married for the third (but not the last) time, and Beckenbauer was his best man. The bride was called Marlies. Through mutual acquaintances, Marlies knew Diana Sandmann, the 26-year-old daughter of a well-known architect. Diana hoped to become a painter, having gone to art school in England, but for the time being she worked – and you can't make these things up – for a Munich picture agency as a sports photographer, which is how she happened to take photos at the wedding. Beckenbauer had had affairs before; for instance, a brief fling with the famous actress and singer Heidi Brühl during the 1974 World Cup made headlines and was never denied. But this time it was different. This time it was serious. As if Beckenbauer's life wasn't already turbulent enough, now it was also getting really complicated.

The same could be said for his club. In March 1976, Bayern received a letter from the Munich tax office. The long and the short of the legalese was that the local authorities, at the behest of the Federal Ministry of Finance, had to inform Bayern that considerable tax payments, which had previously been deferred, would become due. The German historian

Nils Havemann says this note was the result of 'growing opposition to the CSU-led state government's patronage of Bayern Munich'. To this day, we don't know exactly how serious the club's situation was, but it cannot have been good, because Bayern's tax consultant sent a letter of response to the Munich tax office in which he said he would be forced 'to dissolve the club' if the authorities demanded their money immediately and in full.

Bayern's money men – Neudecker, Schwan and club secretary Walter Fembeck – could breathe just a little bit more easily two weeks later. On 19 March, the draw for the European Cup semi-final was made in Zürich's posh Hotel St Gotthard, and Bayern were paired with none other than Real Madrid. It was not only a very lucrative tie that promised to earn the club some 1.5 million marks in gate and television money, it was also a dream come true for the media. For one, the games reunited Bayern with Breitner and his Real team-mate Günter Netzer. Then there was the fact that the Spanish giants had eliminated Bayern's domestic rivals Gladbach – coached by none other than Udo Lattek – in the quarter-finals under scandalous circumstances. (In the second leg, in Madrid, the Dutch referee had disallowed two perfectly legal Gladbach goals.) The outrage in West Germany was so intense that Bayern, of all clubs, were now called upon to help justice prevail.

Breitner missed Real's home leg through an injury, which was just as well as the 1-1 draw at the Bernabéu turned out to be controversial enough: after the final whistle, a Spanish fan ran on to the pitch, hit Müller and threw a punch at the Austrian referee Erich Linemayr, before Hoeness and Maier wrestled him to the ground. Later that evening, Breitner invited just three of his former Bayern team-mates to his villa in Madrid (no prize for guessing who wasn't among the chosen few). Two weeks later, in Munich, he and Netzer were heartily booed for the full ninety minutes, while Bayern won 2-0. Nobody who saw that match had the slightest doubt who the best player on the pitch was. The Dutch newspaper *De Telegraaf* said: 'Franz Beckenbauer – what a technique this man has in his legs! – was the undisputed master of the game.'

Despite the general consensus that Bayern's golden generation had been in steady decline for at least a year, if not more, the team had reached its third European Cup final on the trot, this one against old foes Saint-Étienne at Glasgow's Hampden Park, a location president Neudecker was unhappy about. He argued there wouldn't be enough interest in a match between French and West German sides in Scotland to sell out such a big place (at the time, the ground's capacity was 85,165). Neudecker was also worried about the scheduling. The final was played on 12 May 1976. Only three days later, Scotland were to meet England there in the British Home Championship. Bayern's boss concluded Scottish fans would save their money and rather watch the international. As it turned out, he was right – only 54,000 came out to watch the European final – but his concerns didn't exactly endear his club to the neutrals.

This, of course, was nothing new for the Reds. The same went for the script of the final, because for the third year in a row, Bayern's opponents would consider themselves rather unlucky. The French hit the crossbar twice during the scoreless first half, through Dominique Bathenay and Jacques Santini, which is why the famously bulky Hampden bars entered French football parlance that night as *les poteaux carrés* – the square posts, symbols for an underdog's undeserved defeat. And a defeat it was, because Bayern had the Bull.

On fifty-seven minutes, the West Germans won a free-kick, maybe twenty yards in front of goal. Beckenbauer stood over the ball, Franz Roth was to his right. Both men were thirty years old and had been playing on the same team for a full decade now. 'I often took free-kicks and I often scored,' says Roth. 'So Franz told me: "I'll put it past the wall and then you let rip."' Having thus given Roth his regal instructions, Beckenbauer stood like a Roman statue, erect and gracefully still, calmly waiting for the referee's signal. When it came, he gently nudged the ball to his right. Roth took a short run-up and thumped the ball into the back of the net.

It was the shot that decided the game, because Bayern were – in the words of Geoffrey Green – 'held together and orchestrated by Beckenbauer, strolling at the rear like a boulevardier wandering for his morning aperitif. Scarcely breaking perspiration, he was the hub of their side.' Yet despite such plaudits, it's safe to say this game was not the Kaiser's most memorable match of 1976, not even the most momentous final. Considering he was already a father of three, staring his thirty-first birthday in the face, and had won (almost) all there was to win, the historic games now came astonishingly thick and fast for Beckenbauer.

It started fewer than forty days after Hampden, with the final of the 1976 European Championship in Belgrade against Czechoslovakia. The game made history because it was the first time a major tournament was decided on penalties. This, however, had only been agreed upon a few hours before kick-off at the request of the DFB – which then failed to properly brief the squad. I talked to former Cologne striker Dieter Müller in 2021, whose hat-trick in the semi-final against Yugoslavia had booked the West Germans a place in this game. 'It was 2-2 after extra time, so when I came off the pitch, I was certain there would be a replay two days later. Actually, I'm sure we would have won a second game, as the Czechs were knackered. Anyway, suddenly we were told there would be a shoot-out.'

Maybe that's why Helmut Schön had such problems finding five takers. Beckenbauer, in his 100th international, said his shoulder was hurting but agreed to take the fifth penalty. Hoeness, probably thinking back to a spot-kick he had missed against Poland at the 1974 World Cup, said he would rather not. At this point, goalkeeper Maier volunteered, whereupon Hoeness changed his mind. It was 4–3 to the Czechs when he stepped up. Hoeness blasted the ball over the bar, and then Antonin Panenka beat Maier with his famous trick shot to win the trophy for the outsiders. It also meant the Kaiser never got to take his penalty. At this point, he had no idea that he would play only three more games for his country.

Everybody – including the national coach and the player himself – expected Beckenbauer to lead the team at the 1978 World Cup and only then retire from international duty before slowly seeing out a stellar club career the year after that. In fact, a few months after the Euro 1976 final, Bayern coach Cramer sat down with some journalists in Rio de Janeiro to talk about the year 1979, when the Kaiser's current contract would run out. 'We won't change our style overnight,' Cramer explained, 'though it's a mistake to think we have a second Beckenbauer waiting in the wings. Because there is none. Beckenbauer was the first player in the world who developed a whole new concept of the game. Others will have to find other ways of having success.'

Cramer and his team were in Brazil for the Intercontinental Cup. Bayern had twice declined the offer to contest this trophy, because in both 1974 and 1975, the opponents would

ULI HESSE

have been Independiente from Buenos Aires. Many European teams refused to play clubs from Argentina after some of the finals of the Intercontinental Cup had degenerated into bloody brawls in the 1960s. But now the incumbent holders of the Copa Libertadores were Cruzeiro Belo Horizonte from Brazil, and that seemed safe.

Another reason for past Bavarian reluctance was the fact that the trophy was way more prestigious in South America than in Europe, a discrepancy borne out by the attendances. Bayern's 2-0 win in the home leg was witnessed by just 18,000 people, while 113,000 came out to see the decider in Belo Horizonte four days before Christmas. Although Beckenbauer struggled with a groin strain – and in spite of the team's ridiculously stressful twenty-six-hour journey that left no time for even a nap before the kick-off – Bayern came away with a goalless draw and lifted the one major trophy that had been missing from the Kaiser's cabinet.

Who knows, this triumph may have made all the difference when the results of the Ballon d'Or voting were announced a week later. Beckenbauer finished first, ahead of the Netherlands' Rob Rensenbrink and the great Czech goalkeeper Ivo Viktor. 'I am very happy to have won this award again,' the Kaiser announced. 'I now feel completely compensated for the misfortune I've had with numerous such ballots in the past.'

Glasgow, Belgrade, Belo Horizonte – a trail of trophy games that befitted an international superstar like Beckenbauer. How strange, then, that the most significant game for him personally may have been a match in highly unfashionable Bochum that was played on 16 September 1976. It's one of the few regular Bundesliga games that has its own Wikipedia article, because the hosts were 4-0 up after fifty-three minutes – and yet the visitors won 6–5. It is still the only match in league history lost by a team that held a four-goal lead. That was one of the two reasons why Beckenbauer never forgot this day. The other was a 43-year-old man from Plymouth who followed the wild, crazy spectacle from the stands.

Clive Toye had been the chief sports writer for the *Daily Express* ten years earlier, but he was not in Bochum on journalistic duty. Rather, he was representing a quite unusual football club which he had actually named back in early 1971. The brothers Ahmet and Nesuhi Ertegun, who owned this club, first toyed with the idea of calling it the Blues, but then the man from Devon came up with the snappy 'Cosmos' – New York Cosmos, to be precise. They were currently on their second overseas tour, with stops in Paris and Antwerp, which allowed Toye, the general manager, to check out if there were players in Europe he could lure to Gotham. One player in particular.

In June, while in Yugoslavia for the European Championship, the Kaiser had told a reporter that he 'would love to play soccer for one season in the USA at the end of my career. Pelé is doing that, and it must be great. There are no tactical straitjackets and less pressure than I have here. I could just play my game, show people some imagination and tricks.' Maybe Toye noticed this interview, because the man who had famously talked Pelé into playing for his club with such a clever line – 'You can go to Spain, to Italy, and win a title, but you can come to the Cosmos and win a country' – got in touch with Schwan to test the waters.

The first news about this sensational development reached an incredulous public in early November 1976, when Pelé gave an interview in New York and let it slip that the Cosmos were in talks with Beckenbauer. The Brazilian added the only hurdle seemed to be the money, because the Kaiser's agent had asked for more than 2 million dollars. Schwan quickly quelled the fires by saying that 'there has been no offer. Beckenbauer will definitely stay in Germany until the 1978 World Cup.' He also referred to the report as 'shit news' and mentioned he had been approached by Cosmos 'one year ago'.

Only days before the story broke, Beckenbauer had sold his villa in Grünwald for 1.6 million marks to a property developer. Was it believable that the man they called the Kaiser was indeed just looking 'for something less spacious', as he told the press? Or was he already laying the groundwork for a move abroad? Or, an option not considered at the time, did he have the sneaking suspicion he would be needing cash soon?

Probably the latter. It's doubtful that Beckenbauer seriously thought about leaving Bayern and Bavaria at this point. But then the doorbell rang. It was Monday, 17 January 1977, at exactly eight o'clock in the morning. The housekeeper went to answer the door, then she came back and informed Beckenbauer, who was having breakfast with his family, that 'there are three gentlemen outside. They say they are from the inland revenue. They also say they have a search warrant.' Beckenbauer's villa was only one of sixteen homes all over Munich visited by tax inspectors on this morning, among them Robert Schwan's house and the offices of various business partners.

This in itself was bad enough, though my personal opinion is that Schwan and his client had been tipped off, hence the sale of the Grünwald villa. The bigger problem was that the tabloids had a field day with the story. They had been protecting Beckenbauer for a long time, but the one–two of substantial tax evasion (Beckenbauer eventually settled out of court for 1.8 million marks, then the equivalent of

£475,000) and the flirtation with the Cosmos, the footballing version of high treason, meant the gloves now came off.
This would also explain why the newspaper *Die Welt*, not a
tabloid but controlled by the same publishing house as *Bild*,
finally broke the news that Beckenbauer was cheating on
his wife in April – unless, of course, the rumour is true that
Schwan planted this news item to gently push his client into
welcoming American arms.

When Bayern hosted Kaiserslautern on the day after the
article appeared, the visiting fans greeted Beckenbauer with
chants of 'Whoremonger! Whoremonger!' Of course, he had
heard much worse in his thirteen years as a professional footballer. But this was not only about him. As cosmopolitan as
Munich seems, it's still part of deeply Catholic Bavaria, where
adultery is a much bigger sin than tax dodging – especially
when the guileless, innocent wife is raising three adorable
little boys. Almost half a century has passed, but the lively,
bubbly Diana Sandmann still falls momentarily quiet when
she remembers those days, a time during which people would
call her a whore on the streets of Munich. 'One day I went
shopping,' she says, 'and this woman turned around, looked
me in the eye and then spat on my shoes.'

The Cosmos was beginning to look more and more attractive. Over Easter, Beckenbauer met Toye in New York and
pretty much made up his mind during a spectacular helicopter sightseeing flight. The club were offering him 2.8 million
dollars – minus Schwan's 20 per cent cut of course – to come
and weave his magic for four years in the North American
Soccer League (NASL). However, the player was still under
contract elsewhere. Today, it would be nearly unthinkable
that a club of Bayern's stature would put obstacles in the
way of arguably its most deserving player of all time, but

Neudecker needed money. He asked for a transfer sum of 1.75 million marks. Toye countered with 1.4 million, but Neudecker didn't budge. To break the deadlock, Beckenbauer had to chip in 350,000 marks of his own money.

He played his last game for Bayern on 21 May 1977. Neudecker presented him with the club's badge of honour before the kick-off, but that was the high point of sentimentality. There was not even a lap of honour, let alone plans for a testimonial. Beckenbauer had even declined the offer of a banquet in his honour with a scathing riposte: 'If you have to part with 350,000 marks to get away from the club, you can pay for your own dinner.' It was an unworthy goodbye, but not untypical for Bayern in this era. Fewer than two years later, Gerd Müller would leave without any farewell at all, not even the polite round of applause from the fans which Beckenbauer received. In all likelihood, the Kaiser wasn't too sad about this lukewarm *au revoir*, as it simply proved he had been right in trying to leave all this behind.

The West German press assumed as a matter of course he would leave for the United States together with his family to have some peace and then patch up his marriage oversesas. They were wrong. The Kaiser had no intention at all of taking the past with him across the big pond. Like millions of people before him, Franz Beckenbauer went to the new world to begin a new life.

LIFE II

Chapter Six

On the day that he left West Germany, Franz Beckenbauer saw his father cry for the first and only time. His parents had accompanied him to Munich Airport, where roughly 400 football fans were gathered to bid the Kaiser adieu. The moment Franz Sr, seventy-one years old and suffering from pancreatic cancer, turned his head to one side, the son knew the reason. His mother had long since melted into tears. It was 24 May 1977.

When Beckenbauer landed at JFK International Airport later that day with German punctuality – at 5.03 p.m. local time – there were not just reporters, fans and club officials waiting for him. In the rollicking, if a tad sensationalist, 2006 documentary *Once in a Lifetime: The Extraordinary Story of the New York Cosmos*, Clive Toye remembers: 'We called up our local youth soccer clubs and said "Can you get a bunch of kids out there with a banner to welcome Franz to New York?".' One club that responded was BW Gottschee Soccer from Ridgewood, which is why one of the boys standing under a large flag that read 'Welcome Franz Beckenbauer' was an eleven-year-old Bavarian-born lad who had come to the United States as a baby. His name was Mike Windischmann, and thirteen years later he would captain the US national team at the World Cup in Italy.

Windischmann and the other boys saw not only Beckenbauer walk through customs. Naturally, Robert Schwan had flown with him. Less naturally, Beckenbauer's wife was also in his wake, while the three boys were staying with Brigitte's sister in Ingolstadt, an hour north of Munich. It was probably Schwan's idea to present the Beckenbauers as a wholesome and respectable couple, at least during the crucial first weeks when there would be plenty of media interest. After all, the agent had heard that the US was a prudish country where reputation and appearance were important. He would learn soon enough that New York City was a different matter altogether.

Brigitte must have been happy to play along, as she was hoping there could be a future for her and her husband. In fact, when a German tabloid reporter visited Franz in June, she was still around, informing her guest where you could buy German bread or sausage (on 86th Street) and that she'd been to Broadway with Franz to see the musical *Chicago*. It was true, and yet basically a farce. The Kaiser had all along intended to live in the Big Apple with Diana Sandmann. By mid-July, Brigitte had faded from the scene and was back in Europe, setting up a new home for her and the three children in Sarnen, a Swiss town between Zürich and Berne.

Two days after arriving in New York, Beckenbauer met his new team-mates for the first time when he signed his contract in front of 500 journalists at a posh hotel in Manhattan. There was a press conference during which the club's board mentioned they had first contacted the Kaiser eighteen months before (which would tie in with Schwan's statement), then Beckenbauer answered questions, while an interested Cosmos squad looked on.

Or largely interested. One player was silently and somewhat morosely smoking cigarettes: Giorgio Chinaglia. The burly striker who always kept a bottle of Chivas Regal in his locker had told reporters the team didn't need Beckenbauer. The Italian, generally considered to be the *éminence grise* who really called the shots at the Cosmos, added a sarcastic reference to Franz's famous nickname: 'What's his number – 5? Oh, great. This shirt number is taken by Keith Eddy. He is our libero. He is our king!' Indeed, when Beckenbauer went to pick up his jersey, there were only two numbers left for him: 6 and 25. If Chinaglia gloated when he saw the Kaiser with an alien number on his shirt, it's because the Italian didn't know that the '6' was Franz's lucky number. And there was another good omen: he had a team-mate named Roth again.

The 29-year-old Werner Roth was the Cosmos captain. He nearly didn't make it to the press conference to greet his new team-mate, though, on account of Gotham's notoriously congested roads. 'I almost missed the event due to traffic from the city and getting pulled over for speeding by the police,' he remembers. 'Luckily, I was given a police escort from a sergeant who was a fan.' Roth, who'd grown up in Brooklyn, came from a family of Danube Swabians, an ethnic German population in southeastern Europe. 'I spoke a little German, really *Donauschwäbisch*, a dialect Franz barely understood, and I think we bonded a little over that.'

They certainly did, because even decades later Beckenbauer still recalled fondly how much Roth helped him, especially during the complicated first weeks and months. 'Well, I was the captain,' Roth says modestly. 'Also, I had an apartment in the city, so I could make it a little easier for him to get acclimated. He was on Fifth Avenue, and I was just across the park on West 72nd.' It doesn't sound like much of a distance, but this was New York. The day after the press conference, Roth was supposed to pick up Beckenbauer for his first training session with the team. According to the Kaiser, his new captain was an hour late because he got stuck in traffic yet again.

'I'm not sure how late I was, one minute or thirty, to Franz it didn't matter, but yes, I was late and he was pissed,' Roth remembers forty-five years later. 'And I totally understood. He wanted to make a good impression on his first day, and he didn't see himself as Franz, the superstar, but Franz, the team-mate. And of course he would be upset if any players came late to training, same as I was when that happened.'

The team that didn't need Beckenbauer had just lost four of their first nine games after normal time – and another two through those idiosyncratic thirty-five-yard shoot-outs the NASL had just introduced in order to spice up the boring old penalty shoot-outs, which had been used to decide drawn games since 1975. In other words, after a third of the regular season, the Cosmos (this was the first of the two years the club dropped 'New York' from their name) were in real danger of missing out on the play-offs. This would have been a tragedy rather than merely a disaster, because Pelé was in his final season and still hadn't won a thing in New York, apart of course from the country. Hence the signing of the Kaiser and, probably equally importantly, that of Carlos Alberto in July. The Brazilian played sweeper, which allowed Beckenbauer to move into midfield and do what he had always wanted to do in the US: show the people some imagination and tricks.

'I still remember how fascinated Franz was by the club during those first months,' says Diana Sandmann. 'You have to remember that teams in Europe only had very few foreigners at the time. But the Cosmos had players from ten or twelve countries. Franz told me how the Brazilians would play music and sing and dance on their way to a game, while Germans would only do this after a game, if at all.'

The summer of 1977 may very well have been the wildest, craziest time ever in the wildest, craziest city. There was a heatwave with the highest average temperatures in New York's history – more than thirty-six degrees Celsius over a ten-day span. There was a serial killer by the name of David Berkowitz on the loose, better known as the Son of Sam. There was a dramatically rising unemployment rate, because New York was actually forced to lay off city workers to stave off bankruptcy. And there was a massive, twenty-five-hour blackout in July (on the day that Carlos Alberto arrived in town!), which triggered looting and arson.

Some historians argue that this looting launched hip hop in the Bronx, because it was how some important DJs acquired their equipment. Meanwhile, in Midtown Manhattan, the recently opened nightclub Studio 54 became the place to be and would soon epitomise the disco craze. There was yet another subcultural uprising, when the downtown punk scene nurtured by a music club in the Bowery called CBGB went overground.

Not that those musical stirrings meant anything to Beckenbauer. Here was a man who would soon rub shoulders with Mick Jagger and move into the same apartment hotel that was home away from home for the Who and the Grateful Dead, but who still spent most of the 1970s listening to Tony Christie. Then again, you could say that nobody was hipper than Fab Franz, the Kaiser, during those wild and crazy times, because to this day many locals primarily remember those stifling hot months of 1977 as the 'Summer of the Cosmos' – a season when New York City suddenly and puzzlingly went soccer crazy.

Before Beckenbauer touched down, the club's average attendance for the season was 20,500. Not bad for the still-struggling NASL, but not enough to make the spacious Giants Stadium look even half-full – and not nearly what Warner Communications had hoped for when they signed Pelé (the parent company of the Ertegun brothers' Atlantic Records having taken over control of the Cosmos in 1972). But when in June the team put five past the visiting LA Aztecs, complete with George Best, almost 60,000 were in attendance. And when Gordon Banks, tending goal for the Fort Lauderdale Strikers, conceded no fewer than eight goals against the Cosmos in August, the stadium announcer proudly requested the fans to 'please look around you. Not an empty seat in the house.' The soccer club that nobody used to take seriously had at last managed to sell out Giants Stadium, capacity 77,691!

The Cosmos even began to win those shoot-outs where the player started thirty-five yards from goal and had five seconds to score. In his recently published memoirs about those years, former Aston Villa forward Steve Hunt says that he 'never felt comfortable' during those deeply American exercises, which had been borrowed from ice hockey, but that he received help. 'Franz always advocated using the outside of the foot in a shoot-out, and I took his advice most of the time.' When I ask Hunt what exactly the advantage of this technique was, he explains that 'nearly all players use their inside or top of the foot to shoot, whereas Franz used the outside, which gave him the element of surprise as most goalkeepers would not be expecting that'.

It should be noted that Beckenbauer was serious about this piece of advice. This explanation is necessary because the Kaiser loved to play the court jester in New York City. The man who'd had more column inches devoted to him in his native country than any other living German, without ever being described as a lovable rogue or a practical joker, would now go, in the memorable words of Roth, 'from intellectual to clown as it suited him'. The former Cosmos skipper has a veritable cornucopia of anecdotes about Beckenbauer hand-cuffing team-mates during a pre-game massage or stuffing dead grasshoppers into their socks.

'On one pre-season tour, he had acquired a cache of elec-tric pens, which gave you a shock when you clicked the top to write,' Roth recalls. 'And he concocted all sorts of tricks to get people to take the pen and click the top. He asked me to write my address down for him at the airport, and I nearly took someone's eye out when I flung the pen across the wait-ing area.' Those pens also came in handy when somebody approached him to ask for an autograph. 'He would take out one of his electric pens with a flourish and ask the fan to write his name so Franz could personalise the autograph,' Roth says. 'And we all watched and waited for the screaming fan's reactions. And Franz just laughed like a little kid. No autograph, but an even better story.'

Back home, they had been seriously worried about Beckenbauer's move to the US. They said he would ruin his reputation, not to mention his career; they said he would make a fool of himself in this Mickey Mouse league; they said New York was a dangerous place, they were afraid of this madman, Chinaglia . . . and now here was Beckenbauer, having a total blast. Football-mad Henry Kissinger, born in Bavaria, became his fanboy, once barging into the Cosmos' dressing room while Beckenbauer was lying in the bathtub.

The Kaiser met Muhammad Ali on the day after the boxer's bout with Earnie Shavers, when The Greatest was still in no condition to get up from his hotel bed, which resulted in a series of bizarre but charming photos. Every Monday night, the Kaiser partied with his team-mates at Studio 54, where the Cosmos and their sizeable entourage had a table reserved for them. As the reporter David Hirshey describes, 'the players sprawled on leather banquettes instead of stools; glassy-eyed supermodels, rather than sweaty, overweight sportswriters, vied for their attention; Dom Perignon flowed instead of Gatorade . . . and Grace Jones often rode naked on a white horse'.

The many tales of the Cosmos' bacchanalian nights often forget to mention that these parties were not only an expression of the players' exuberance and their status in town, but also of their camaraderie. You would have expected a clear division between the superstars and the many lesser known American (or indeed British) players in the squad, but it wasn't there, apart from the occasional Giorgio-ism from macho man Chinaglia. In his book, Hunt mentions not once but twice that his mother thought the world of Beckenbauer because of his kindness and hospitality.

All you have to do to become aware of this close bond is to study footage of the Cosmos' 1977 season and watch out for the goal celebrations. They were so boisterous and – considering the times – elaborate that I actually felt forced to ask Hunt if the players had been intentionally overdoing it, perhaps in an attempt to give those Americans in the stands the show they had come to see. 'No, they were purely spontaneous,' he says. 'There were no elements of showbiz, it was purely a team celebrating. There was a huge togetherness in the team and this showed in our goal celebrations.'

And there was a lot to celebrate. Shortly after arriving in New York, Beckenbauer was interviewed on television. 'I think my challenge here in the United States is much bigger than it was in Europe. Maybe I can help a new sport here. Soccer is a new sport in the United States. That was a reason why I came,' he said. 'And Pelé, of course. I'm his biggest fan. The only sportsperson you can compare him to is Muhammad Ali. I'm very proud to play on the same team as Pelé.' Everybody at the Cosmos felt that way, and everybody, says Roth, gave a little bit more just to make sure Pelé could go out on a high.

Thanks to their scintillating form in the second half of the season, the Cosmos reached the championship final known as Soccer Bowl for the first time since 1972. Beckenbauer was not only voted the season's 'outstanding defender' by his peers, but also lifted the league's Most Valuable Player award, for which he received a Toyota Celica Liftback on the day before the final in Portland, Oregon, against the Seattle Sounders. 'Thank you very much,' he politely told Toyota's regional manager Bill Miller. 'I'm very happy to drive such a beautiful car.' (It wasn't true. The Kaiser remained faithful to his metallic-blue Mercedes-Benz.)

Hunt opened the scoring with a truly legendary opportunistic goal. Seattle's Canadian goalkeeper Tony Chursky collected the ball and then put it on the ground. But since he was deaf in the right ear, he didn't hear his team-mates' warnings, as Hunt was sneaking up on him and then nudged the ball across the line from seven yards. Yet the Sounders, fielding nine Britons in the starting XI, tied the game soon afterwards. It was left to – who else? – Chinaglia to win the match. On seventy-eight minutes, he headed home a Hunt cross from the left wing. The third Cosmos player to celebrate the winner by wrapping his arms around the Italian was Beckenbauer, who even planted a kiss on Chinaglia's cheek. So much for being bitter rivals.

The team's victory party, held in a lounge in Portland, put even the wildest Studio 54 night to shame. At one point, Beckenbauer asked Pelé for a dance, whereupon two of the three most famous footballers on the entire planet (Cruyff would have completed the *pas de trois*) performed what David Hirshey described as 'a little samba, laughing, stepping on toes'. During the party, Pelé told a friend: 'You know, I feel like a baby, like a baby that wants to cry.' When the team arrived on a chartered plane at JFK one day later, some 5,000 ecstatic fans greeted the players at the airport. A freaking soccer team! New York City had never seen anything like it.

If 1966 was the most important year of Beckenbauer's professional life, then 1977 was probably the most amazing, possibly the most deeply satisfying and certainly the most instructive year for Franz. Like a great many other European athletes who had gone abroad, he found the American approach to sports not only refreshing but healthy. It was an approach that said you don't have to prove to anyone that you are totally committed and focused, because if you aren't, you'll be found out when the game starts. It was an approach that assumed athletes have to be loose and relaxed to be on top of their game, not tense and dogged. It was an approach that argued this whole thing only made sense if everyone, in the stands and on the field of play, was enjoying themselves. Finally, it was an approach that never mistook supreme elegance for arrogance. It was as if Franz Beckenbauer had found his very own promised land, the place where he had been meant to be all along.

Also, for the first time in his life as an adult, he was not constantly supervised by his agent – Schwan came to New York only on very rare occasions – and not gently monitored by his wife. Now he had to make his own decisions, and somehow the results spoke for themselves. Yes, there was Diana, but she let him run free, not least because she became as enamoured by New York City – if not more – than Franz was. She attended a private art school and today works as a painter.

'In New York, Franz went to a supermarket for the first time in his life,' she says. 'That would have been impossible back home, but in New York, everybody left him alone. People did recognise him, but all they said was "Hey, Franz! Good to see you, great game." Athletes had this incredible status in America and were treated with deep respect. And so our life was very relaxed. When Franz came home from training, we often went directly to the beach at St George on Staten Island and had a picnic, sometimes with Werner Roth.'

One of Franz's first guests in New York was his brother Walter, who stayed for more than three weeks. 'Over the previous years, Franz had become somewhat detached from his family,' he remembers. 'Of course, Robert Schwan only meant well. He wanted the best for Franz, but he did shield my brother from everyone, and that included us. Now, in New York, it was different. I remember we sat down in Central Park and talked for three or four hours. I think it was the first time I really told him what I did for a living.' He pauses for a moment. 'You know, I have always been my own man with my own life. But I'm my brother's biggest fan. I love him. That's why New York was great.' Still a very vibrant man, he lets out a bellowing laugh. 'And, of course, it totally blew my mind. Here I am, a simple Giesing lad, and now we go and see Cassius Clay at the Madison Square Garden and I get to meet him the next day! I'm no boxing fan, but I had always been fascinated by Ali. What a man. What a meeting.'

But the year still wasn't over. First, there was Pelé's farewell tour, which saw the Cosmos travel from the Caribbean to Japan, from India to Brazil. In between, there was even a visit to communist China, then a very unsual destination for Western teams. Although Chinaglia refused to taste shark fin soup, the players were in high spirits. 'All the incredible pressure to win in Pelé's last season was off,' Roth remembers, 'and we could finally relax, at least emotionally.'

Beckenbauer's plan was to spend his holidays in the US when the tour ended in mid-October with a game in Rio de Janeiro. But he had to cut his holidays short. On 1 November, his father was hospitalised, and the prospects were not encouraging at all. Beckenbauer went home to Europe to support his mother and see his sons after all those months. He also spent a lot of time at his father's sickbed, though he was in Switzerland with his family when Franz Sr passed away on 28 November. Beckenbauer drove back to Munich through the night for the last goodbye. Almost twenty years later, he would tell an interviewer that it was 'one of the most beautiful moments of my life. I was alone with myself and my father, who was no longer alive and yet somehow lived on. His soul was still in the room.'

'On Pelé's farewell tour, Franz and I talked endlessly about the past season and the importance of the next one, our first of the new era without Pelé,' says former Cosmos captain

Roth. 'And I remember we had such a debate over whether we could win back-to-back championships. I was confident we could win again in 1978, and Franz was sure we couldn't, that we made a bet for dinner at the Four Seasons, including wine and alcohol. Franz even wrote it down in a one-page agreement we both signed.' Roth pauses: 'I still have it somewhere – and now that I think of it, he still owes me that dinner.'

Perhaps Beckenbauer doubted that the Cosmos could defend their title because he had no idea whether or not he would be there to help his team-mates during the crucial weeks of the regular season. There were two pressing problems: the World Cup in Argentina and his shoes.

In the Kaiser's absence, West Germany's national coach Helmut Schön had made Hamburg's right-back Manfred Kaltz the new sweeper. Since the results were not disastrous, at least initially, public opinion was divided over whether the DFB should make an effort to have Beckenbauer available for the 1978 World Cup. There was nothing in Beckenbauer's contract with the Cosmos about this, and since the NASL didn't pause for the tournament in Argentina, an agreement had to be reached with the club. Schön pleaded with the DFB; he desperately wanted the Kaiser in his squad if it was at all possible.

And Beckenbauer himself? Good question. While his father was dying, he was constantly asked about the World Cup and had a different answer every time. He said he would love to play for West Germany in Argentina. He said the national team was over and done with. He said he was undecided. When a reporter confronted him with all those contrasting statements in November, he replied: 'You know, I'm at a stage in my life where I change my opinion from day to day. I just don't know what I want.'

However, some people knew exactly what they wanted. Alf Bende, then a high-ranking Adidas man, told the newspapers: 'Of course we would be happy to see Beckenbauer back in the national team.' The Kaiser was still the company's most important testimonial, his contract valid until 1985. Adidas were very much interested to have him wear their boots on the biggest stage of all, the more so since his successor as West Germany captain was Berti Vogts, a Puma man. And so Beckenbauer agreed to see what he could do. In early December, he even noted that 'if the Cosmos allow me to take part in the World Cup, perhaps it's best if I stay in Germany and play the next six months for Bayern Munich'.

His old flame could have certainly used him, as Bayern were right in the middle of their worst-ever Bundesliga season. But during a telephone conversation with Schön, Beckenbauer explained that, post-Pelé, he was the biggest draw the Cosmos had and that he didn't think the club would want him to miss a large chunk of the season. He was right. In January, Cosmos president Ahmet Ertegun confirmed this. 'Of course we would love to see a Cosmos player captain a side that could win the World Cup, and there have been serious inquiries from the German FA. But they want him to be there for the preparations as well. And we just can't do without him for three months during our season.' Still, the DFB debated the matter for another six weeks, a clear sign that Schön still thought the world of Beckenbauer without having actually seen him play for ten months. But on 21 January, the governing body officially announced that 'Beckenbauer's participation in the World Cup is not feasible under the conditions set by Cosmos'. In late February, the Kaiser flew back to New York.

It was just as well, as you had the feeling his heart wasn't in it any more. Beckenbauer would have played for his country out of a sense of duty, not because he wanted to. His priorities now lay with the Cosmos, as he made clear in November when he travelled to London to assist Ahmet Ertegun with his sheer presence alone.

Steve Hunt had gone back home and was unsure whether he should play another year in the NASL. Suddenly he got a call from Ertegun, inviting the 21-year-old to watch England's World Cup qualifier against Italy at Wembley with him. When Hunt explained that he was in Birmingham, not London, the president sent a limo that picked him up and took him all the way to Ertegun's flat in the capital, where Ertegun was not alone. 'Franz Beckenbauer was waiting with him,' Hunt said. 'It was quickly apparent that I was wanted at Cosmos. I may be easily flattered, but with a music legend and the world's greatest defender in the room, how could I refuse?'

As early as August 1977, Beckenbauer had told a German reporter in his deepest Bavarian accent *'Jo mei, I bin a Ami'* – well, I'm an American now. At the time, it will have been a mixture of flippancy and chagrin (Beckenbauer had just been told that a famous weekly sports TV show in Germany had referred to him as 'a tax fugitive'). Now it was becoming a self-fulfilling prophecy. He moved out of the St Regis Hotel and into the Navarro on Central Park South. It was technically still a hotel, but had the feeling of an apartment building like the famous Dakota (where John Lennon lived and died). Franz and Diana were on the 21st floor, in an apartment that ran across the entire floor, so that they could see both Central Park and, from the rear windows, the Empire State Building.

The Navarro was popular with artists, from rock bands

like the Kinks and the Rolling Stones to singers like Plácido Domingo or Luciano Pavarotti. When Rudolf Nureyev came to the Metropolitan Opera with the London Festival Ballet, he lived next to Beckenbauer for some time and the two got on like a house on fire. The Kaiser has often told the story of how one day Nureyev put a hand on his knee with clear intentions. It either happened at the River Café, a restaurant in Brooklyn, or in a yellow cab. In any case, the incorrigible ladies' man Beckenbauer could convince the ballet dancer that their friendship had to remain platonic.

He was going native so quickly that the Cosmos declared 21 May, the day of the home game against the Seattle Sounders, who had Bobby Moore in their line-up, to be 'Franz Beckenbauer Day'. On the Thursday before the match, the writer Alex Yannis sat down with the German for a piece that would appear in the *New York Times* under the headline 'The Americanization of Beckenbauer'. The Kaiser told him that 'it was the best decision in my life to come to New York.. Here it is so private. I go places without people recognising me. In Germany it was bad. I guess that if West Germany loses the World Cup, they will blame it on me.' Then he enthused about Madison Square Garden and Greenwich Village, Carly Simon and Liza Minnelli.

Three days later, it was not so private any more. Another huge crowd of close to 72,000 listened to Berndt von Staden, the West German ambassador to the United States, who lauded Franz's 'contribution to German-American friendship', and also to a mass choir under the baton of the Swabian choral conductor Gotthilf Fischer, which must have pleased Beckenbauer but will have left New Yorkers bemused. Then the Kaiser stepped up to the microphone to address the cheering masses. 'I'm very proud, and it's a big honour for me to have this wonderful day and to celebrate with the beautifulest people and the beautifulest crowd in the world.'

There were two people among this most beautiful crowd who couldn't understand a single word of what he was saying, but they were beaming with pride nonetheless. Antonie, his mother, had boarded a plane for only the second time in her life to visit Franz on the other side of the big pond. A friend of the family called Paula kept her company, and if the photos that were taken during this trip are any indication, both were having the time of their lives. Diana even took them to the White House in Washington on, wonders of wonders, a shuttle flight. Antonie especially radiated health and good spirits only six months after losing her husband.

In these weeks and months, the fun just never seemed to end. Beckenbauer had befriended Jascha Silberstein, the German-born principal cellist of the Metropolitan Opera. Now the Kaiser would constantly and, as was his wont, effortlessly switch from Studio 54 to the Met and back again, with a trip to Carnegie Hall in between, where he and Diana sat in Frank Sinatra's VIP box while Ol' Blue Eyes was on stage, singing his recently released version of 'New York, New York'. Each summer, Franz's three boys would come to the Big Apple to spend their school holidays with their dad, which turned them into devoted fans of American sports.

Life on the pitch was a blast, too. On 16 August, four Cosmos players in a row failed to find the target during the sudden-death shoot-out against the Minnesota Kicks. With elimination as early as the conference semi-finals looming large, Carlos Alberto scored with a trick shot and then Beckenbauer converted the last and deciding attempt of a long night – with the outside of his right foot.

Fewer than two weeks later, almost 75,000 filled Giants

Stadium for Soccer Bowl 1978, and the Cosmos made the most of their home field advantage, beating the Tampa Bay Rowdies 3-1 to lift their second straight title. Infinitely more spectacular, even titillating, was a friendly played a mere three days later, on 30 August, when the Cosmos hosted an all-star team featuring the likes of Zbigniew Boniek, Teófilo Cubillas and Roberto Rivellino. But all eyes were on the home team. More precisely, on the Cosmos player wearing the unfamiliar number 30. His name was Johan Cruyff.

King Johan had retired from the game in May – or so thought everybody who didn't know that he was haunted by even bigger tax problems than the Kaiser had faced. The Dutch superstar couldn't quite agree on a proper contract with the Cosmos, because the Americans wanted him for three years instead of the one he had in mind, and also because Cruyff was reluctant to go on those endless post-season tours that earned the club a great deal of cash. So in return for an undisclosed sum of money, Cruyff agreed to play two friendlies with the Cosmos and promised the club he would only sign with them if and when he really returned to competitive football.

The Cosmos drew the game 2-2. Beckenbauer set up the first goal and Cruyff made the second. The two men were supposed to play together again only a few days later, in a game that was billed as 'The Cosmos & Cruyff vs Atlético Madrid'. But Cruyff abruptly left the US and wouldn't fulfil his obligation until the end of September, when the Cosmos played Chelsea at Stamford Bridge. Two Englishmen – Steve Hunt and Dennis Tueart – combined to bring the touring Americans ahead, before Ray Wilkins equalised in the final minute. It would not be the last time Beckenbauer and Cruyff were on the same team, but it was the last time that this team was the Cosmos. When the Dutchman at last decided to join the NASL in May 1979, he signed for the Los Angeles Aztecs.

One of many reasons why he reneged on his promise to the New Yorkers was that the league had misgivings. While the Cosmos were drawing more than 47,000 fans on average, many other clubs were struggling. No fewer than ten teams, among them the Aztecs, had failed to break the 10,000 barrier in 1978. With gates like that, how could these clubs play the Cosmos game and sign star players to drum up interest? And yet they had no other choice.

There were more signs that not all was well, once you looked beyond Manhattan's glitter and glamour. Discipline at the Cosmos, for instance, appeared to be eroding. Clive Toye once said that after he had been removed from his post at the end of the 1977 season (most likely at the behest of Chinaglia), 'the lunatics took over the asylum'. It was more than just sour grapes. When the club began their 1978 post-season tour of Europe, a German writer followed the club around for the first weeks and called the team 'the most expensive bunch of slobs in the world'. He said the German hotel near the French border where the Cosmos set up camp for three days had 'rarely served so much whisky' and quoted coach Eddie Firmani as saying his players were 'the best in the world – at cards'.

Maybe the writer's damning description was exaggerated for effect so that his readers would shake their heads at the sort of company the Kaiser was now keeping. But maybe it wasn't. Ten months later, a group of Cosmos players would be involved in a brawl with the cleaning staff at Giants Stadium which got so out of hand that eight people – five of them players – suffered injuries, one of whom had to be taken to the hospital. The fight apparently broke out when Chinaglia went into the stands to retrieve a ball and had objects thrown at him. A few weeks later, during a home game against the Vancouver Whitecaps, a free-for-all scuffle on the pitch lasted for no fewer than fourteen minutes and saw four players ejected, Chinaglia among them. Ahmet Ertegun claimed the altercation happened because the referee was discriminating against the hosts, while Whitecaps coach Tony Waiters said Carlos Alberto had been kicking people left, right and centre.

Even worse was the team's form on the pitch. In September 1978, some 75,000 people filled Munich's Olympic Stadium in order to welcome home their prodigal son – and to finally see this Cosmos team they had read so much about with their own eyes. For the Kaiser, it was a disaster of epic proportions. His old adversary Paul Breitner, now back in red, played like a man possessed as Bayern dismantled the Americans 7-1. 'You have to feel sorry for Franz, the footballer,' Breitner said after the final whistle. He wasn't even smirking; he meant it. Even Beckenbauer's old friend Hans Schiefele called the Cosmos 'a comet that has burned out' and said the visitors had been 'humiliated'.

Unbeknown to everybody at the time, this painful, sobering night would establish yet another intriguing parallel between the careers of Beckenbauer and Cruyff. Just fifty-six days later, Bayern travelled to Amsterdam for the Dutch master's testimonial – where they were even more ruthless, inflicting a historic 8-0 defeat on the hosts that would cause hard feelings in the Ajax camp. It was no consolation for Beckenbauer, of course, and the same went for the fact that the Cosmos earned a staggering 500,000 marks from the Munich debacle. Robert Schwan, no longer Bayern's business manager but still Beckenbauer's adviser, had bargained on behalf of the New Yorkers and struck an excellent deal.

It was not that the Cosmos had come up against an overpowering and fired-up Bayern side (after all, the Reds themselves were about to suffer a legendary ignominy, a 5-4 defeat at home against second-division Osnabrück in the cup). Seven days after the collapse in Munich, the American ambassadors conceded six goals against VfB Stuttgart, a mid-table Bundesliga team remarkable only for the fact that Uli Hoeness's younger brother Dieter was playing up front. 'Many of his excellent passes were all for nothing, because he lacks the right environment for his game,' *Kicker* magazine said about Beckenbauer. 'Once more, he became resigned early. You really have to pity him.'

Of course, Beckenbauer was well aware that his team was not in the same class as Bayern, not even as Stuttgart. But being pitied on his return to his home country? Breitner feeling sorry for the Kaiser? Ouch. At the time, the German-American journalist Ben Wett, who knew Beckenbauer well, was producing a thirty-minute film about him for the NBC network. They shot some footage in an empty Olympic Stadium, for which Wett asked Beckenbauer to casually climb up the steps to the stands. 'Wouldn't it be better if you shot me walking down the stairs?' Franz replied with a grin. 'Just to show that it's all going downhill for me.'

He may have been half-joking, but one thing that certainly went downhill in those months was his health. A particular problem for Franz, the athlete, were the plastic pitches so common in the NASL. For his first weeks in the US, Adidas had given him custom-made boots with 144 round rubber studs, but even they couldn't cushion the impact or ease the constant strain on knee joints and hip sockets. These pitches were all early generations of astroturf and cannot be compared to the smooth carpets of today. Some fields were hard as concrete, others full of holes hastily filled with sand. Beckenbauer soon felt the effects of unforgiving playing surfaces on his body. His Achilles tendons hurt so much that only lying down could ease the pain.

Looking back, Steve Hunt says that he enjoyed playing on this surface, as 'it favoured the more skilful players because it was a true run of the ball', before adding that 'I've suffered myself, which I believe is to do with playing on astroturf'. He and Beckenbauer were by no means alone. Another reason why Cruyff refused to sign with the Cosmos was his aversion to the artificial surface at Giants Stadium, which he blamed for 'enormous blisters on the soles of your feet'. (The Aztecs, by contrast, played on natural grass.) In *Soccer in a Football World*, his book about the history of the game in North America, Dave Wangerin explained that 'others wrestled with shin splints, ingrown toenails, and ugly abrasions. But it would be years before ailments such as "turf toe" passed into the American sporting vernacular, and gridiron and baseball teams had not yet begun to attribute serious injuries to their playing surfaces.'

In mid-April 1979, Beckenbauer suffered an injury in the opening game of the new season. At first, it looked like a simple strain, but then it turned out he had damaged his meniscus. In May, he underwent an operation on his right knee. It was the Kaiser's first truly serious injury since October 1967, when he was hospitalised because a bruised toe had become infected (and then turned out to be fractured). Back then, he had missed only four games and was out for just thirty-five days. But now he was sidelined for almost exactly three months. Beckenbauer never doubted astroturf was to blame.

Lamentably, he also had to sit out the rematch against

Bayern Munich, of all games. It was unfortunate because the Cosmos were much improved, not least because of some good and comparatively young acquisitions, among them US phenomenon Rick Davis and the Brazilian Francisco Marinho, plus the Dutch duo Wim Rijsbergen and Johan Neeskens; none of them older than twenty-eight and thus still close to their prime. The New York Cosmos, their full name restored, even held their own against World Cup winners Argentina – featuring a teenage Diego Maradona – for eighty-eight minutes, before Daniel Passarella scored the only goal of the night. Against Bayern, Beckenbauer performed the ceremonial kick-off, then watched from the bench as his team suffered a creditable 2-0 defeat.

However, the lengthy lay-off also meant that Beckenbauer was in fine physical shape when he went back to West Germany after the Cosmos' customary post-season tour, this time to Asia and Australia. So Franz decided to play some football. On 28 December, a World XI travelled to Dortmund to raise money for UNICEF with a charity match against Bundesliga club Borussia. Once again, Beckenbauer played with Johan Cruyff, who captained the side, and both men went the distance. Truth be told, the Kaiser didn't cut the best of figures two minutes from time, when Dortmund scored the 3-2 winner, but he was still the star of the night and rightfully showered with praise.

Former national coach Helmut Schön, who had handed over the team to Jupp Derwall, observed that 'given a good preparation and some proper training, Beckenbauer could still play for any Bundesliga club, even for the national team. What others have to work really hard for, he does just like that.' Beckenbauer was all smiles even before he had heard these and many other plaudits. For the first time in almost three years, he had been allowed to play in the libero position and enjoyed it immensely.

Playing for the World XI that night was Hamburg's right-back Manfred Kaltz. After the game, he remarked that the Kaiser was still an outstanding player and joked that his club should make him an offer. Almost the same comment was then made by one of the two men who had been coaching the World XI: Beckenbauer's former Bayern boss Branko Zebec. Just like Kaltz, Zebec was now under contract at Hamburg. And who was the man who negotiated those contracts for the club as their business manager? Why, none other than Franz's old friend Günter Netzer.

Netzer approached Zebec to learn if the coach had been serious about Beckenbauer. Could the Kaiser really still cut it in the Bundesliga? When Zebec replied in the affirmative, an idea began to take form in Netzer's head. He conferred with Hamburg's new president, a lawyer called Wolfgang Klein, and then did some maths. Finally, Netzer placed a transatlantic phone call to New York and asked Beckenbauer if he could imagine playing for Hamburg after his contract with the Cosmos ran out in October 1980. The question seemed to greatly amuse the Kaiser, who cracked a few jokes and larked about. But as Netzer noted in his autobiography, there was something in Beckenbauer's voice that told him the competitive fire was still burning. There was a chance. Netzer said he would come to New York with Klein to talk this over. Beckenbauer replied that it couldn't hurt. On 30 April, Netzer travelled to England to watch Hamburg's opponents in the European Cup final, Nottingham Forest. Two days later, he boarded Concorde.

On the face of it, Netzer's wild idea didn't seem to make any sense. Beckenbauer would be thirty-five before he could

even don Hamburg's shirt. He hadn't played at the highest
level for more than three years; the World XI game had
showcased his vision and composure, but also his lack of pace.
Finally, he wasn't supposed to join some nondescript team
that could use his experience alone. This was the Hamburg of
Kevin Keegan, Felix Magath and the fearsome striker Horst
Hrubesch. They had just demolished Real Madrid 5–1.

But now all those accusations from ten years before entered
into the equation on the plus side. Beckenbauer had indeed
spent a large part of his career in a position where you could
conserve energy. Unlike midfield maestros or goal-scoring
threats, he had not been kicked to pieces again and again by
ruthless man-markers. Netzer was sure the Kaiser had another
two years of football in him, especially if he could play in his
favourite position and build from the rear as the libero.

In New York, Netzer and Klein sat down with Beckenbauer
and Schwan to discuss the details. The Cosmos had offered
the player a new and financially very interesting deal;
Hamburg, on the other hand, would need the help of their
main sponsor, BP, to come up with the 1.2 million marks per
year Schwan was putting on the table. After some prelim-
inary negotiations, Beckenbauer took his guests to Régine's,
a posh restaurant-cum-discotheque on Park Avenue and 59th
Street, where Mick Jagger had once been turned away for not
wearing a tie.

All of a sudden, their table was surrounded by photographers, who snapped away and then vanished as quickly as
they had appeared. Netzer wondered what that was all about.
Schwan, Klein and himself were total unknowns in New
York, while even Beckenbauer was just a minor celebrity in
such a place. Netzer suspected that Schwan was behind it.
The agent wanted some photos for the tabloids back in West

Germany, who would make a big story out of this. Public opinion could then put some pressure on Beckenbauer to sign the Hamburg contract.

If Netzer is right (and perhaps he's not, because his club's interest in Beckenbauer had already been reported back home), why was Schwan so keen on bringing his client back to the Bundesliga? A good guess is Adidas. There were signs that the company would be reluctant to extend Beckenbauer's contract beyond 1985 if he decided to stay in the NASL. It's not clear how seriously the Kaiser had to take such threats, because he now had so many ties to Adidas that their business relationship seemed to be in for the long haul. For instance, as recently as April 1979, Beckenbauer's and Schwan's Swiss lawyer Hans Hess had set up a company called Rofa – short for Robert and Franz – that was meant to target the rapidly growing market for sports television and advertising rights. Beckenbauer and Schwan owned a third of this company (a share they would sell three years later), but the brain behind the whole operation was someone else. Even though his name was deeply hidden in the list of partners, the mastermind was Adi Dassler's son Horst.

Horst Dassler had gone abroad in 1959 to oversee a small factory in Alsace. From these modest beginnings, he built his very own empire, the massively successful Adidas France, which at one point threatened to become bigger than the parent company. Following his father's death in 1978, Horst returned home. For the time being, Adi's widow Käthe was the company's chairman, but Horst would soon follow her in this post and become, as *Die Zeit* put it in 2014, 'the inventor of modern sports corruption'. Dassler's 'system of extortion, bribes and espionage', said *Bild* in its review of a 2018 investigative documentary about the dark side of Adidas, 'made the former family company the number one sportswear manufacturer'. Perhaps the most important jigsaw piece in Dassler's shadowy system was a company by the name of International Sport and Leisure (ISL), which the *Stuttgarter Zeitung* once described as 'world sports' cancerous growth'. It was officially formed in 1982, but it can be traced back directly to Rofa.

So Beckenbauer could have been fairly sure that there was a future for him with Adidas, even if he accepted the lump of money Warner Communications were willing to throw at him, reportedly 5 million marks for two more years in New York. Then again, better safe than sorry. 'You can say that Adidas held the trump card until the end,' the Kaiser explained to the *New York Times* in July, when he had announced his return to West Germany. 'I was told I always had a job with Warner, but as what? As Mickey Mouse?' He paused for an instant. 'Or is it Bugs Bunny?' It was blatant overacting, because he had come to know his cartoon characters very well. Bugs Bunny was the official Cosmos mascot.

Still, a part of him probably would have liked to stay. He certainly wasn't wanting for respect or admiration, even love, and people were genuinely sad to see him go. 'Franz came to us a well-oiled Swiss watch of a professional,' says Werner Roth. 'I learned a lot from him in the course of our time together about taking personal responsibility for my development and performances ... I think his time in America softened his corners a little and took the edge off.' Diana Sandmann explains that she 'would have preferred to stay in New York, but it was Franz's decision to make. He thought about it very long and very hard. I'm sure he would have never gone back to Munich, but Hamburg was a different matter. It was and is more cosmopolitan than Munich, so we felt it wouldn't be too much of a culture shock after New York.'

There was one thing left to do – win another championship, which brings us back to that charity game in December 1979. The World XI's second coach on that day, sitting next to Zebec on the bench, had been Hennes Weisweiler, then in charge of Cologne. Barely four weeks after the match, he left that club because he didn't see eye to eye with the president, and signed a contract with . . . the Cosmos. Weisweiler promptly guided the team to another Soccer Bowl and another final victory, 3–0 against the Fort Lauderdale Strikers in Washington.

Three days later, on 24 September 1980, the Cosmos said goodbye to the Kaiser with a 'Franz Beckenbauer Farewell Game'. The opponents were an NASL select team, but the one player whose participation set Beckenbauer's pulse racing wore the Cosmos shirt with the number 10. Pelé had come out of retirement one last time to play with and for his friend. He even scored a very fine goal in the 3–2 loss. Watching it all and paying their dues were 71,413 New Yorkers, whom Beckenbauer addressed before the game. He would later admit that he was very nervous about speaking in front of so many people, but he kept a stiff upper lip. 'Thank you for everything you have done for me in the last four years. You have always let me feel that you liked me. Good luck to you, I love you all!'

LIFE II

Chapter Seven

Not long after his return to the Bundesliga, Beckenbauer delivered a classic one-liner: 'As soon as I heard the catcalls, I knew I was home.' I suspect he said that because he knew it was a classic. Or maybe he still harboured ill feelings about the receptions he had all too often encountered across the country prior to exploring the Cosmos – because it wasn't like that at all the second time around, at least not during the first year.

Maybe he was peeved because there were shrill whistles during his first home game for Hamburg, but that was a disastrous 5-0 defeat at the hands of AS Saint-Étienne in the UEFA Cup that would have enraged even the most forgiving fan. Or maybe he was annoyed that he was constantly booed during a friendly match away at Werder Bremen, then in the second division, in March 1981. But Werder were Hamburg's bitter rivals. In other words, he was now abused for being a Hamburg player, not for being Franz Beckenbauer. True, it helped that he was no longer playing for Bayern Munich. But it was also because people had found out they somehow missed him.

This isn't to say that Beckenbauer wasn't in for some unpleasant surprises when he returned to West Germany. A fortnight before Netzer had travelled to New York City to discuss the Kaiser's homecoming, Branko Zebec had fallen asleep on the bench – during a Bundesliga game in Dortmund. It was now impossible for the club to hide or tolerate Zebec's boozing any more; the coach was living on borrowed time. In mid-December, Hamburg soundly beat 1860 Munich 4-1. Beckenbauer, playing in his 400th Bundesliga game, was in stellar form. Zebec less so. He made two strange substitutions during the match that had the players scratching their heads. His post-game press conference was incomprehensible. Two days later, he was relieved of his duties with immediate effect.

When Beckenbauer learned about this, he stormed into Netzer's office and complained profusely. The way he saw it, a major reason why he signed for the club had just been removed. 'I was really surprised that Franz was so enamoured of Mister Zebec,' says Ditmar Jakobs, then a 27-year-old defender in his second season with the club, 'because the training sessions and the pre-season preparations were very, very tough. Conditioning was important for Mister Zebec. People today would never believe how much running we had to do. Actually, that is the reason why Kevin Keegan left us. He just couldn't stand Mister Zebec's training methods any more.'

Of course, Beckenbauer was only too familiar with those methods himself. Perhaps he felt that getting into top phys-ical shape was exactly what he needed after almost four years without truly top-level action. 'He was a sensational player,' remembers Jakobs. 'But he was also the consummate profes-sional, the first man on the training pitch and the last. He was a role model for us all. Did he complain to Netzer? I wouldn't know about that. In the dressing room, he was just one of the lads, no airs and graces. In any case, he then also got along just great with Ernst Happel.' The legendary Austrian coach, whom Beckenbauer would later call 'a genius, if these exist in football', took over Hamburg in the summer of 1981. But at that point, the great Beckenbauer comeback had long since stopped being the fairy tale it should have been.

Jakobs, who now works as an insurance broker (including advising professional footballers), explains that 'Franz began to have these minor ailments. He blamed them on all those years playing on astroturf, and he could very well be right.' During this first season back home, the Kaiser didn't miss many games, but he was also never really fit. A seemingly endless series of small muscular problems plagued him, typically groin strains or his old problems with the heel cord. It was rarely enough to sideline him, but always enough to cause a dull, subliminal pain.

The season ended with a June tour of Guatemala, Mexico and the west coast of the United States. In Los Angeles, the players met Muhammad Ali, who pointed at Beckenbauer and yelled: 'You! You are the greatest!' Laughingly, the Kaiser replied: 'No, Pelé is the greatest.' Whereupon Ali furrowed his brow in jest and said: 'Who is that? When did he box?'

A few weeks later, Beckenbauer met another great, the coach he would later call the best of them all. There is a famous but probably apocryphal story about Ernst Happel's first training session with the Hamburg team. According to this anecdote, the Austrian asked Hrubesch to place a can of Coca-Cola on the crossbar. Then he put a ball on the ground, twenty metres in front of goal, and knocked the can off the bar with his first attempt. He asked his new squad to do the same. Allegedly, the only player who hit the can was, no prize for guessing, Beckenbauer.

This story is usually told to explain that Happel, who had spent the last couple of years working in Belgium, had to earn the respect of his players – and that he did so without resorting to some tired old disciplinarian methods. But it also illustrates that there was an unspoken bond between Happel and Beckenbauer. The Austrian would always bemoan the lack of technique, finesse and brains in the German Bundesliga, which he felt was dominated to an unhealthy degree by sheer physicality.

Happel was greatly, deeply and genuinely fond of the Kaiser, but of course he never said so. That's because Happel didn't speak very much to begin with, not least because there was always a Belga cigarette dangling from his lips. And if he talked, he did it in his very own patois, a mixture of Austrian, Dutch and French, plus dialects that linguists are still trying to identify. At first the other players asked Beckenbauer, the Bavarian, to interpret for them, but the Kaiser had to profess he was as clueless as they were.

The Austrian promptly led his new club to the 1981-82 league title, but for Beckenbauer it was another frustrating campaign. After a promising opening game in mid-August that saw him in fine form, the club travelled to Brussels for an international tournament. The West Germans reached the final against hosts Anderlecht, which went to penalties. When Beckenbauer took his spot-kick, he felt a sudden pang of pain in the groin. He had torn an adductor muscle in his right leg and would be out of action until well into October, a month after his thirty-sixth birthday. Demoralised and frustrated, Beckenbauer announced plans for his testimonial after the end of the season. He said he hoped for profits in the region of 1 million marks, which he would then donate to charity. In the end, someone close to him came up with a different and even better idea.

By all accounts, Happel was still hoping at this point that Beckenbauer's injury curse would sooner or later be lifted and that the player might reconsider his stance. If that's the case, then the next weeks and months convinced the Kaiser he had been right. In early March 1982, when Hamburg played the Swiss club Neuchâtel Xamax in the UEFA Cup, a Beckenbauer gaffe gifted the hosts a goal in the first half, and suddenly you could hear boos and 'Beckenbauer out!' chants from the stands. During the interval, the Kaiser told Happel he should be substituted because he couldn't breathe properly on account of a bruised rib. Beckenbauer watched the second half not from the bench but, standing alone in the cold south-west wind, from the gate through which marathon runners would enter the stadium for their final laps. The next day, he asked Happel to not play him any more unless there was an emergency. 'I'm in no shape to help this team,' he said.

That emergency promptly arose later that month, when Hamburg were missing some key players. Happel gave Beckenbauer the number 6 shirt and played him in midfield against Stuttgart, which must have rekindled his attacking instincts. The Kaiser hit the post with a shot and then, five minutes after the break, went up for a header in the opposition's box. In so doing, he collided with his team-mate Hrubesch and suffered a kidney rupture. There were no two ways about it: somebody or something was trying to tell him it was over.

One person who unavoidably spent a lot of time with Beckenbauer during those months was Hamburg's physio, Dr Friedrich Nottbohm. An energetic man who was about to win the city's parachuting championship for the ninth time, 38-year-old Nottbohm asked Beckenbauer about his plans for the proceeds from the testimonial. When the Kaiser replied he was thinking about donating them to UNICEF, Nottbohm said: 'Have you considered the option of setting up a foundation?'

It was an inspired idea. The profit from the testimonial eventually came to 800,000 marks, which Beckenbauer increased to 1 million out of his own pocket. This was the starting capital for the Franz Beckenbauer Foundation, which today annually contributes twice that amount, roughly 1 million euros, to charitable enterprises and groups, families or individuals in need. Nottbohm had a seat on the board of trustees until he succeeded Hamburg's former president Wolfgang Klein as the foundation's managing director. (The two men, Klein and Nottbohm, died within two months of each other in 2017.)

Beckenbauer's testimonial would not only go down in the annals as the starting point for a player's foundation, then a novel idea, but also for one of his specialities we have so far neglected to mention. There was a Bayern Munich team meeting in early 1975 during which marking responsibilities at corners were discussed. Suddenly Sepp Maier piped up. 'Mister Cramer, shouldn't Katsche rather be taking care of their most dangerous man?' With many questioning faces on him, he identified the 'most dangerous man': 'That's Franz, of course.' People who were there say that Beckenbauer shot him looks that would have instantly killed lesser men than Maier, but the goalkeeper had a point. The Kaiser was known for sometimes putting the ball into the back of the wrong net.

And, you guessed it, he even did that when his Hamburg team met a West German national team that was preparing for the 1982 World Cup. On that day, 1 June, Beckenbauer scored an astonishing own goal from almost eighteen yards out. However, he also found the target at the proper end with a slick volley, as Hamburg lost the match 4-2. After the game, everybody was talking about the Kaiser, and not because the DFB had made him only the third honorary captain of their national team after Fritz Walter and Uwe Seeler. Rather, he had been playing really, really well. Hennes Weisweiler declared that 'Franz was quite obviously the best player on his team'. His old Bayern team-mate Werner Olk added that 'he doesn't play football, he celebrates football. He did things today that players won't be able to duplicate in ten years.' Even the national coach Jupp Derwall chimed in. 'I can understand why Ernst Happel wants him to continue.'

That evening should have been the end of Franz Beckenbauer, the football player, and indeed almost all books and articles that have been written about him (or even supposedly by him) devote at best a single line to what happened in 1983. But the thing is this: one year after his testimonial and 4,000 miles away from Hamburg, Beckenbauer scored another stunning own goal from eighteen yards! This time he didn't just simply put the ball past his own keeper, but lobbed him. Shaking his head, he walked back to the halfway line and looked so dejected that two opposing players – Jeff Durgan and Perry Van der Beck – walked over to him to console the Kaiser.

Durgan and Van der Beck were squad members of a very peculiar NASL club known as Team America. It was the brainchild of NASL president Howard J. Samuels to save a sport that was on its last legs. In the 1982 season, no fewer than seven NASL clubs had folded, the Los Angeles Aztecs among them, and even the mighty Cosmos were sometimes drawing only 18,000. Samuels deduced that people were no longer interested in watching ageing foreigners, and so he set up a team based in Washington that consisted only of US citizens. It was doomed to fail from the beginning. A star like Rick Davis preferred staying in New York and being on a team with Neeskens, while strong players who did show an interest were not released by their clubs. Team America finished with the worst record in the league and actually needed own goals from fading legends to get on the scoreboard.

If anything, the sad story of this club illustrates how terrible things stood for American soccer in 1983. Enter Beckenbauer. He had returned to New York briefly in September 1982 to star in Carlos Alberto's farewell game, when he told reporters that he wouldn't rule out playing for the Cosmos again. After all, he was still under contract with Warner Communications to do promotional work for them. And what could be better promotion than playing for the team Warner owned? In April 1983, it was announced that Beckenbauer would come out of retirement to play football again. He signed a contract for five months, worth an estimated $250,000. His new coach, the Brazilian Júlio Mazzei, was quick to point out that this was not a publicity stunt to lure the fans back to Giants Stadium. 'I think the public will see the best Beckenbauer they have ever seen,' Mazzei said. If that sounded a bit over the top, he had an explanation at the ready. 'He will play sweeper. That is his position. The man revolutionised the position. He played midfield with the Cosmos before because Carlos Alberto was here.'

Beckenbauer missed the first game of the new league season, because back home he was now also a newspaper columnist for the *Bild* tabloid and, as such, in April he had to cover West Germany's two qualifiers for the 1984 European

Championship. But on 1 May 1983, he was back on the pitch. 'Come and ask me in October if the decision to play again was the right decision,' he told the *New York Times*. 'I want to help the team. I feel like I never left, but it takes time to get into the rhythm.'

Against Montreal Manic, he set up the Cosmos' fourth goal before being substituted ten minutes from time. 'I could have played ninety minutes,' he explained, 'but I noticed that the muscle was getting tight, and we were leading 4-0.' When Cosmos beat writer Alex Yannis asked him which muscle he was referring to, the Kaiser pointed to his head. After all those months spent skiing in Austria – he had bought a house in Kitzbühel in Tyrol – or jetting to the Carnival in Rio de Janeiro with his girlfriend Diana, it took some time to realise he was now wearing shorts again and running across that dreaded astroturf.

'He was still fantastic – whenever he was on the ball, a murmur went through the crowd,' remembers the German-born Hubert Birkenmeier, then the Cosmos' first-choice goalkeeper. 'He had always stayed in touch with us. When he played his testimonial for Hamburg, Carlos Alberto, Giorgio Chinaglia and yours truly were in the stands, because we happened to be in Europe and he invited us. When he came back, it was a difficult time for the club. Warner were haemorrhaging money because the Atari was no longer selling, wages were cut and everything. But Franz was still Franz. An idol for the kids, a great mate on and off the pitch, and the perfect gentleman.'

Guided by Beckenbauer, the Cosmos won their division again, but then went out in the play-off quarter-finals against Montreal. There was one very memorable day, though. On 16 June, the New Yorkers played host to the team that had just won the European Cup against Juventus. It was none other than Ernst Happel's Hamburg side. A slightly disappointing crowd of 31,000 came to Giants Stadium to witness what turned out to be one of the greatest and most legendary nights in Cosmos history.

At half-time, the West Germans were leading 2-1, but there were already clear signs that they would not be playing the Americans off the park. Happel was one of the pioneers of the pressing game and a well-oiled offside trap was an integral part of those tactics. But time and again the Cosmos got behind the backline, such as when Neeskens and Vladislav Bogićević were both one on one with goalkeeper Uli Stein, who saved brilliantly both times. After the game, Beckenbauer declared that 'the Cosmos are not a bad team. We adjusted well after the first twenty minutes or so. We were too afraid of them, but then we realised we can play with them.'

Chinaglia levelled the score after the break, and when it was still 2-2 with fifteen minutes to go, the visitors resigned themselves to the fact that this wouldn't be the walkover they had been expecting. They must have been quite jet-lagged, too, having landed in New York only the day before. It was also very hot, and their holidays would begin in a few hours. So the Hamburg players decided to just run down the clock and draw the game. Mistake.

'Many teams that came to play us underestimated the conditions,' says Birkenmeier from his New Jersey home. 'That astroturf could be tricky. We defeated many strong teams. We only had problems with Anderlecht, because they cottoned on to it and actually practised on astroturf before playing us.' But few teams collapsed as thoroughly as Beckenbauer's former club. An unmarked Neeskens put the

Cosmos ahead, then Chinaglia converted a penalty, before Davis and Roberto Cabañas each scored after mazy runs through the Hamburg backline. Finally, Bogićević made it 7-2 with a simple tap-in. Günter Netzer was aghast. 'The team's holidays begin when we say they do, not a single day earlier,' he said. 'They'll find excuses for us in Germany, but the truth is that we were embarrassed.'

The Cosmos had been knocked out of the play-offs on 12 September, the day after Beckenbauer's thirty-eighth birthday. Still, he had made the league's all-star team yet again and the club offered him another contract. The Kaiser mulled this over for quite a while but eventually decided against it, probably following the old adage that when you discover you are riding a dead horse, the best strategy is to dismount. Sixteen months later, the NASL suspended operations.

Just a handful of months after Beckenbauer had hung up his boots for good, the slightly younger Johan Cruyff did the same. It was another in a long line of parallels between the Kaiser and the King. The Dutch author Marcel Rözer, who published a book about the two legends in 2007, has a few more in store. 'They both had absent fathers,' he begins. 'Johan's dad passed away when he was still a boy. Franz's father was alive, but not really available for him as a dad. So both of them were looking for father figures and found them in their respective agents, who also happened to be about the same age. Both players had one older sibling, who would somehow have to come to terms with the fact that he was forever going to be just "the brother of".' Rözer sees one distinction, though. 'I think one of the major differences between Beckenbauer and Cruyff is that Franz grew up, while Johan never did.'

Beckenbauer himself has repeatedly stated that he didn't have to grow up until he first moved to New York. On the other hand, there are those who say that the Cosmos was the greatest kindergarten in football history and that Beckenbauer didn't really grow up until 2015, when he was dealt a blow of fate you wouldn't wish on your worst enemy. In any case, there are some more differences between him and Cruyff, starting with the fact that the Dutchman was a steadfast Puma acolyte. Another is that Cruyff had visions and always knew what he wanted – be it money, as his detractors would say, or a better football world. But Beckenbauer, in stark contrast, was never a visionary. He also never seemed to truly care about money or material goods. He admired fluent, offensive football, but he could be extremely pragmatic, both as a player and a coach. And most importantly, he never really knew what he wanted.

When Beckenbauer was asked shortly before his seventy-fifth birthday about all those sudden and thorough changes of heart that have littered his career, all he could say was: 'I guess that's symbolic of my life. It was all a bit of a mess, really.' What he meant by this was that he had never planned anything beyond joining a club and becoming a footballer. Everything else somehow just happened to him, usually because – as his friends will put it – he can't say no.

Sometimes he couldn't say yes, either. There are plenty of stories about Schwan supplying the press with inside information just so that the resulting coverage would force his client to make up his mind about one thing or another and come to a decision, hence Netzer's immediate suspicion about the photographers at Régine's. The most famous of all these cases gradually developed over the months after Beckenbauer's second return from New York, until reaching boiling point in the summer of 1984.

It's part of the Beckenbauer-as-shining-light myth that the man who went on to become only the second footballer to win the World Cup as both player and coach never wanted to go into coaching. It sounds good but it's not true. As early as August 1981, he told *Die Welt* newspaper about his plans for his second career. 'I'd like to stay close to sports. Maybe work as a journalist, maybe as a club's business manager. I will also acquire my coaching badges at the Sport University in Cologne.' In the same interview, he bitterly complained about his treatment at the hands of the journalists after his return from the US. 'Hennes Weisweiler warned me about the public,' he explained. 'He said the media are more and more looking for negative sensations. Gosh, I'm not a dreamer, I knew what I would be in for. Still, it was irritating to be pounced on like that.'

The same media that pounced on him when he was struggling on the pitch during his time at Hamburg were now keen to talk him up as the next West Germany manager. It never fails to amaze non-Germans that Jupp Derwall was so monumentally unpopular after winning Euro 1980 and then reaching the 1982 World Cup final that the press (and, truth be told, the fans) were calling for his head. It's quite easy, though. After the World Cup, there was a widespread feeling that the national team was morally corrupt and almost an embarrassment, despite the success on the field of play.

From a West German standpoint, the tournament in Spain was not only marred by the notorious Patrick Battiston incident (when goalkeeper Harald Schumacher brutally and cynically knocked out the French defender in the semis). There was also an annoying atmosphere of arrogance, such as when Derwall admitted after a sensational loss against Algeria that he hadn't warned his players about the opposition because 'they wouldn't have taken that seriously'. The team also behaved dreadfully towards their own fans.

Finally, the lack of discipline put even the Cosmos in the shade. Schumacher would soon publish a tell-all book in which he revealed shocking details about the preparation camp in Schluchsee, destined to go down in German football lore as *Schlucksee* – Lake Swig. He said that some players gambled 'like addicts' and that others 'screwed until dawn and then came crawling to the morning training session looking like damp cloth, while still others downed whisky in the manner of binge drinkers'.

In October 1983, just weeks after Beckenbauer's last game and before he had even turned the latest Cosmos offer down, a reporter from the illustrated news magazine *Quick* bluntly asked him: 'Wouldn't you like to coach Germany? Millions of football fans secretly want this. They yearn for somebody who knows everything about the game, who has seen the world. Somebody even stars can learn from, who knows all the tricks on the pitch and behind the scenes. Somebody with experience and authority.' Beckenbauer replied: 'This subject is most certainly not on the agenda for another four years. In any case, I don't have the necessary coaching badges. But I will get them at some point in the coming years.' Then he let slip that he had been in talks with the Sport University in Cologne, which handed out those badges, about 'special conditions', meaning a shortened course, without success.

As lame ducks go, Derwall proved to be tenacious. A few weeks after the *Quick* profile, West Germany went into their remaining two European Championship qualifiers needing just two points to go through. They promptly lost the first game at home against Northern Ireland. When an eighteen-year-old Norman Whiteside beat Schumacher from close range, Billy Bingham's side were suddenly topping the table. The West Germans still seemed to be on the safe side, because their final group game was another home match, against minnows Albania. Shockingly, the visitors went ahead after twenty-two minutes. Karl-Heinz Rummenigge soon tied the game, but his equaliser was followed by almost an hour of intense nail-biting, until Cologne's libero Gerd Strack, wearing the Kaiser's number 5, headed home a late winner.

National coach Derwall had cheated the gallows once more, and he came very, very close to doing it all over again at the Euro 1984 finals in France. West Germany needed only a draw from their final group game against Spain to reach the semi-finals. The team got off to a flying start, hitting the crossbar twice and the post once before half an hour was up. But Spain's goalkeeper Luis Arconada played a blinder, and so the encounter was still scoreless going into the last minute. Then Juan Señor whipped in a cross from the right and Antonio Maceda headed the ball past Schumacher. He, too, was his team's libero.

On the next day, the 39-year-old *Bild* reporter Jörg F. Hüls was shooting the breeze with his new colleague, columnist Beckenbauer. Both men knew that Derwall was now history, but who was even qualified to follow him? Not in terms of coaching badges or job experience, but sheer standing. After all, the next national coach had to restore not just the quality of the West German game but its reputation. The French newspaper *Libération* had just celebrated Derwall's side's exit from the Euros. 'German football, this brute animal, deserved to be drowned in its own urine. The German monster has survived for too many seasons, too many international tournaments. The Germans were suffering from the distressing delusion that history was on their side, that fate would always deliver a happy ending for them.' Mincing words was clearly not the newspaper's style.

'Erich Ribbeck,' Hüls suggested.

'Come on!' Beckenbauer said.

'Berti Vogts.'

'You must be kidding.'

'What about Helmut Benthaus?' Hüls offered, referring to the 45-year-old German coach who had just guided VfB Stuttgart to an unexpected Bundesliga title. Benthaus, a trained teacher, was a pleasant and sophisticated man. And the DFB's number-one target.

'In that case everybody will pass their A-level exams,' the Kaiser quipped, 'but still not play proper football.'

'Well, then you have to do it yourself.'

'Now you've gone bonkers!'

Try as he might, Hüls couldn't really get anything more substantial out of Beckenbauer than that he was willing to enter into talks with the DFB and that 'responsibilities will have to be discussed'. The writer then constructed an interview out of the conversation and sent it to over to the Hamburg desk so that it could be published the next day, 22 June. But the sub-editor in Hamburg must have felt that the article lacked some real punch, because he came up with the headline 'Derwall gone – Franz: I am ready'.

Even by the standards of the most notorious of German papers, this was audacious. It had to be cleared by someone, and so the tabloid's go-getting head of sport, Werner Köster, made a phone call. Some people say it was placed to the Hotel Pavillon Henri IV in Saint-Germain-en-Laye, where Beckenbauer was drinking red wine with Hüls and the other *Bild* hacks. According to this version, it took quite a lot of cajoling (and many drinks) until the Kaiser gave the headline the green light.

Another theory, which is the more likely one, says that the phone call from Hamburg was made to Kitzbühel. Robert Schwan, the great white bird, had found a ready-made nest and was now living in the flat above Franz and Diana in the house Beckenbauer had recently bought in the small Austrian town. This version is more likely because Beckenbauer always maintained that the headline caught him unawares. In his 1992 autobiography, he explained that 'this *Bild* headline came thanks to Robert Schwan and the newspaper's head of sport'. Beckenbauer's only reliable biographer, Torsten Körner, says that the Kaiser was 'genuinely surprised' by the headline.

To this day, people from *Bild* pat themselves on the back and claim their paper was instrumental in making Beckenbauer the national coach. Whether or not this is true largely depends on the definition of 'make' – not to mention 'national coach'. The headline, and its ensuing brouhaha, did indeed force two somewhat reluctant parties – Beckenbauer and the DFB – to enter into negotiations. However, at first neither expected this to be more than just a temporary stop-gap solution. The DFB still wanted Benthaus, but the problem was that he couldn't even be reached for comment during those fast-paced days in June 1984, because he was holidaying somewhere in the Canadian wilderness. A writer for *Kicker* magazine managed to get through to Benthaus's sister-in-law, who was living there on a remote ranch, but all she could say was that she had seen the coach a couple of days ago and that he might return tomorrow or next week. The writer asked her to tell Helmut Benthaus that Jupp Derwall had been sacked; he would then guess the rest.

One person who could not only be reached for comment

but who was eager to get a word in was Stuttgart's president, the high-ranking politician Gerhard Mayer-Vorfelder. 'We will not release Mr Benthaus from his contract, which runs until 1985,' he stated. 'Where are we supposed to find a new coach so quickly, anyway?' This forced the DFB's hand. Of course, it was not unheard of for ruthless coaches to get out of contracts, but Benthaus was so popular precisely because he wasn't that kind of coach. If Stuttgart stood firm on this, Benthaus would never renege on his word.

On the day before the Euro 1984 final, DFB president Hermann Neuberger sat down with Beckenbauer to discuss the situation. The president must have been wary, because this was not the first time he had talked with the Kaiser about a post with the national team. In 1977, shortly before Beckenbauer signed for the Cosmos, Neuberger had urged him to stay in West Germany and held out the prospect of one day becoming national coach. Five years later, on the occasion of Beckenbauer's testimonial in Hamburg, the president renewed his offer. And according to *Kicker* editor Karl-Heinz Heimann, Neuberger had made a third attempt barely a month ago in Zürich, when West Germany played Italy to celebrate FIFA's eightieth birthday. Having been rebuffed three times, Neuberger was now on his guard.

Still, the two men came to an understanding. Beckenbauer would be made the national team's 'technical director' until Benthaus was available. During that one year, the Kaiser would be assisted by a DFB employee who held the necessary coaching badges. 'I probably don't realise what I've gotten myself into now,' Beckenbauer told a reporter, adding: 'As soon as a new national coach has been found, I will back-track.'

So why did he agree to help out in the first place? As

observers would soon point out, he was a man of contradictions. Many found him to be taciturn, others garrulous. He had a naturally friendly disposition, but his tongue could be vicious. He was often lethargic, then suddenly impatient. Someone so unstable, to use his own word, was temperamentally unsuited to this particular vacancy. And yet he took the job. Was it really just because he couldn't say no? Was it out of a sense of duty? Was it because he needed to feel the competitive juices flowing again? Was it, as he told *Kicker*, because he was sick of his non-German friends making fun of the national team? Was it, as he told the *New York Times*, because someone had to do something to stop the rot and everybody said he was the only one who could do it? As the Irish comedian Dave Allen would have said: yes.

The deal Beckenbauer and Neuberger had struck needed to be amended only two days later. On the last Thursday in June, Benthaus came back from his overseas holidays and had a thirty-minute phone conversation with the DFB president. If Neuberger had expected the coach to be jubilant, he was in for a surprise. The way Benthaus saw it, he could be in big trouble if he committed himself now. What if the Kaiser proved to be a smashing success? Conversely, what if Stuttgart had a disappointing season? Too many things could happen during the next twelve months. So Benthaus told Neuberger that he would wait until April 1985 to decide whether or not to take over the national team. Of course such uncertainty was not ideal for the DFB, especially in the build-up to a World Cup. And so Neuberger asked Beckenbauer if he would also sign for two years instead of just the one, to which the Kaiser agreed.

There was another change to the agreement when Neuberger came up with a job title he liked better than technical director. He suggested *Teamchef*, in the sense of the team's boss ('chef' having no culinary meaning for Germans). Beckenbauer replied he couldn't care less about what his actual title was – manager, coach, director. So why not chef?

Neuberger then also suggested two potential assistants with those all important badges: the experienced Erich Ribbeck or the 36-year-old Horst Köppel, a former Gladbach player who had become Derwall's right-hand man as recently as the summer of 1983. Beckenbauer chose Köppel. 'The DFB asked me if I was willing to work under Franz, and of course I said yes,' Köppel recalls. 'So he gave me a call. I don't think we talked for more than five minutes. My understanding was that Erich Ribbeck wasn't interested in being an assistant coach, but I could be wrong about this. Either way, Franz and I hit it off right away.' That must have been the case, because Beckenbauer publicly stated: 'I'm doing this with Köppel – or I'm back on the course.' He was referring to golf, a sport he had picked up thanks to Diana Sandmann (more about that later) and which he would one day play quite decently, boasting a handicap of seven, as well as playing a round with Tiger Woods.

In mid-July, during a regular board meeting of the West German game's governing body, Neuberger officially announced what everybody had already read in the papers. Until the World Cup in Mexico, Franz Beckenbauer would be the new national coach by any other name. It was Friday the thirteenth, and the agreement would have consequences for Beckenbauer's life on many levels. That's because his travels abroad would from now on be organised by a 38-year-old DFB secretary called Sybille Weimer. The Teamchef found her rather attractive.

LIFE II

Chapter Eight

The two quotes which are most closely associated in the public mind with Beckenbauer's years at the helm of the national team are '*Schaun mer mal*' and '*Geht's raus und spielt's Fussball*', both spoken in an understated but noticeable Bavarian dialect. The first means 'Let us see' and was his stock reply for nosy reporters clamouring for details about the line-up or the tactics. The second translates as 'Go out and play football' and was the Kaiser's legendary parting remark before his team left the dressing room to meet Argentina in the 1990 World Cup final.

The popularity of these lines has created a misleading image of the Teamchef. Today, many people think that Beckenbauer ran the team in a relaxed, almost casual manner, secure in the knowledge that his god-given talent for coming out on top would rub off on his charges. The hard work, people think, was done by his assistants, while the Kaiser mainly used his charisma to motivate or stimulate the players.

It's nonsense. If anything, until the very late stages of his managerial reign, Beckenbauer was probably not relaxed and casual enough, and was working too hard. He spent endless hours scouting and analysing whatever team his side would be up against, almost pathologically afraid that he would overlook a crucial detail and not prepare his players as comprehensively as possible. 'You wouldn't have thought he was so meticulous,' says Horst Köppel. 'He had this image of being a hands-down guy, but instead he was very thorough. I remember our discussions about the squad for the 1986 World Cup went on for ever. We had narrowed the list down to twenty-six names, meaning four players needed to be cut. That was also the only real difference of opinion we ever had. I was all for taking Guido Buchwald to Mexico. Franz said in jest: "You only want to pick him because he is a Swabian like you."' (Buchwald was born in Berlin, but moved to the Stuttgart area as a toddler.)

It's tempting to argue that Beckenbauer was so obsessed with dissecting how other teams played because he had been a defender. His mindset was to assume that the opposition had the ball, and he took it from there. His friend Johan Cruyff – who had gone into coaching eleven months after Beckenbauer, also as a 'technical director' because he lacked the required diplomas – was the total opposite. He took possession as the starting point and created an entire philosophy out of it, one that permeates football to this day.

Beckenbauer the coach has left no such legacy. During his time with the national team, he became greatly interested in philosophy and would soon devour books on the subject, quoting Confucius in conversation with puzzled writers. But he was no deep thinker, no innovator, no philosopher himself. Quite the contrary: the Kaiser was the most calculating proponent of *realpolitik* among German World Cup-winning coaches.

If he had a grand unified theory at all, it was a sobering one. After the 1986 World Cup, a reporter accused him of having failed to do what had been expected of him – overhaul the team, change the football, build an attacking side. Beckenbauer coolly replied that 'a defensive stance corresponds to German nature, so that's how we play football. We get stuck in, we destroy the opponent's game and then force our game onto him. That's all we know how to do.' Probably realising that it was hard if not impossible to align these cold, cruel words with the way he himself used to play the game, Beckenbauer added: 'I have to adjust to my possibilities. The last time we had a really great national team was in 1974. That was when we could be active. But, after that, it all went downhill with German football.'

Put differently, it was not his character, his personality or his former position on the pitch that informed his football – it was the footballers at his disposal. There were very few technically gifted, creative players around. Two of them, Hamburg's playmaker Felix Magath and Barcelona's midfielder Bernd Schuster, had fallen out with Jupp Derwall and refused to play for the national team. The Kaiser managed to lure his former team-mate Magath out of that self-imposed exile, but somehow his regal charm didn't work on Schuster, who'd just been voted the best foreigner in Spain's top flight. Or rather, it didn't work on someone close to him.

In late March 1986, Beckenbauer called Schuster in Barcelona, while a chartered plane was waiting at Munich Airport, ready to take the Teamchef to Catalonia, even though it was Easter. However, the phone was not answered by the player but by his wife Gaby, who doubled as her husband's agent. She told Beckenbauer that Bernd would play at the World Cup . . . for 1 million marks. It tells you how desperate the Kaiser was for some real talent in his team that he replied he was willing to discuss the matter in person in a few hours' time in Barcelona. But when Gaby Schuster told him he needn't bother to come down if he didn't have a cheque with him, Beckenbauer hung up. The 26-year-old Bernd Schuster, the best German footballer of his generation, never played for his country again.

And so Beckenbauer travelled to the 1986 World Cup in Mexico with a squad he secretly feared had the potential to really embarrass the country. Or perhaps not quite so secretly. First, he publicly called the Bundesliga 'a scrap heap', which didn't endear him to the clubs' representatives. Then he rubbed the journalists who covered the national team up the wrong way by saying that their articles were 'as irrelevant as a bicycle falling down in Beijing'. Finally, he came close to alienating his own team when he predicted that 'we just cannot win this World Cup. And while we're at it, we're not going to win the 1988 European Championship either.'

But thoughtless remarks like these were only the beginning of Beckenbauer's mistakes before and during the tournament. First, he allowed the reporters to set up camp in the same hotel as the players, the La Mansión Galindo near Santiago de Querétaro. It was a strange idea, considering how thin-skinned and irritable Beckenbauer had become in his dealings with the media, even with journalists he had known for years. Within weeks the Kaiser would admit that 'allowing the press into our hotel was the worst decision I've ever made'. With at least fifty writers from various countries constantly lurking around the premises and looking for stories, it was a disaster waiting to happen.

And it happened early. Before the tournament had even started, the daily Mexican newspaper *Excélsior* carried a piece by a journalist called Miguel Hirsch about a lack of discipline in the West German camp. *Bild* then quoted from this article and, in time-tested tabloid style, vastly exaggerated the content. Beckenbauer went berserk when he read this and fell back upon strong language. When he was asked if he had confronted the writer directly, the Kaiser said: 'No, because if I had, he would be dead now. With a little Mexican like that, a squeeze is enough and he's gone.' A few days later, Beckenbauer sheepishly sent *Excélsior* a letter of apology, arguing his Bavarian dialect was the reason why a statement that was meant to be funny had come out sounding very harsh. 'I accept this apology without humour,' said Hirsch, 'but the damage has been done, Franz.'

The next person Beckenbauer probably would have liked to squeeze a little harder was Uli Stein. When Beckenbauer's former Hamburg team-mate realised that he was only going to be the reserve goalkeeper, he went into full pouting mode. Before West Germany's opening game, he told the press: 'If someone has a spare airline ticket, I'm going home.' Ten days later, a writer claimed Stein had drunk himself into such a stupor that he fell off a barstool, which the player vehemently denied. Still, on the day of West Germany's round-of-16 game against Morocco, a reporter spotted him at four o'clock in the morning, fully dressed and fresh as a daisy.

Two days after that, Stein was one of four players (the others being Ditmar Jakobs, Klaus Augenthaler and Dieter Hoeness) who missed the curfew by three hours. Beckenbauer gave them a good dressing-down for this 'idiotic' behaviour, whereupon Hoeness shot back: 'You can call me anything – but not an idiot. I know how brainy I am and I know how brainy you are. That's why you don't call me an idiot.' Beckenbauer eventually fined Jakobs, Augenthaler and

Hoeness 5,000 marks each. Stein, however, was supposed to pay 10,000 marks. When he heard this, the goalkeeper once again threatened to travel home immediately. At this point, Schalke's Olaf Thon, barely eighteen years old, suddenly raised his voice to announce he would like to leave as well, because 'there is nothing to learn here'.

The Kaiser had just about managed to quell this mutiny when the next scandal broke. The newspapers back home were reporting that Stein was calling Beckenbauer *Suppenkasper* behind his back and in front of the other players. (It was a reference to the character from a German children's book known as Soup Kaspar in English – and, of course, to the Kaiser's legendary 1960s TV ads for Knorr.) The DFB demanded a severe punishment, and so Stein was finally given the airplane ticket he had craved so much – against Beckenbauer's wishes. Unless the apocryphal story that defender Sigmund Haringer was banned from the 1934 squad for eating an orange is actually true, Stein became the first German player ever sent home from a World Cup. No wonder *Stern* magazine would dub Beckenbauer's merry men 'la Cage aux Folles'.

Taking all this hoopla into account, it comes as little surprise that Beckenbauer, according to his 1992 autobiography, offered DFB president Hermann Neuberger his resignation after the end of the tournament. The Kaiser couldn't just say thanks and walk away because he had extended his contract until 1988 only a few months earlier. But Neuberger said no, and Beckenbauer didn't insist – for two good reasons. The first was that, as he confessed to his old Cosmos acquaintance, the writer Alex Yannis, during the World Cup, 'I'm beginning to like coaching'. He enjoyed being around the players and nurtured a good relationship with his squad. Even

Stein never bore a grudge, and first-choice goalkeeper Harald Schumacher even marvelled about the 'patience of a saint' which Beckenbauer displayed towards the team. It was only the media that found him touchy and aggressive.

The second reason why Beckenbauer tendered his resignation just perfunctorily (in case Neuberger had changed his mind about him) was that, against all odds, the World Cup had been a sporting success. The Kaiser may have been a walking public relations disaster, but he didn't put a foot wrong in his day job, except perhaps for insisting on giving Karl-Heinz Rummenigge playing time even though the Bayern forward was carrying a knee injury and never became really match fit. Beckenbauer's pedestrian but well-organised and resilient team squeezed past Morocco, defeated hosts Mexico on penalties and then won the semi-final 2-0 against reigning European champions France. 'We have managed all this without any young players developing,' the Kaiser told the *New York Times*. 'We have to rely on the veterans.' As far as he was concerned, his team had not disappointed but overachieved. While the West German press was on his back, saying his side lacked panache and valour, he looked at the final ninety minutes of the tournament and had to conclude that being courageous and taking risks had cost the team the trophy.

West Germany fell behind in the final against Diego Maradona's Argentina because Schumacher completely misjudged a cross from a free-kick. Being a goal down, the team was forced to become uncharacteristically adventurous and was promptly hit on the break ten minutes into the second half. But then Beckenbauer's gamble paid off when, of all people, Rummenigge pulled one back, before Rudi Völler suddenly tied the game nine minutes from time. It was a classic Teutonic comeback, stunning the Mexican crowd and shocking the Argentinian players. Either because the Germans were now too euphoric after their equaliser or because they smelled blood, thinking this was a golden opportunity to knock out a punch-drunk opponent, Beckenbauer's men pressed forward. Fewer than three minutes after Völler's goal, eight West German players were in Argentina's half, three of them crowding in on Maradona. But still the Golden Boy found an unmarked Jorge Burruchaga with a magnificent through ball to decide the game.

'Argentina deserved to come out on top in the final, and they are worthy World Cup winners,' the Teamchef said after the game. 'We were overjoyed to even make it this far.' Years later, he would argue that a West German victory in 1986 'would have been a defeat for football', though of course such self-critical verdicts roll off your tongue so much easier when you've bagged the biggest prize of them all.

The World Cup in Mexico was a steep learning curve for the Kaiser. He was only eight years older than some of his players – Jakobs, Magath, Hoeness – and he had been on the same team as quite a few of them, including the side's captain, Rummenigge. He would have to make some adjustments, and the good thing was he could do so without undue pressure. West Germany was going to host the 1988 European Championship, so there were no must-win qualifiers ahead. Beckenbauer could go about learning how to be a little less lenient towards his players and a bit more forgiving with regard to the press pack at his own pace. Not that it was easy, though. Not at all. One can think of many places on this earth where the country's greatest player of all time could work in peace if he had just taken the national team to the World Cup final. Alas, Germany is not one of them.

First, Beckenbauer lost his trusted assistant, as Horst Köppel asked the DFB in December 1986 to be let out of his contract at the end of the season. Sources claim he did so when he realised that Beckenbauer would stay on until 1990, that Köppel didn't want to remain in the Kaiser's shadow. 'No, not really,' he says today. 'That was, if anything, a side issue. The main thing was that I wanted to spend more time on the training pitch, working with players. But you only have that in club football. Instead I was attending all those boring meetings of regional DFB associations. Franz refused to do that – I couldn't blame him! – but somebody had to represent the national team. Suddenly I received an offer from a club in the Bundesliga, Bayer Uerdingen. I had to make a decision.'

Next, it was a player who put a spanner in the works. In February 1987, Harald 'Toni' Schumacher published his tell-all memoirs about life in the Bundesliga. The book was filled with all the right ingredients to make it a bestseller: sex, gambling, in-fighting, money and drugs (in the form of doping). It also derailed his career. His club, Cologne, immediately suspended the player because he had broken his contract by not clearing the book with the board first. Beckenbauer – you know, '*Schaun mer mal*' – was calmer and more prudent. He first read the book, then discussed the matter with Neuberger, finally with Schumacher himself. It was only in March that Beckenbauer declared the goalie's international career to be over. In the span of fewer than nine months, he had now banished two outstanding keepers, but luckily the West German reservoir was deep. Stuttgart's Eike Immel (a future Manchester City player) and young Bodo Illgner from Cologne were now vying for the number 1 shirt.

Finally, his old chums from the tabloid press made life difficult. *Bild* had signed two new columnists and both had a history of sparring with Beckenbauer: Udo Lattek and Paul Breitner. In the spring of 1988, with the European Championship on home soil barely two months away, Breitner accused Beckenbauer of 'digging German football's grave' with his defensive 'horror tactics', while Lattek argued the man in charge of the national team secretly 'despised' his players because he could detect none of his own talent in any of them. The Kaiser hit back, of course, also via *Bild*, and called Breitner 'a nutcase' who must have been drunk while composing his column.

It was more than just a storm in a teacup; the tabloids were speaking for many regular fans. After a lacklustre game against Sweden in late March, *Kicker* magazine's letters pages were teeming with complaints from disgruntled punters. One, Mr Woitaschek from Maintal near Frankfurt, grumbled that 'since football is not a science, you don't need to carry coaching badges to see that the "singularly lucky find Beckenbauer" (Neuberger) is turning this team into a second-rate side if nothing is done about it.' Many observers felt the tabloids were testing the waters to see if they could already position Beckenbauer's successor, presumably Lattek, the way they had done it four years earlier when they wrote Derwall out of a job and promoted the Kaiser. 'Breitner, the watch dog, was let loose to bark,' as the *Süddeutsche Zeitung* put it. Beckenbauer himself must have suspected something like this, because he openly toyed with stepping down, saying: 'They are not going to treat me like they treated Jupp Derwall.'

However, as it would turn out, this furore was not the beginning of his end, but the end of his beginning. Perhaps it was the much-quoted comment from a more seasoned coach that helped the Kaiser put things into perspective. When Bobby Robson, who as England manager knew a thing or two about the most thankless job a football country had to offer, was asked if he had any idea why Beckenbauer was criticised so heavily, he replied: 'It's because the best sailors are always to be found on the beach.' Within a few weeks, Beckenbauer would be able to joke that the man who was penning the columns of all three men – Breitner, Lattek and himself – 'must be earning millions, considering the amount of intellectual diarrhea he has to process'.

Or maybe he stopped shouting at the wind and started to ride the wave because he realised that football was a piece of cake compared to his love life. After more than three years of labouring like a sixth-former for his first date – his own words, not mine – Sybille Weimer had finally done what all women sooner or later did, succumb to the boyish charm of the chosen one. In his 1992 book, Beckenbauer would defend his next clandestine affair by saying that his relationship with Diana Sandmann had been doomed from the start due to his feelings of guilt towards his family – which was a bit rich, considering he was now cheating on the woman he had cheated on his wife with. Oh, and with a married woman.

Before the one game from the 1988 European Championship which every German (and Dutchman) remembers, Beckenbauer tried a little gamesmanship. He sat down with captain Lothar Matthäus, midfielder Pierre Littbarski and Dortmund forward Frank Mill, informing the trio that he had an idea for the following day's semi-final against the marvellous Dutch. After years of being told that his football was too cautious, the Kaiser was now going to start three centre-forwards – Jürgen Klinsmann, Völler and Mill. This would surprise the men in orange and force them to be a bit more defensive, which was not their style. The key to success,

Beckenbauer explained, was the element of surprise, which is why he asked the three players to not reveal the line-up.

On the next day, Littbarski's name was printed on the team-sheet that was distributed to the press in Hamburg, the site of the game. Only minutes before kick-off came a news bulletin from the DFB that said the player was suffering from an upset stomach and would have to be replaced by Mill. When the Dortmund striker tired late in the game, he was taken off – and Littbarski came on. 'It can happen that a player falls ill very shortly before a game,' the Dutch coach Rinus Michels said sarcastically. 'But it's stupefying that the sick player is then brought into the game.'

Yet the silly ploy almost worked. On fifty-four minutes, Klinsmann was brought down in the box by Frank Rijkaard, West Germany were awarded a penalty, and Matthäus put his team ahead. It was not the clearest penalty the Romanian referee Ioan Igna had ever awarded, but it was much, much clearer than the spot-kick he granted the Dutch twenty minutes later. Marco van Basten lost his balance under a challenge from Jürgen Kohler, but tried to get up quickly again to collect the loose ball. Only then did he realise that Igna had blown his whistle and pointed to the spot. Ronald Koeman put the penalty away, then Van Basten scored a famous winner two minutes from time.

Fourteen years after Munich, the Netherlands finally had their revenge for the traumatic World Cup defeat, and they thoroughly enjoyed it. Reports suggest that 9 million people took to the streets of the Netherlands to celebrate – in a country of 15 million. In Hamburg, meanwhile, there were some disturbing scenes. The Dutch fans burned German flags in the stands, while Koeman pretended to wipe his backside with Thon's shirt. Matthäus revealed that the Netherlands'

Former US secretary of state Henry Kissinger, born in Germany
and a massive football fan, liked to rub shoulders with the Cosmos in 1977.
The man in the tub with Beckenbauer is the team's captain Werner Roth.

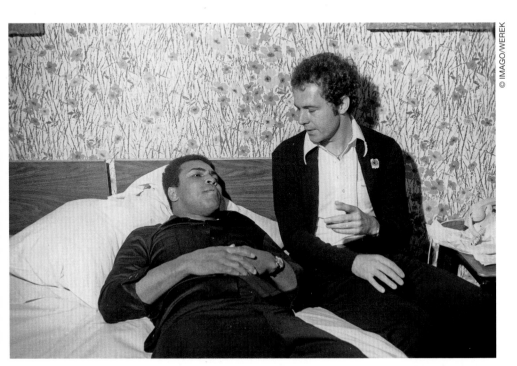

The Kaiser met The Greatest for the first time after the latter's bout with Earnie Shavers
in September 1977. Muhammad Ali had won the fight but was still feeling its effects. Also
in the room, though not pictured, was Beckenbauer's older brother, Walter.

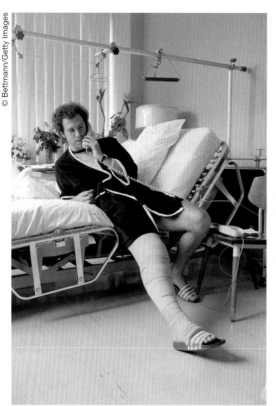

In May 1979, Beckenbauer underwent knee surgery at Lenox Hill Hospital in Manhattan. 'Franz began to have these minor ailments,' said his former Hamburg team-mate Ditmar Jakobs. 'He blamed them on all those years playing on astroturf, and he could very well be right.'

The treacherous playing surfaces in the US informed Beckenbauer's decision to return to Germany. When he arrived in Hamburg on 31 May 1980 in a private jet, he was mobbed by the club's fans.

Beckenbauer's debuts often went wrong, so he cannot have been surprised to lose his first game in charge of the national team 3–1 against Argentina on 12 September 1984. Next to him is his assistant Horst Köppel.

It was his long-time girlfriend Diana Sandmann who introduced Beckenbauer to one of his greatest passions: golf. Here the couple share a round in October 1985, not too long after Beckenbauer had met his second wife, Sybille.

In 1986, Beckenbauer took West Germany to the World Cup final, although goalkeeper Harald 'Toni' Schumacher was one of the few truly classy players in the side.

At the tournament in Mexico, Beckenbauer was very popular with the local fans, who remembered his heroics during the 1970 World Cup.

Berni, the Euro 1988 mascot, didn't faze Beckenbauer: after all, he had often appeared alongside Bugs Bunny during his days with the Cosmos.

It was at Italia 90 that the Kaiser's country finally learned to love him for good. He was now a charming, serene man at ease with himself.

Of course it helps if you win the whole thing. When the final ended,
Beckenbauer was beaten to the pitch by sub Paul Steiner (*right*).

By the end of his tenure, Beckenbauer was adored by the public,
the press – and particularly by his players.

Beckenbauer with Monaco coach Arsène Wenger during the Kaiser's rather brief stint at Marseille. A few years later, in April 1994, the Frenchman would be offered the Bayern job.

At the time, Beckenbauer was about to lead Bayern to the league title – but only on an interim basis.

On 6 July 2000, Beckenbauer proudly presents the trophy he won as a player and as a coach, because his country has just been awarded the 2006 World Cup, for which he led the bid committee. It's the high point of the Kaiser's career – and the beginning of his downfall.

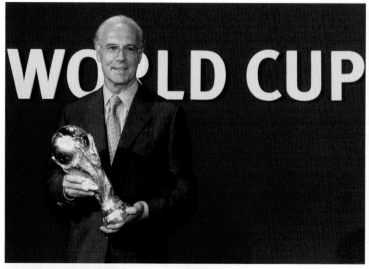

Beckenbauer with Chancellor Angela Merkel a few days before the 2006 World Cup final. Whatever he was aiming for with his shot, chances are he will have hit it.

On the twentieth anniversary of the World Cup triumph in Rome, Wolfgang Niersbach returned the winner's medal Beckenbauer had gifted him back in 1990. Little did Niersbach, then the German FA's secretary general, know how many headaches Beckenbauer would cause him in the years to come.

goalkeeper Hans van Breukelen had said to him: 'I hope you die like an animal.' (Van Breukelen admits this, adding he is not particularly proud of his behaviour during that game.) Until this day, the West Germans had not quite realised how deep the Dutch resentment really ran. They would make a mental note of it, though, which led to the strange situation that while the matter was now more or less closed for many people in the Netherlands (Van Breukelen says that, for him, 'the trauma was over'), the Germans were ready and willing to fill this latest rivalry with life.

As far as football was concerned, however, most observers agreed that sheer talent had prevailed. 'The clearly better team has won deservedly,' said Neuberger. 'We should be happy with having made the semis.' He had a point, because in those days the European Championship was widely considered a stronger tournament than the World Cup. (To make the last four, West Germany had to progress from a group with Denmark's golden generation, Italy and Spain.) Still, one man begged to differ. Two years after predicting his team stood no chance whatsoever of winning the trophy, Beckenbauer complained that West Germany had just suffered their 'most unlucky defeat in decades'.

If you look beyond the Kaiser's famous propensity to exaggerate ('in decades'), it was not a totally unreasonable statement. His team had given the favourites a good game. In fact, Klinsmann had missed the target only by the narrowest of margins when it was 1-0, and the Netherlands' penalty was indeed softer than anything Bernd Hölzenbein had ever hustled. Still, two days after the game, a member of the Kaiser's immediate family was sitting in a Munich beer garden (drinking water, of course) and declared that 'the Dutch were far superior'.

Stephan Beckenbauer, nineteen years old, would be meeting his father later in the day because it was grandma Antonie's seventy-fifth birthday. Stephan was half-expecting to hear some critical words from the man who was now known as the Teamchef. After many years in Bayern's youth set-up, Stephan had just left the Reds and joined none other than the Blues, 1860 Munich. His dad had never really been happy that Stephan desperately wanted to play professionally, knowing very well how difficult it would be to live down the Beckenbauer name. Stephan's brothers had no sporting ambitions. Thomas, the oldest, had run a restaurant in Costa Rica for a couple of years, while Michael was studying medicine. But Stephan was at least as crazy about the game as his father had been. Not that this formed a bond between the two. Much later, Stephan would say that 'in the twenty-five years that I played football, my father watched maybe five of my games'.

The relationship between the Kaiser and his three boys was destined to suffer another setback only weeks later. In July 1988, a celebrity gossip magazine broke the story of Franz and Sybille. It was not a scoop, though. Robert Schwan had carefully orchestrated this disclosure, selling exclusive photos for 120,000 marks. Considering that the lovebirds had elaborately posed for these photos, it doesn't shed a good light on the Kaiser that he yet again failed to clear the situation with the woman who still thought she was his partner before the tabloid juggernaut gathered pace. For someone who was striving for harmony so much that he couldn't prepare Diana for the imminent headlines (or, for that matter, his legal wife Brigitte, who was still certain her husband would one day come back), Beckenbauer was certainly inviting disharmony into his private life on a regular basis.

No sooner had the story been published – and Diana moved out of the house in Kitzbühel – than Franz asked Brigitte for a divorce, as he intended to marry Sybille (herself still bound to a husband who was refusing to let her go, just to keep this interesting). Brigitte flatly refused to co-operate, calling her husband's request 'rash' and suggesting he had just 'blown a fuse'. But of course she must have known she would never stand a chance in court, considering she had been separated from Franz for more than a decade. This multiple tug of war would go on for well over a year, which only proved how serious Franz was about his plans with Sybille. Who knows, Beckenbauer's private turmoil may have even influenced his decision about his job, because being the *de facto* national coach was not exactly conducive to peace of mind and a quiet family life.

In late October 1989, Neuberger approached Beckenbauer during the DFB-Bundestag, the large national meeting of the West German game's governing body that is held every three years. The DFB president pleaded with the Kaiser to stay on in his role beyond the coming World Cup in Italy, but Beckenbauer refused to commit himself. Neuberger told him he needed an answer in late November or early December, and the Kaiser promised to make up his mind. Barely two weeks later, he would be given a scary reminder how fickle this coaching job was and how thin the line that separated glorious success from abject failure.

By now, Beckenbauer had a pretty good team together, a really fine balance of muscle and vision, brawn and brains. Nobody embodied this better than Beckenbauer's favourite player, Lothar Matthäus. For many years, Matthäus had been labelled a failed talent and was almost habitually accused of bottling. When he joined Inter in 1988, at the age of twenty-seven, *Der Spiegel* acerbically said the nation 'has lost an ageing child star who never dared to develop'. But in Italy, the midfield dynamo at long last grew into the exceptional performer Beckenbauer had always seen in him.

And yet this outstanding West German national team had come pretty close to messing up the qualifying campaign for the World Cup. Beckenbauer's men drew three of their first five games (twice against the Dutch and once in Cardiff against Wales). Suddenly they had to win their final group match to go through as one of the best second-placed teams. Ahead of the return game against Wales in Cologne in mid-November, Beckenbauer spoke of 'the most important match of my coaching career'. For once, he was not exaggerating. For West German fans, failing to qualify for a major tournament was inconceivable to begin with. Doing it with the best national team in fifteen years would have forced Beckenbauer's immediate resignation and rendered Neuberger's plea irrelevant.

This being football, bloody hell, right-back Stefan Reuter gave the ball away after just eleven minutes and Norwich striker Malcolm Allen put the visitors ahead. Völler made it 1-1 from a corner but, at half-time, the atmosphere was palpably tense. The game was a matter of such national importance that Beckenbauer's new assistant, an eloquent man named Holger Osieck who had studied history before becoming a football coach, was interviewed live on television during the break. 'We're still relatively calm,' he said. 'We know we have forty-five minutes left. Starting to panic would be the worst thing we could do now.'

Three minutes into the second half, local hero Littbarski crossed from the left and his Cologne team-mate Thomas Hässler scored with a famous volley from ten yards. The hosts were the better team and quite firmly in the driving seat – yet they didn't add an insurance goal. When Littbarski even failed to convert a penalty, hitting the inside of the post, Beckenbauer and Osieck silently looked at each other and shook their heads. They were no longer sitting on the bench but standing on the running track that circled the pitch. With 150 seconds left on the clock, Wales mounted an attack. Clayton Blackmore raced down the right wing and whipped in a cross. Six yards in front of goal, Colin Pascoe outjumped his marker with ease. His header cleared the crossbar. 'Oh, my heart was in my mouth,' the German TV commentator said. 'I haven't had the jitters like that in a long time.'

Within two minutes of the final whistle having been blown, Beckenbauer was in front of the cameras, being quizzed. 'You always said you would only continue if the team qualifies for the World Cup,' the reporter said. 'So what did you feel when Wales took the lead?' The Kaiser replied: 'In such moments, you don't think of your own personal future. You only think about the team.' Then the reporter said: 'We've been watching you. You were very strung up. Will you relax now?' Beckenbauer smiled. 'I don't have any time to relax.' Ten days later, he informed Hermann Neuberger that he would step down as Teamchef after the World Cup in Italy.

In mid-January 1990, Franz and Brigitte Beckenbauer were officially divorced after twenty-three years. Needless to say, the tabloid reporters were waiting for the Kaiser the moment he stepped out of the Munich Family Court. 'I don't feel any different,' Beckenbauer told them. 'But that's no surprise, considering we've been separated for nearly fourteen years.' (Shouldn't that have been 'nearly thirteen years'? Ah, let's not be petty.)

Almost exactly four weeks later, on Easter Sunday, Franz married Sybille Weimer, née Mehl, now Beckenbauer. Again, the party was a rather low-key affair. Of course, Robert Schwan was there, and also one of Franz's oldest (in both senses of the word) friends, the 76-year-old Rudolf Houdek. The wealthy meat producer had been a Bayern member since 1961 and first met Franz two years later, when the boy was still playing for the under-19s. Houdek not only sponsored the Reds, but also the West German national team, and was on first-name terms with anybody who was somebody, from Helmut Schön to Hermann Neuberger.

The party was no big affair because Beckenbauer had been only half-kidding when he told the TV reporter that he didn't have any time to relax. Eight days after the festivities, West Germany played Uruguay to prepare for the World Cup. Since Augenthaler was injured, Beckenbauer used Thomas Berthold as his libero, but the wild 3-3 draw convinced him that the defender was not an ideal solution in this position. The preceding September, Augenthaler had talked Beckenbauer into trying something revolutionary in a 1-1 draw against the Republic of Ireland in Dublin: a flat back four. But the boss remained unconvinced. He preferred the classic German 3-5-2 formation, with a sweeper supported by two man-marking centre-backs and two marauding wing-backs.

That was another difference between him and Cruyff. Although the Kaiser had seen so much of the football world and, of course, created a new position on the field, when it came to tactics, he was a conservative. 'This is our character, this is our system,' he said about the libero set-up, sometimes adding in so many words that Germans were too stupid to understand how a flat back four worked. When Erich

Ribbeck became Bayern Munich coach in 1992 and began to experiment with a sweeper-less formation, Beckenbauer was instrumental in getting him sacked. And when the Kaiser coached a team for the very last time, six years after the World Cup in Italy, he was still fielding a libero.

But more important than the names and the positions was the mood. Four years after the tournament in Argentina, Beckenbauer was a changed man, or at least a changed Teamchef. Perhaps it was the knowledge that he would be walking away from it soon, perhaps it was the experience gained over six difficult years as the most important coach in the land. He may not have been serenity personified, but he was so much more at ease that the writer Christoph Bausenwein would later say the atmosphere at the West German camp reminded him of 'a Boy Scout troop' on an outing. It also helped that no fewer than five of the players were active in Italy. They felt literally at home: Inter player Andreas Brehme took team-mates to his favourite restaurant in Carimate, half an hour south of the German hotel near Lake Como; Matthäus chatted about the World Cup in Italian with his local *barbiere* while getting his hair cut.

Crucially, this time the journalists were kept out. They could only stare at the windows of the Castello di Casiglio in Erba from a distance, reporting back home that the lights were often on until the early hours of the morning in Beckenbauer's room. He was still painstakingly preparing for every game, though this time he did not share every detail with his players. He trusted them and knew they were good enough to win this thing. On at least one occasion, all the boss would tell them was 'Go out and play football'.

The key game of the World Cup for the West Germans was another hot-blooded, even scandalous encounter with the

Netherlands, this time in the round of 16. The reason the two rivals met so early was that the Dutch had their fingers firmly on the self-destruct button. They had progressed from their group only by the skin of their teeth because it was sometimes difficult to ascertain if they were fighting against the opposition or each other. This is why their coach Leo Beenhakker didn't quite know what to reply when the Kaiser walked over to him before the game and said: 'Leo, I'm going to tell you something. The one who wins this game will be champions.'

This was the infamous game in which Frank Rijkaard spat at Rudi Völler – twice; first during the match and then, after both men had been sent off, while leaving the pitch. It was also Klinsmann's best performance for his country, as he not only ran himself ragged alone up front but also scored the crucial opening goal from a Buchwald cross. Five minutes from time, a ridiculously unmarked Brehme made it 2-0, before the Dutch pulled one back from the penalty spot in the dying moments. As Beenhakker told author David Winner, Beckenbauer repeated his prediction after the game: 'He said: Now watch me. Now we will be the champions.'

Of course, Beckenbauer had no way of knowing that his team would not score from open play again at this World Cup. Or that they came so close to botching the quarter-final against Czechoslovakia that he would throw a legendary temper tantrum. 'This has entered the annals of the game because I had never seen Franz like that,' Littbarski remembered even a quarter of a century later. Beckenbauer kicked the dressing room door, and when that refused to give in, he kicked a bucket with such brute force that dozens of ice cubes rained down on his non-plussed players. He yelled at the team, until the goalkeeping coach intervened. This man was none other than Sepp Maier, Beckenbauer having asked his old team-mate to assist him back in October 1987. Now Maier tried to bring everybody back down to earth. 'Franz, are you even aware that we have won the game 1-0? We're through to the semi-finals.' Beckenbauer shot him an angry glance and replied: 'I don't give a fuck about that, not if we play shitty football.'

Three days later, Beckenbauer was the complete gentleman again, well-dressed and well-behaved. After 120 minutes of football, he stood on the pitch next to the coach who had taught him that the best sailors are always to be found on the beach. Beckenbauer and Bobby Robson almost seemed to enjoy themselves, as their players prepared for a penalty shoot-out. The result stood at 1-1, after Brehme's freakishly deflected free-kick and Gary Lineker's clinical finish. Both men in charge were smiling. In his 1992 book, Beckenbauer describes the moment thus: 'I told Bobby Robson: "That's it. We've done our job. The rest is now a question of luck or the absence thereof."' However, when Robson died in 2009, the *Daily Express* quoted the Kaiser as saying: 'After the final whistle, he came over to talk to me before the penalty shoot-out. He said: "Franz, both teams have done their best." Then he pointed up to the sky as if to say it was now up to the gods. I will never forget that gesture, a human touch when the pressure was so high. I don't know anyone else who could have done that.'

Regardless of who said what, it has become a tired old cliché that luck and the gods don't play a role when Germany and/or England are involved in a shoot-out. But things weren't yet so clear in 1990. As a player, Beckenbauer had lost a major title on penalties in 1976. And as a coach, he had lost a shoot-out against Sweden in early 1988 that was unimportant but not inconsequential: it was the match that triggered so much tabloid criticism of Beckenbauer that Robson came up with his seafaring metaphor to support his younger colleague.

When Chris Waddle's penalty followed a trajectory reminiscent of Uli Hoeness's moonshot back in 1976, Beckenbauer jumped into the arms of the first man to come his way, which happened to be substitute Paul Steiner, before racing on to the pitch to celebrate with his players. But he didn't forget the other coach. As everybody, winners and losers alike, slowly trotted off the pitch later, Beckenbauer walked next to Robson and put his left arm around the shoulder of the England manager. At the press conference, the Kaiser said: 'It was a fantastic evening. I can't remember many games as good as this one. It is regrettable that such a match is decided on penalties.' What he didn't say was that he knew he had just won the World Cup. Yes, there was one more game to be played. But for him as the Teamchef, it would be international number 66. His lucky number. Nothing could go wrong.

'Football is Pelé's beautiful game,' Pete Davies wrote about the semi-final in Turin, 'and with the Germans we'd played it beautifully – with strength and speed, with courage and skill, with honesty and honour.' Hardly any of that was on display during the anticlimactic last game of the tournament, the reason being that only one team came to the Stadio Olimpico in Rome on 8 July 1990 to play football. That was, of course, West Germany. Opponents and incumbent champions Argentina, their squad ravaged by suspensions or injuries, were seemingly intent on taking the game to a penalty shoot-out, having already beaten Yugoslavia and then hosts Italy in this manner.

Consequently, Beckenbauer's team dominated the game to an absurd degree and had twenty-two shots on goal to Argentina's one. But clear-cut scoring opportunities were few and far between. Libero Augenthaler, in his last game for the national team, was getting bored at the back, so he joined in the attack – and was tripped in the box by goalkeeper Sergio Goycochea on fifty-eight minutes. The Mexican referee, who stood not even two yards away from the incident, made a strange gesture as if to indicate that the sweeper had dived. If that's what he meant by pointing his finger at the German, Augenthaler's incredulous stare must have told him he had made a mistake. At least that would explain why he blew his whistle five minutes from time, when Völler accepted an invitation from defender Roberto Sensini to go down in the box.

The South Americans, down to ten men after Pedro Monzón had become the first man to be sent off in a World Cup final for his very late tackle on Klinsmann, understandably went ballistic. Kohler, meanwhile, might have muttered the words 'poetic justice' under his breath, because Sensini's challenge was uncannily reminiscent (right down to the spot in the penalty area where it happened) of Kohler's supposed foul on Van Basten two years earlier.

Matthäus, the captain, was West Germany's designated penalty taker, but Beckenbauer had told his players that he wouldn't mind if the team altered the protocol on the pitch. Since Matthäus had had to change into new boots at half-time and felt slightly uncomfortable in them, his good pal Brehme stepped up instead. The full-back was almost naturally two-footed, using his left foot for power, the right one for precision. Now it was time for precision. Goycochea guessed the right corner, but the ball crossed the line just inside the left-hand post.

Eight minutes, ten seconds and one more red card for Argentina later, the final whistle came. This time Beckenbauer remained calm. The first thing he did was take off his glasses, before smiling at Holger Osieck. Only then did it seem to sink in. He hugged the men around him, one of whom was the chief press officer, Wolfgang Niersbach. Barely five minutes later, the Kaiser gave his first post-match TV interview, right there on the pitch in Rome. 'Congratulations, Franz Beckenbauer,' the German reporter said. 'World Cup winner as a player, World Cup winner as the Teamchef!' The Kaiser shrugged and, flashing his trademark mischievous schoolboy grin, replied: 'Well, there you go. Isn't life full of amazing coincidences?'

However, even this was not yet the moment the nation fell in love with him. That came after Niersbach had dragged him away to the awards ceremony, after he had received his winners' medal from Francesco Cossiga, the president of Italy, and after his team had gone on their well-deserved lap of honour. Suddenly, the German TV commentator drew attention to the fact that while the team was parading the trophy around, Beckenbauer stood on the pitch all by himself. The director quickly cut from the celebrating players and fans to the Kaiser, who was slowly walking across the grass in the dark, his hands thrust in his pockets, the shiny medal hanging around his neck, seemingly lost in thought while all around him pandemonium raged. For almost half a minute, people at home felt like intruders who were sharing some very private moments with the most public of all Germans. In those thirty seconds, he finally became a national icon.

Of course, he helped his own case enormously by being quiet during those precious moments. A few minutes later, during the official press conference, his unfortunate tendency to say the first thing that came to his mind was on display again. With Niersbach sitting next to him but unable to come to the rescue, Beckenbauer declared: 'We're number one in the world, we have been number one in Europe for some time. Now we'll add all those players from the East. I believe the German team will be unbeatable for years to come. I'm sorry for the rest of the world.'

It has to be noted that there was a reason he allowed himself to be goaded into this famous and foolish prediction; he was replying to a question from an American journalist. The Berlin Wall had fallen eight months earlier and reunification was on the cards. The writer wanted to know if Beckenbauer expected an all-German team to be even stronger than this West German side. Needless to say, the Kaiser's honest reply would not make things any easier for his successor, none other than Berti Vogts.

Later, in the dressing room, Beckenbauer took off his medal and gave it to Niersbach. When the press officer protested, saying he couldn't accept this gift, the Kaiser assured him: 'Take it, we've got enough of those.' For almost two decades, the gold medal hung above the fireplace in Niersbach's home. In 2010, when the entire squad and staff came together for the twentieth anniversary of the triumph in Rome, Niersbach returned the medal, arguing it was Beckenbauer's reward for the Italian job, not his.

Fewer than two years later, in March 2012, Wolfgang Niersbach was elected the eleventh president of the DFB. Little did he know that he would soon suffer the ignominy of having to step down amid allegations and accusations, most, if not all, of which were laid at the feet of Franz Beckenbauer.

LIFE II

Chapter Nine

On the day before the 1990 World Cup final, FIFA president João Havelange held a press conference at the Forum Italico in Rome, a building owned by Italy's national public broadcasting company RAI. The Brazilian lauded the tournament the way FIFA presidents always do, conveniently overlooking the obvious fact that it had been the most dour and defensive tournament since Chile 1962. Havelange finished the press conference at 1 p.m. and then asked the assembled journalists from all over the world to hang around because a German company was about to break 'important news'.

Helpers scurried around to remove the FIFA backdrop and replace it with a giant Adidas logo made of blue neon tubes. Then a man called Gerhard Ziener took the microphone. He was the spokesman for Adi Dassler's four daughters. Three years earlier, in April 1987, Horst Dassler had died from cancer, whereupon the fate of the company was put into the hands of his sisters. By 1990, things weren't looking good. After decades of fighting Puma on all fronts, Adidas had been blindsided by an upstart named Nike and was losing a lot of money.

That is why Ziener now told the press that a controlling interest in the quintessential German family business had been sold to a – what could be a non-litigable adjective here? – colourful French entrepreneur, who also happened to own Olympique de Marseille: the 47-year-old Bernard Tapie. Ziener didn't mention that Tapie had paid only 440 million marks (a sum the Frenchman himself would later call 'laughable') and of course he didn't say that he personally doubted Tapie was on the level. He just gave the floor to him.

Tapie told the auditorium that the World Cup final would be an all-Adidas event: 'Both teams are wearing shirts and shorts and shoes from Adidas. Even the ball is an Adidas ball. Only the referee's whistle doesn't come from Adidas.' Like so much of what left his mouth, it sounded good but was baloney. Some Argentinians, like Oscar Ruggeri (Diadora) or Gustavo Dezotti (Lotto), wore Italian boots, while Diego Maradona, still the most famous player in the world, was Puma's great posterboy – not to mention that some of the German reporters in the audience will have known that Lothar Matthäus was a near-fanatical Puma man because his father and his older brother used to work for the company. (In fact, Matthäus once said: 'I was Rudi Dassler's third son.') In the end, of course, the non-Adidas referee whistle decided the final and 'Maradona's tears fell on to his Puma boots', as Barbara Smit memorably put it in her book about the two German companies. It was an outcome that may have planted yet another crazy idea in Tapie's head.

During the last week of the World Cup, Beckenbauer had told writer Ludger Schulze that he nurtured some very nice plans for the coming months. 'I'll be lazing around in Kitzbühel for eight weeks. Then Sybille and I will retreat to the solitude of the mountains, rent an alpine hut with no telephone connection. I'll also play some golf. It takes time to recharge the batteries.' He wasn't wanting for offers, of course. As early as March 1990, Fenerbahçe had tested the waters to see if he would be interested in working in Istanbul as their director of football. (He was.) There was also some interest from the United States Soccer Federation, because the country had been awarded the 1994 World Cup and needed a figurehead, or what *Kicker* referred to as a 'locomotive'. But first, holidays.

Or so he thought. But within a week of winning the World Cup, the Kaiser found himself in Zürich, talking to Tapie. The Frenchman later told the Marseille paper *Le Provençal* the meeting had been only about Adidas and that he had signed Beckenbauer to a 'ten-year contract' (which was immediately denied by a company spokesman, who pointed out that Beckenbauer already had a long-term contract). Soon there were rumours that Tapie had in fact asked Beckenbauer to replace the popular Marseille coach Gérard Gili.

This wasn't a totally far-fetched idea. In April, OM had lost the European Cup semi-final on away goals when Benfica striker Vata knocked the ball across the line from six yards out – with his right hand. The incident convinced Tapie that the referees favoured the big clubs. A scandal like that, he reasoned, would have never happened with a superstar like Beckenbauer at the sidelines. But the Kaiser declined his offer. So Tapie changed his tactic. Now he asked Beckenbauer to become technical director in Marseille.

In August, there was another meeting in Switzerland. According to Gili, there were not only Tapie, Beckenbauer, Osieck (who spoke French) and himself present, but also the Swiss René Jäggi, the general director of Adidas. Only two weeks later, the Kaiser signed on the dotted line to become

Marseille's director of football for two years for an annual salary of 2.8 million francs. *Au revoir*, alpine hut. *C'est la vie*.

So why did he go on the next adventure so soon when what he really wanted was to recharge the batteries? Did Adidas play a role? Or was it simply because – as he confided in his friend, the writer Hans Blickensdörfer, before signing the contract – 'Tapie is a man you just can't say no to'? That was certainly the case. The man who'd once sold television sets door to door had an infectious personality and could convince anyone within minutes of even the wildest schemes.

The Kaiser began his new job at Olympique de Marseille on 18 September 1990, exactly a week after his forty-fifth birthday. The following day, the team played Dinamo Tirana in the first round of the European Cup (the result was 5-1, Eric Cantona scored one of the goals). During the half-time break, Beckenbauer went into the dressing room to say a few words to the players in English. As he later told *Kicker*, he also made a few tactical changes. The next morning, coach Gérard Gili resigned.

It is inconceivable that Beckenbauer had not foreseen this. Why else had he prised Osieck out of the contract his trusted assistant had signed back in May to work in Schalke's youth set-up, so that he could come with him to France? Had Beckenbauer declined the original offer to coach OM only because he knew it would look very bad if Tapie sacked Gili after back-to-back league titles? 'To be honest, we weren't really surprised when Gérard stepped down,' defender Manuel Amoros said a few years ago. 'We all knew that Tapie would change the coach, the physio, the assistant, the doctor. He changed many, many things.'

Beckenbauer and Osieck promptly lost their first game in

charge, 1-0 against lowly Cannes. It was OM's first defeat of
the season, with a team that included class acts like Dragan
Stojković, Chris Waddle and Jean-Pierre Papin. Shrill catcalls rang around the Stade Vélodrome. A French newspaper
headlined: 'Beckenbauer *kaputt*'. Thus began the Kaiser's 263
tumultuous days in Marseille, arguably the most misunder-
stood stage of his career.

Germans have an impression of Beckenbauer that is perhaps
best summed up by an anecdote Diana Sandmann tells. 'I
had spent some time in England as an exchange student in
1966,' she says when I ask her if it's true that she is responsible
for the Kaiser's obsession with golf. 'So I had had some contact with the game as a young girl. However, I only started
playing myself when Franz and I were in Hamburg together.
I took lessons at a club in Hoisdorf, where the pro was a
Briton called Barry Rookledge. One day, when Franz was
nurturing a groin injury and couldn't train with the team,
he said: "Let me come with you, I'll be your caddy today."
We went to the driving range and he grabbed one of my
clubs. He held it like a broomstick, because he'd never been
on a golf course before. Then Franz swung – and launched a
rocket. Barry came running towards us and said: "Who hit
that amazing shot?"'

Rookledge remembers the day differently, but Sandmann's
account is in accordance with Beckenbauer's image as a complete natural destined to be successful at whatever he does
or tries. There was, for instance, the day in May 1994 when
Bayern were celebrating the Bundesliga title in a Munich
restaurant. Late in the evening, the team appeared live on a
sports TV show to give interviews. One of the regular fea-
tures of this show was a shoot-out at the *Torwand* – literally,

a goal wall – a contraption with two holes roughly the size of a football. When Beckenbauer was challenged to try his luck, a tipsy Lothar Matthäus intervened. He joked that hitting one of the small holes from ten yards was too easy a task for the Kaiser, there had to be a handicap. So the ball was placed on a wheat beer glass. Beckenbauer pulled up his right trouser leg to protect his formal wear from the inevitable spill, struck – and hit the bottom hole at the first attempt. He was still six years away from his most famous Lazarus act, but the image of that strike cemented his role as The Man Who Never Fails.

This is why Germans are fascinated by Beckenbauer's French enterprise. From a distance, it appeared to be a chaotic fiasco. In October 1990, the German press reported that Tapie had sent the Kaiser a fax to the team's hotel in Tirana to demand that Alain Casanova should be made reserve goalkeeper instead of Gaëtan Huard. Beckenbauer humoured him; the game against the Albanian minnows finished scoreless. Next, the Kaiser tried to impose the libero system on his new team, which didn't really work out. Then OM lost in Sochaux and conceded three goals in four minutes at Auxerre. Oh, and there was also a tax investigation going on. Some of Beckenbauer's players would miss training sessions because they were summoned by the examining magistrate.

In December, Beckenbauer told *Kicker* that he was 'unhappy with the whole situation'. That was even before rumours began doing the rounds that Tapie wasn't paying him on time or that he was about to resign and move to the US to assist Eberhard Herzog, a Mercedes-Benz manager who had been appointed a member of the 1994 World Cup organising committee. A few days before Christmas, French newspapers claimed that Sybille had already packed her bags and was ready to move back to Kitzbühel. *France Soir* said the only reason her husband hadn't already been fired was the Adidas connection; 'breaking with Beckenbauer would mean alienating a big slice of the market'. Instead, Tapie signed a new coach, the chain-smoking Raymond Goethals. Asked if and how he would be working together with the Kaiser, the 67-year-old Belgian replied: 'We'll distribute the roles in early January. I'm not afraid. I've been in situations worse than this.'

And so, when the Berlin monthly *11Freunde* joined forces with the Paris-based magazine *So Foot* to publish a joint issue about the two countries' football relations in 2018 (100 years after the end of the First World War), the Germans had a specific request: could the French deliver an inside account of *la grande Beckenbauer catastrophe* and talk to people who were right there in the thick of things the one single time the Kaiser didn't succeed?

When the article arrived in Berlin, the Germans couldn't believe their eyes. It was basically a 4,000-word piece about how amazing Franz Beckenbauer is. 'As a human being, he was the best guy you can imagine,' former midfielder Laurent Fournier told *So Foot*. 'There was absolutely none of the coldness you would expect from a German.' Defender Basile Boli declared that 'my square feet became round because of Franz' (meaning he worked harder and became a better player). Bernard Pardo, a French international, even felt sorry for all the turmoil Beckenbauer had to endure in Marseille. 'Oh man, the things we did to the Kaiser! One day I was standing on the training pitch when I saw a policeman coming towards me. He said "Monsieur Pardo, let's not make a fuss over this, but you have to come with me together with Pascal Olmeta and Bernard Casoni". Franz looked at me and went: "What? The police?" I replied, "Sorry, coach, but we've got to go."

It was late at night when the police finally released us. Franz was really disillusioned about Marseille after that.'

All the players also remembered how brilliant a footballer he still was. 'When he joined in the *toros*, he would never ever be in the middle,' Fournier said, referring to the popular drill known as piggy-in-the-middle or *rondo*. 'This guy just let the ball bounce off his foot,' Boli added. 'The moment he got the ball it was gone again – whoosh! And when he played a proper game with us, Abedi Pelé and Chris Waddle could never get past him. It's not as if they didn't try!'

Goethals, or so it seemed, got Marseille back on to an even keel – the team defended their league title, reached the final of the *Coupe de France* and also made the European Cup final. But the players and club representatives who talked to *So Foot* all insisted that this success was just as much Beckenbauer's. 'He let grandpa Raymond do his thing,' Olmeta said. 'But he talked a lot to us, gave us advice. He has to be credited with the results we achieved.'

When OM played away at Spartak Moscow in the semi-finals of the European Cup in April 1991, Beckenbauer visited Lev Yashin's grave at Vagankovo Cemetery, accompanied by Valentina, his old friend's widow. During the game, he (and Osieck) sat on the bench next to Goethals, a habit he had picked up from Robert Schwan, who used to do that when he was business manager at Bayern Munich. At one point, Goethals jumped up to tell one of his players off, knocked his head against the roof that covered the subs' bench and fell down on to the running track, the omnipresent Gitanes finally leaving his mouth. Everybody on the bench broke down laughing, except for the Kaiser, who tried to keep a straight face, knowing too well that all cameras would be on him. They always were.

It was the highlight of the season. No, not Goethals' *faux pas* but the game. Marseille won 3-1 and had, barring a meltdown in the return leg at home, reached the final for the biggest trophy in club football. Beckenbauer had been signed by Tapie – whether as coach or technical director made no real difference here – to make his club the number one in Europe. Now the German was only one step away from reaching this goal after all of just nine months.

However, that last step didn't happen. OM lost the final in the Italian city of Bari against Red Star Belgrade on penalties, even though the Kaiser did everything that was in his powers. During the half-time break, he even changed the studs on Boli's shoes while the player was getting a massage. After the shoot-out, Tapie said: 'Today I learned that money can't buy you everything.' This has to be taken with a grain of salt, considering his club would be severely punished for match-fixing a mere three years later.

Shortly after the game, Beckenbauer told Tapie that he didn't want to continue in his current role, saying it was so time-consuming that he was neglecting all his other business interests – whereupon Tapie came up with an astonishing idea. On the first day in June, he asked the Kaiser to become Marseille's vice-president. Seven days later, OM also lost the French Cup final, 1-0 against Monaco, and Beckenbauer went home, in this case meaning Austria, to consider his options. They are still waiting for him in Marseille to fulfil the second year of his contract, not least because he did become vice-president in 1991 – though not in France.

Beckenbauer never returned because the number of his options was growing almost by the minute. While Tapie was still hoping that the Kaiser would come back and sit, figuratively speaking, at his feet, Neville Southall made one of the best saves in the history of Welsh football to deny Jürgen Klinsmann. A few minutes later, referee Bo Karlsson of Sweden blew his whistle, and Ninian Park in Cardiff erupted. Thanks to an Ian Rush goal, Wales had won their Euro 1992 qualifier against World Cup holders Germany 1-0. In other words, they had defeated the very team none other than Beckenbauer himself had declared, only ten months earlier, to be invincible 'for years to come'. Almost inevitably, the tabloid *Bild* headlined: 'Franz, come and save us!'

He didn't and he couldn't because there was a team even dearer to his heart that needed him more. Bayern Munich were struggling on many fronts. The club had just lost the 1991 Bundesliga title to an unfancied Kaiserslautern team, but that was only the beginning of the Reds' unfathomable woes. On 5 October, Bayern were beaten 4-1 at home by Kickers Stuttgart and sank to twelfth place. Two days later, the club's board, led by president Fritz Scherer, met Beckenbauer at the Sheraton Hotel in Munich. They asked him if he would consider taking over the team from coach Jupp Heynckes. 'When?' he asked. 'Now,' they said. The Kaiser declined, arguing there were too many appointments to keep, too many promises to honour.

But it was not the end of the matter. Now Schwan entered the picture again, or maybe that should be the arena. He was a few weeks away from his seventieth birthday, but as busy as ever. (Among other things, he handled money matters for Markus Wasmeier, then one of the continent's best alpine ski racers.) Schwan's tongue hadn't slowed down, either. In an interview with *Kicker*, he tore into Scherer for having offered the coaching job to Beckenbauer, arguing it was just a PR measure orchestrated by a president desperate 'to save his own position'. Schwan added Beckenbauer would be willing to help his club – but in another role: 'He is ideally suited for the post of president.' Having thus proclaimed a coup to bring down Scherer, Schwan suggested another rolling head for good measure. 'I can imagine some alternatives to Mister Hoeness as well – for instance, a man like Karl-Heinz Rummenigge.'

Uli Hoeness had become Schwan's successor as Bayern's business manager in 1979 and had done a great job so far. However, during those wild weeks in 1991, his future at the club seemed to be in danger. On the day after the meeting with Beckenbauer, he sacked his good friend Heynckes and gave the job to former Bayern player Sören Lerby. It was not his most inspired idea. Suffice it to say that the Dane lasted only 154 days and never coached another team.

One of Lerby's first games in charge turned into a historic train wreck, a 6-2 loss in the UEFA Cup at the hands of the Danish club B 1903 from Copenhagen. It was a drama for Bayern, so there won't have been cries of joy upstairs in that house in Kitzbühel. But the great white bird must have felt that he was getting closer to seeing yet another plan through – Beckenbauer as Bayern Munich's president, with Rummenigge as the business manager. However, Scherer and Hoeness weren't to be pushed aside quite so easily. Either because they agreed that true club icons could always bring something to the table or, more likely, because they adapted an old adage and decided that if you can't beat them, make them join you, Hoeness and especially Scherer invited Beckenbauer and Rummenigge on board.

However, the duo could only wield some influence if they sat on the club's executive committee. That was made up of the president (Scherer), the vice-president (Hans Schiefele, the former player and journalist), the treasurer (Kurt Hegerich, a local businessman), the secretary (Karl Hopfner) and business manager Hoeness. Put differently, there were no vacant posts. During Bayern's AGM in late November, the board thus asked the members to agree to a change to the statutes that allowed them to appoint two additional vice-presidents who would be responsible only for the professional football division.

And so, almost exactly one year after he had moved into his own apartment in Marseille with Sybille, a spacious flat overlooking the Mediterranean, Beckenbauer was suddenly back in Munich and a Bayern executive. Michael Meier, business manager of soon-to-be-rivals Borussia Dortmund, predicted problems: 'Now the whole club will be shaking whenever Franz coughs.' He was exaggerating, but only slightly. The moment Beckenbauer and Rummenigge walked into corridors of power that were already ego-filled and constantly reverberating with statements from one talkative board member or another, Bayern were well on the way to earning their most famous nickname: Hollywood FC.

While Beckenbauer was getting closer to achieving the aim Schwan nurtured for him – after all, it's not a big leap from vice-president to president – his French chum was reaching the pinnacle of his own career. Bernard Tapie, raised in a poor Parisian suburb, was named minister of urban affairs by the French prime minister in April 1992. However, as *The Economist* would soon say: 'Why on earth did Pierre Bérégovoy ever appoint the flamboyant Tapie to a government pledged to root out all suspicion of public corruption and scandal? Mr Tapie, self-made multi-millionaire, boss of the leading Olympique de Marseille football club, and brilliant self-publicist, has many admirable qualities, but unimpeachable integrity is not usually counted among them.'

Tapie held the coveted post for only seven weeks. In May, a French judge charged him with fraud (relating to a business deal that dated from 1985), and suddenly he was on the back foot in many walks of life. Soon he sent out signals that he was interested in finding someone who would take Adidas off his hands. This is how his fellow countryman Robert Louis-Dreyfus eventually stepped into Beckenbauer's life. In late November 1992, the banker Jean-Paul Tchang pitched the idea of acquiring Adidas to the 46-year-old Louis-Dreyfus, who was getting bored with running advertising giants Saatchi & Saatchi. Fewer than three months later, in February 1993, it was announced that a group headed by Louis-Dreyfus had acquired a controlling interest in Adidas from Tapie for 370 million dollars.

By comparison, Bayern Munich spent a lot less money in those weeks and months – and yet more than they ever had before. By international standards, Hoeness's thirteen-year reign as the man in charge of buying and selling had been marked by frugality. This radically changed with the two new vice-presidents, one of whom had seen the star system at work in both New York and Marseille. 'All the millions in the bank are of no use if you don't have any points,' Beckenbauer stated. Rummenigge agreed: 'In the old days, we may have had debts, but we were successful and popular.'

When the disastrous 1991-92 season finally ended, Bayern hurled 23.5 million marks at the transfer market to acquire players like winger Mehmet Scholl (from Karlsruhe), defender Thomas Helmer (Dortmund), the Brazilian Jorginho (Leverkusen) and ... Lothar Matthäus (Inter). Matthäus was still Franz's favourite player, and although he was now thirty-one years old and limping back across the Alps with a torn cruciate ligament, Beckenbauer's faith in him never wavered. If Matthäus had really lost a step or his trademark dynamism — and it was a big if — well, he could still play libero, couldn't he? This is another reason why the Kaiser blew his top when Bayern's latest coach, Erich Ribbeck, started experimenting with a flat back four. One could say the Kaiser coughed, and the whole club shook. And so Bayern did play with a libero (Olaf Thon) when they travelled to newly promoted Saarbrücken in October 1992. Of course, the hosts were rank outsiders. 'At the end of the day, it doesn't really make any difference,' one of their defenders predicted before the match, 'if Bayern win the league by ten points or by only eight points.' The name of this young man was Stephan Beckenbauer.

At twenty-three years of age, the Kaiser's youngest off-spring (at the time, at least) had become a bona fide Bundesliga player. No strings attached, no nepotism necessary. He would make just twelve appearances in the top flight, as Saarbrücken were relegated at the end of the season, but he had achieved what he set out to do, an accomplishment that was, and perhaps still is, not widely enough appreciated. Not all sons of truly great footballers who take up the game become this successful. Yes, Johan Cruyff's son Jordi played for Barcelona and became an international. But Pelé's son Edinho ended up in jail for money laundering and drug trafficking.

Stephan Beckenbauer defended flawlessly against Bayern, and it was the Munich giants who could consider themselves lucky to come away with a 1-1 draw, not the upstarts, which was also an early indication that Stephan was a better player than fortune-teller. Bayern did not win the league by ten points, nor by eight; in fact, for the third year running, they didn't win it at all. The writing was now on the wall. In November 1992, the same month that DFB president Egidius Braun announced that Germany would launch a bid for the 2006 World Cup, Franz Beckenbauer published his latest autobiography. It caused nowhere near as many headlines as Harald Schumacher's book, but there was one passage everybody quoted from. 'I believe that we live on after death, in another existence. That is why I wish for a conscious death, so that I can prepare for my soul leaving my body and returning in another shape.' Reincarnation would happen sooner than expected for him, because Bayern Munich's vice-president was about to return as the club's coach.

This wasn't planned, though. Beckenbauer had more than enough commitments already. Not all of them, incidentally, were totally in line with his role as a leading Bayern official. In late 1992, for instance, he entered into a four-year agreement with the Japanese automobile company Mitsubishi, worth 4 million marks. Nothing wrong with that, of course, except maybe that Opel were Bayern's main sponsors at the time, meaning the club's vice-president was now personally endorsing a rival product. This would set a trend that eventually turned comic – although the club could never see the funny side of it. In 2001, Bayern signed a deal with the electric utility service providers E.ON; Beckenbauer starred in commercials for their competitors Yello. In 2002, German Telekom became Bayern's new shirt sponsor; Beckenbauer pledged allegiance to O_2. In 2003, Bayern announced a partnership with the Paulaner brewery; Beckenbauer began to endorse Erdinger wheat beer.

Perhaps even more problematic was the Kaiser's latest incarnation (sorry, couldn't resist) as a television personality. In March 1993, he worked as the colour commentator during a game between Bayern and Frankfurt for Premiere, Germany's first pay-TV station. He liked it so much that he also covered the Masters golf in Augusta in April and then agreed to host an entire regular show during the World Cup in the following year. Oh, and he also signed a deal with RTL Television to become the station's Champions League pundit during the 1994-95 season. On top of all that, he agreed to succeed his old foe Paul Breitner as the main columnist for *Bild*, plus all its offshoots, starting in August 1994. In other words, the man who could never think of a flippant remark without actually uttering it would soon be commenting on his own team's games on the screen and in print. As the Cosmos mascot Bugs Bunny once remarked: 'Of course you realise, this means war.'

In May 1993, Beckenbauer's son Michael became a father himself, which meant that the 47-year-old Kaiser was now a grandad. Not that he could make up for all the time he failed to spend with his kids by doting on the grandson, though. Being knocked out of the UEFA Cup by Norwich City was nobody's idea of fun in Munich, and so Ribbeck's position became untenable. In December, Beckenbauer finally gave in, telling Schwan: 'Okay, Robert, if you clear this with all my business partners, I'm going to do it.' Schwan didn't have to ask what 'it' was. He went to make some phone calls. Four days before the end of the year, Ribbeck accepted an offer from president Scherer to step down immediately in exchange for 500,000 marks severance pay. Then the club announced that Beckenbauer would coach the team until the end of the season.

Of course, he lost his first game in charge. After all, this was the man who had been defeated in his Bundesliga debut with Bayern in 1965 and his first game for the Cosmos in 1977, who had lost his first match as West Germany's Teamchef in 1984 and his debut as Marseille's gaffer in 1990. However, that VfB Stuttgart managed to win the first game after the end of the winter break in Munich, 3-1 in mid-February, was worrisome. Bayern were now in fifth place, with barely a dozen games left in the season.

At one point, the Kaiser complained his team were playing 'like a schoolboy side'. But somehow his players were never offended by such slips of the tongue – because it was his tongue. (Many years later, Beckenbauer would criticise the team even more harshly after a game in Lyon, but some players later argued this speech won them the Champions League.) On the last day of the season, Bayern needed a win at home against Schalke to lift the 1994 title. It was such a nervous, sluggish game that Beckenbauer kicked a large metal box that stood on the running track in total frustration, nearly fracturing his foot in the process. Then his libero Matthäus bent a free-kick around the wall to break the spell. Much later on this day, Beckenbauer would be challenged to that shoot-out live on television where he scored from a wheat beer glass. He went to bed around three in the morning but could only sleep for a few hours, because he had to get up early to visit Antonie in Schwabing. It was Mother's Day.

On 14 November 1994, Bavaria's public-service broadcaster did something unprecedented. It covered the annual general meeting of a football club live on television. Granted, this was not any old club but mighty Bayern Munich, a team named after the state. Still, what sort of ratings could you possibly expect from boring speeches and the election of a new treasurer, followed by statements of accounts and reports on the activities of the various club divisions (for the first time in six years, Bayern's chess team had failed to win the national championship)?

Oh, the ratings were good, because this was not a normal meeting, it was what the newspapers inevitably referred to as 'the Kaiser's coronation'. On this day, Bayern's 33,000 members – or, more precisely, those of them who were present – elected Franz Beckenbauer the twenty-eighth president in the club's history, which dated back to January 1900. Of course, there was no other candidate. Who would have dared to run for office against The Man Who Always Won?

The story of how this latest promotion came about was astonishing even for a man who had turned stumbling on a new job into an art form. This time it was neither his agent Robert Schwan nor the tabloids who pushed Beckenbauer into a new role; it was a politician. Only weeks before his enthronement, the Kaiser had been determined to step down as vice-president because the club's affairs were becoming muddled. In September, he took part in a secret meeting of only three people: himself, Fritz Scherer and Karl-Heinz Rummenigge. The latter announced that he would run for president in November, whereupon Scherer said he would do the same. When details of this meeting were later leaked to the press (not by Beckenbauer), the two candidates engaged in a very public verbal spat. It was all very entertaining for neutrals, but as Beckenbauer put it, the struggle threatened to 'tear the club apart'.

That's when Edmund Stoiber, the minister president of Bavaria, asked Beckenbauer to see him in his office. The 53-year-old conservative politician had become a Bayern member as early as 1966 (five years before he joined the Christian Social Union) and now he was concerned about the state of his club. If the question was Scherer or Rummenigge, he explained, the only possible answer was Beckenbauer. Stoiber, a seasoned expert in such matters, explained that he had put out his feelers and was sure that both candidates would gladly withdraw their applications to make room for the Kaiser. It was the only way to restore peace.

And so Beckenbauer allowed himself to be made president – and immediately told everybody who would listen that the whole concept was rubbish. 'Our football clubs have become economic enterprises, some have budgets of close to 100 million marks,' he said, 'yet they are still run by honorary, unsalaried part-timers. And these people who sit on the board are not only responsible for the club, they are legally liable. This is nonsense! Being the president of a Bundesliga club is a full-time job. I can see only two options for the future. Either our clubs are turned into limited companies, or we come up with a system under which the members elect only a supervisory board, which then appoints a group of professional, salaried executive directors.'

He wasn't the first official, and wouldn't be the last, to bemoan the old-fashioned German club model as outdated. But of course his word carried a lot of weight. Still, Beckenbauer had to wait another four years before finally getting his way. In October 1998, the DFB changed the rules and allowed its member clubs to turn their professional football divisions into limited companies. The DFB wasn't the first German sports association to fundamentally alter its structure, as ice hockey had done something even more radical in 1994. The winter game, quite popular in many parts of the country, had not only made the clubs companies but even created a US-style league without promotion and relegation. Football didn't go that far. In fact, it installed a peculiar safety net. To thwart scary scenarios like foreign billionaires buying up German football clubs as if they were commodities or rich men's playthings, the DFB created a statute which stipulated that 50 per cent of a plc's voting shares plus one share had to remain in the possession of the parent club. (Yes, this is the now world-famous – or infamous, if you should happen to be a foreign billionaire – '50+1 rule'.)

However, even this rule change would not make it any easier for the clubs to get the one thing right that counts for so much in football: signing the best coach for the team. This would remain a problem of absurd proportions for Bayern until the arrival of Ottmar Hitzfeld in 1998. Take Beckenbauer's first season as the president. In April 1995, five months after his coronation, the Reds won an away game at Frankfurt in great style, 5-2. However, there was a problem. Deep into the second half, with three points seemingly in the bag, Bayern's Italian coach Giovanni Trapattoni had brought on a young Dietmar Hamann. At the time, Hamann hadn't yet signed a professional contract, so he was what DFB rules defined as an 'amateur player'. A professional team could field only three such players; Hamann was Bayern's fourth on the pitch. 'I'm the only one who is to blame,' Trapattoni said after learning the club had forfeited the game. 'I should have known the German rules.' Then he dryly added: 'In Italy, they would have given me a bonus for winning an away game with four amateurs.'

Bayern finished the season in sixth place, and Trapattoni didn't extend his contract, although he was popular with the players, the fans and the board. He confessed to the *Süddeutsche Zeitung* that 'my biggest problem was the language. I told the club: If I can't be 100 per cent Trapattoni, we should stop it here.' The club briefly considered replacing Trapattoni with

Ajax boss Louis van Gaal. But then the triumvirate that ran Bayern hit upon a spectacular idea.

In early February 1995, shortly after Trapattoni had informed the club he would leave in the summer, Rummenigge, Beckenbauer and Scherer (now a vice-president) travelled to a town near Munich called Ottobrunn, right next to Neubiberg, where the young Beckenbauer may have been slapped in the face by an 1860 player. Their destination was the house of Uli Hoeness, where they were going in the dark of the night to secretly meet two surprise guests from up north: Otto Rehhagel and his wife Beate.

As early as the beginning of 1992, Beckenbauer had clamoured for Werder Bremen's coach Rehhagel to take over at Bayern. The idea hadn't become any more reasonable in the intervening three years. Since 1981, Rehhagel was governing Werder – and, people said, the city of Bremen – in a manner that was inevitably dubbed 'Otto-cratic'. His word was law, and newspaper reporters were little more than his messengers. In Munich, he would not only dive into the shark-infested waters of the gutter press, but could hardly be expected to boss around a board made up of men who had played in five World Cup finals. In other words, the combination could never work.

Then again, it very nearly did. Rehhagel delivered one of the most famous wins of this Bayern era, when his team triumphed 2-1 at the Nou Camp over Barcelona in April 1996 to reach the two-legged UEFA Cup final. The Catalans were coached by none other than Johan Cruyff. Beckenbauer had last seen him during a charity golf tournament in Barcelona almost one year earlier. Asked about his relationship with the Dutchman, Beckenbauer disclosed that he had tried to sign Cruyff as the new Bayern coach in the summer of 1994.

Cruyff on the bench, with Beckenbauer, Rummenigge and Hoeness on the board – what a Gang of Four that would have been! Taking into account how Rehhagel fared in this snake pit, it would at the very least have been entertaining, because the main reason even this legendary night in Barcelona was not enough to save Rehhagel's job was that he couldn't stop an ego-studded team from publicly disintegrating.

The problems began when Matthäus tore his Achilles tendon a few months before Rehhagel's arrival. With the 34-year-old Matthäus labouring towards a comeback that might never happen, Helmer became Bayern's replacement sweeper, while new signing Jürgen Klinsmann tried to take on the mantle of team leader. When Matthäus sensed that two other alpha males were trying to usurp his position, he went on a media rampage. Soon, accusations and complaints were flying back and forth. The club was unable to stop this bickering in public, not least because both Beckenbauer and Rummenigge were well-paid tabloid columnists themselves. For the Kaiser, this chaos may have been business as usual, but Rehhagel was like a vessel lost at sea.

Just eleven days after the famous win away at Barcelona, Bayern were beaten at home by Hansa Rostock. They now trailed league leaders Dortmund by three points with four games left in the season. The club decided to pull the emergency brake. Many years would pass before Beckenbauer and Hoeness admitted that sacking the coach with so few league games left and the UEFA Cup final coming up was unfortunate. The more elegant solution would have been to let Rehhagel win the UEFA Cup and then pull off the feat that was being discussed in the boardroom at least since March – invite Trapattoni to come back. Denying Rehhagel the opportunity to go out with his head held high, and a

European trophy tucked under his arm, would inevitably lead to bad blood.

Seemingly the only person in Munich that Rehhagel wasn't mad at was the man who replaced him on the bench. A few days after his dismissal, Rehhagel told a reporter that 'Franz was against sacking me, the others talked him into it', before adding that Beckenbauer had never once meddled with his team selection or tactics. Perhaps he was a bit forgetful here. Many reporters remembered how the Kaiser, who loved Mehmet Scholl almost as much as he loved Matthäus, had stormed into the VIP lounge before the home game against Gladbach in October to declare: 'Do you know what that madman wanted to do? He wanted to put Scholl in the stands! I prevented that.' (Scholl was the best player in red on that day, but Bayern still lost.)

For ten thrilling days, it looked as if the Kaiser could yet again weave his magic. Beckenbauer won his first two games in charge, which included the first leg of the UEFA Cup final against Girondins de Bordeaux. League leaders Dortmund, meanwhile, suffered a shock collapse, losing 5-0 away at Karlsruhe. Suddenly Bayern were back in the race for the Bundesliga title, the more so when the team then took an early and commanding 2-0 lead in Bremen, against Rehhagel's old club. But even men born under a lucky star can suffer a black eye – literally.

Bremen somehow managed to turn the game around, winning 3-2. The next day, Beckenbauer was participating in a five-against-two *rondo* during training, when Helmer mishit the ball, knocking the glasses off his coach's head. For the next game, away at Schalke, the Kaiser sported an all-too-visible shiner. Squinting at the pitch, he saw his former player Olaf Thon collect the ball deep in Schalke's half. Thon picked up speed, left all Bayern players in his wake and finished his fifty-yard solo run with a tremendous shot into the top corner. It was not the goal that decided the game (this came in the final minute, when Bayern were throwing everything forward), but it was the moment when you just knew that for once the Kaiser would finish second.

Still, on the last day of the season, a group of Bayern fans held up a banner that said 'Thanks, Franz'. There were reasons to be thankful. In midweek, Bayern had won the UEFA Cup for the first time in the club's history. It was also the Reds' first European trophy in twenty years, and the 5-1 aggregate score against a team from Bordeaux that boasted future World Cup winners Zinedine Zidane, Bixente Lizarazu and Christophe Dugarry (plus goalkeeper Gaëtan Huard, whom Beckenbauer knew from his Marseille days) was no mean feat. But those pesky press people just would not let him forget that he had rechristened this competition 'the Losers' Cup' a couple of years earlier. That's not to mention that it felt strange to celebrate a title he had practically inherited from Rehhagel. During the victory party in Bordeaux, he at first refused to hold the cup aloft, saying: 'I've got nothing to do with this thing.' The players felt differently. At one point, they even began to sing: 'Franz, please don't go!'

But he did go. His second stint as Bayern coach was also his last. However, this didn't mean he would now have the time to further improve his golf skills. Someone like the Kaiser was always in demand. In November 1996, there were rumours he would run for the FIFA presidency when the elderly João Havelange stepped down in 1998. ('If FIFA want something from me,' he said evasively, 'they know where to find me.') And just a few weeks later, in December, Egidius Braun had a plan. 'No German footballer is more highly regarded in the world than Franz Beckenbauer,' the DFB president announced. 'I hope he will be my ambassador for the German World Cup bid.' Neither man knew that this sentence, uttered two days before 1996 ended, would lead to Beckenbauer's greatest triumph. And to his fall from grace.

LIFE III

Chapter Ten

Remember that embarrassing day in April 1995, when Giovanni Trapattoni forfeited a game against Frankfurt by bringing on Dietmar Hamann? At the time, Hamann was registered with Bayern Munich's reserves, who were competing in the third division. Hamann wasn't the only player on that team who would be going places; the side also boasted future Champions League winners like Samuel Kuffour or Alexander Zickler.

Back then, such teams were referred to in Germany as a club's 'amateurs'; today they are normally called Bayern II or Bayern under-23s. They are in large parts made up of players who have just outgrown youth football but are not yet quite ready for the senior game. However, since these sides play competitive games at a fairly high level in a regular league, they usually include a number of older players with a special psychological make-up.

These latter players have to accept that their own professional careers are either over or will never really get off the ground. They have to be content with helping young talents develop and pass on their knowledge. One such key senior figure for Bayern's amateurs in 1995 was the 35-year-old Hans Pflügler, who had made roughly 300 appearances for the first team and was now slowly winding down his playing days. Another was Stephan Beckenbauer.

The Kaiser's son had returned to Bayern in the summer of 1994, and also to Munich where he was sharing a house with his mother, Brigitte, while he was going through a painful divorce. These living arrangements may have saved her life, or at the very least her mobility, when she suffered a serious accident in October 1995. While cleaning the windows, Brigitte lost her footing and fell down the basement shaft, where Stephan found her a couple of hours later. Brigitte was unable to move, as two vertebrae were broken. The doctors feared she would be paralysed for the rest of her life. Almost miraculously, she eventually recovered and learned to walk with a stick. Brigitte lived until 2021, when yet another accident resulted in a fatal femoral neck fracture.

One reason why Stephan Beckenbauer never really broke through at the highest level was his propensity to pick up nagging injuries. Sadly, this tendency didn't stop upon his return to his father's club. In late 1995, he had to undergo disc surgery that sidelined him for a while. Shortly after making his comeback, in March 1996, he tore his cruciate ligament during a third-division game in Kassel. He came back again, playing sweeper for Bayern's reserves, but his knee was never quite the same again. Before the year was over, he decided to pack it in. He was only twenty-seven when his great football dream ended. A few months later, in August 1997, Stephan Beckenbauer – together with another, slightly older 'amateur' called Roman Grill – officially switched from being a player to joining the coaching staff.

Nobody knew it at the time, least of all club president Franz

Beckenbauer, but his son's misfortune turned out to be a crucial moment for Bayern, because Grill and Stephan Beckenbauer would soon become the two most influential and successful coaches for Björn Andersson, the new head of youth development. The Swede – the player whose leg Terry Yorath broke in the European Cup final between Leeds and Bayern – had been brought in to address a problem that was not only affecting Bayern but the entire German game: an alarming lack of talent.

According to Berti Vogts, Beckenbauer had called him only an hour after making that fateful statement in 1990 about Germany having become invincible. 'Berti, I think I have just said something very stupid,' he supposedly confessed. 'I'm really sorry.' In marked contrast to the Kaiser, Vogts had earned his coaching stripes by working with the DFB's youth teams for more than a decade, which is why he was acutely aware of the fact that his predecessor had had the great fortune of being able to work with the last fine footballing crop for one or perhaps even two generations of German players.

That the country still insisted on using the libero system was not necessarily to blame for this dearth, but it was certainly emblematic of a backwardness born out of complacency. When Vogts nominated his squad for the 1998 World Cup, a full third of the players had worked under Beckenbauer in Italy eight years earlier (and add to this Ulf Kirsten and Olaf Marschall, who were so old they had made their international debuts for a country that ceased to exist in 1990). Vogts's qualities as a coach may be the subject of debate – they certainly are in Scotland, where he coached the national team between 2002 and 2004, failing to qualify for either the European Championship or the World Cup – but his patchy record with the German national team was to a large degree simply due to a lack of quality players.

Of course, it all ended up in tears and Vogts had to resign barely two months after the World Cup in France. This started what a newspaper later termed 'a grotesque win-a-manager tombola', because DFB president Egidius Braun just couldn't find a successor for Vogts. He even phoned the Englishman Roy Hodgson, offering him the job. A day later, he called again and told Hodgson he had changed his mind. Then he rang Paul Breitner. Breitner, who had never coached a senior team in his life, agreed to take over. Fifteen hours later, Braun contacted him again, now with the news that there was opposition within the DFB and that he had to take his offer back. It was all hugely embarrassing, which is why Braun himself now came under a lot of criticism. Karl-Heinz Rummenigge suggested a radical reformation of the governing body – and even a new president: Beckenbauer.

The next DFB-Bundestag was only six weeks away and suddenly Braun had to fear for his re-election. That's when a phone call from a hotel in Copenhagen, where Bayern were about to face Brøndby IF in the Champions League, came to his rescue. On 19 September 1998, at five minutes past three, Braun broke sensational news to the DFB's board of directors. Franz Beckenbauer had called earlier in the day to offer the beleaguered president his support. The Kaiser had even agreed to run for the post of DFB vice-president to help Braun clear up this mess, bring some professionalism to the table and improve the reputation of the German game.

It was a gift from heaven for the president. With the man whom none other than Vogts had dubbed 'the shining light of German football' as early as 1990 in his camp, Braun's re-election was suddenly a mere formality. Plus, one of the DFB's harshest and most vocal critics was suddenly forced to put his money where his mouth was. Just a few weeks ago, the Kaiser had referred to the DFB's league committee – a panel made up of representatives of the thirty-six professional clubs – as 'a laughing bag'. Now he could help set changes in motion.

Beckenbauer, for his part, had come to appreciate Braun as a man of honour. True, the 73-year-old DFB president could sometimes appear a bit naïve and quaint – he was known as 'Father Braun' – but he was a gentleman and always true to his word. Beckenbauer knew this because he and Braun had been working together for the last nineteen months to bring the World Cup to Germany. This was also the reason why joining the DFB in an official capacity was no longer the giant step for the Kaiser it would have been a few years earlier. In a way, he already was representing the DFB by being the main ambassador for the World Cup bid.

After some initial misgivings, mainly because he felt the bid was doomed to failure, the Kaiser had embraced his latest calling with all the fervour of a recent convert. In March 1997 he explained his involvement by declaring that 'the chance to host a World Cup is a gift to us all. The country can present itself to the world. The advertising value is priceless.' Provided the German bid had the backing of UEFA, he even saw a chance to actually defeat competitors like South Africa or Brazil. 'Our application has to be more convincing,' he said. 'But we must never give the impression of trying to force things. A certain looseness, that's what we aim for.'

The man who was born loose celebrated the first stage win of what would be his very own Tour de Charme four weeks later, when UEFA president Lennart Johansson denounced England's rival World Cup bid as the crass breach of a gentle-man's agreement. The Swede was referring to an unwritten but well-documented deal between Braun and FA chairman

Bert Millichip dating back to 1993: Germany would back England's bid for Euro 96 if the English would in turn support a German World Cup bid.

However, there was also a setback. In June 1998, Sepp Blatter was elected the new FIFA president. Beckenbauer knew the Swiss well, because there was an Adidas connection. None other than Horst Dassler had helped Blatter get a job with FIFA and the two men used to be so close that Blatter once spoke of 'soul mates'. During his early FIFA days, Blatter even worked from an Adidas office in France and was paid through an Adidas account. On the downside, Egidius Braun was very critical of Blatter's methods and had refused to grant him the support of the DFB. In the end, the Swiss had won the election mainly thanks to the African delegates – which meant he would definitely vote for the South African bid. Still, Blatter had only one vote on FIFA's twenty-four-man executive committee, so there was still a lot to play for.

Until October 1998, the German World Cup bid committee was made up of five men. Beckenbauer took care of the nitty gritty and his old ally Wolfgang Niersbach was in charge of the media work, while the trusted DFB soldiers Braun, Horst R. Schmidt and Wilfried Straub did all the boring, less glamorous work. Then a key figure joined them. On the first day of the DFB's Bundestag, it was announced that the 54-year-old Fedor Radmann would become a member of the bid committee as 'chief co-ordinator'. What this meant was simply that Radmann would be the guy who actually knew how to navigate the often rocky waters of sports politics and go about being awarded a major tournament.

Radmann had not only predicted that Blatter would win the FIFA election, he had come within four votes of the actual result, which mightily impressed the other people on the committee. By most accounts, it was the DFB's general secretary Schmidt who got Radmann on board. Schmidt had been a member of the team that organised the 1972 Summer Olympics in Munich, and Radmann had cut his teeth during this event in various capacities. Some twenty years later, he then organised the ice hockey world championships in Germany.

However, Beckenbauer was also very familiar with the man, because in between the Olympics and the ice hockey showpiece, Radmann had worked for Adidas, mostly under Horst Dassler. In fact, Radmann had held a leading role at International Sport and Leisure, the company that had grown out of Rofa (Robert Schwan and Franz Beckenbauer's firm) and which a Swabian paper once called 'world sports' cancerous growth' because it was behind so many 'dirty affairs and dubious deals'.

The DFB's Bundestag in October 1998 was a historic event, because it was at this meeting that the delegates voted to allow clubs to become limited companies. They also re-elected Braun and made Beckenbauer vice-president. The Kaiser's ride was a little bit bumpy, though, because seventeen of the 203 delegates refused to lend him their vote. The reason, he felt, was a speech given by VfB Stuttgart president Gerhard Mayer-Vorfelder earlier in the day. Mayer-Vorfelder told the assembly: 'In the last weeks, people have voiced criticism of the DFB that was often shallow and superficial, yet they were lauded as unorthodox thinkers. But some of those unorthodox thinkers were just bullshitters. Being clueless makes it very easy to mouth off.'

There was not the slightest doubt that Mayer-Vorfelder was talking about the Kaiser, who indeed didn't know an awful lot about the inner workings of a huge body like the

DFB – and who would never count being patient and diplomatic among his virtues. This is why Braun mentioned in his own speech that there would be time to teach Beckenbauer 'some expertise'. Charmingly, he added: 'However, I can't rule out a certain spontaneity now and then.'

Beckenbauer was hurrying out of the convention hall in Wiesbaden, 260 miles northwest of Munich, even before the votes had been counted. He was already quite late for an event he had been invited to long before anyone knew that he would have to spend a large part of 24 October in the company of DFB officials and delegates. His son Stephan was getting married for the second time.

According to the *Kölner Express* newspaper, Fedor Radmann knew more than half of the FIFA bigwigs who would vote on the World Cup bids personally. A week after the DFB Bundestag, Radmann told the reporters his recipe for success. 'There's us, England, South Africa, perhaps Morocco and then in all likelihood Brazil – it means you will have to show yourself. Be present but be discreet, that is my motto.' The journalists interpreted this to mean that 'Radmann will chase Beckenbauer across the globe'. And that's most certainly what he did.

The duo's trek around the world began in February 1999 with a trip to Doha, the capital of Qatar, followed by stays in Dhahran in Saudi Arabia, Muscat in Oman and Kuwait. In April, the two men travelled, via Stockholm, to the World Youth Championship in Nigeria, where Germany were knocked out at the group stage, again underlining the country's problems with talent development.

Next on the itinerary were the Copa América in Paraguay and the Women's World Cup in the USA. In July,

Beckenbauer and Radmann were seen at the Confederations Cup in Mexico, where Germany were beaten by the United States and failed to make the knockout rounds. In October 1999, the Kaiser reckoned that he had racked up 'approximately 350,000 miles' for his airline loyalty programme in fewer than eight months. That was before he left for New Zealand, Thailand, South Korea, China and Japan.

In contrast to most professional observers, who assumed that the World Cup would go to South Africa, Radmann always exuded optimism. 'I go on the theory that we'll be very happy on the day the World Cup is being awarded,' he said in the summer of 1999. The main reason for his unshakeable confidence, he explained, was Beckenbauer. 'With all due respect to Nelson Mandela or Bobby Charlton, Franz is unique in the world of football,' Radmann said. 'Without him, our chances would be critically slimmer. His humble demeanour is just amazing.' He recalled how Beckenbauer had spontaneously donated 70,000 marks to an orphanage in Mexico, and how he would chat with youth team players in Africa as easily and unaffectedly as with US president Bill Clinton during the G8 summit in Cologne.

In December 1999, a *Kicker* poll revealed that more than 77 per cent of the magazine's readers believed their country would be awarded the World Cup. One, Emil Otto from Regensburg, probably spoke for many when he quipped: 'Franz Beckenbauer could bring the World Cup even to the moon, so why shouldn't he be able to pull this feat off with Germany?' Manfred Hofmann from Gemünden argued that 'he is quite simply a darling of fortune'. Adalbert Bosheck from Krefeld said Beckenbauer was 'success personified. Whatever he tackles will work out.'

Stunningly, amid all his constant jet-setting and rounds

of golf with Asian politicians and American entrepreneurs, Beckenbauer somehow still found the time to work for the club he presided over. He did so, in the truest sense of those words, above and beyond the call of duty. In late 1999, either during a business trip to Hamburg or after Bayern's Christmas party, Beckenbauer fathered another child. The mother was a 33-year-old club employee by the name of Heidrun Burmester. She had come to Munich nearly ten years earlier from her home in the north of Germany, in Lower Saxony, where she had grown up on a farm. Through a temp agency, Heidi found a small job at Bayern, but since she was bright and reliable, she soon worked her way up to being the chief secretary in charge of merchandise.

Munich may be the third-largest city in Germany, but it can feel like a small town. News of Beckenbauer's latest affair spread quickly, but the local press kept shtum, apart from the occasional insider jokes. (The cartoonist for the *Süddeutsche Zeitung* began to add baby soothers or rattles when drawing the Kaiser.) It was an out-of-town newspaper that finally broke the story in mid-November 2000, almost exactly three months after Beckenbauer's fourth son, Joel Maximilian, had been born. Robert Schwan, only a week away from his seventy-ninth birthday, did his job and immediately denied the story, calling the article 'a fairy tale'. But eventually the Kaiser owned up in his own inimitable way: 'God is happy about every child that comes into this world.' He also explained he had confessed to his wife Sybille, adding that 'our marriage is strong. We will stay together. Everything will be the way it used to be.' As Berti Vogts knew all too well, Beckenbauer was never very good at making predictions.

The notoriously gossipy Munich press had probably closed ranks around the Kaiser all through the first months of 2000 because he was on a mission of national importance. Nobody wanted to be the journalist who derailed the German World Cup bid by dredging up a scandal, while St Franz was criss-crossing the planet like a footballing Phileas Fogg.

Beckenbauer had help, of course. First, there were the seven major German sponsors, powerful companies: Lufthansa, Telekom, Bayer, Deutsche Bahn (German rail), DaimlerChrysler, Dresdner Bank and, needless to say, Adidas. Then there was his club, Bayern Munich. During a trip to Bangkok, the Kaiser had discussed a potential friendly between the Reds and Thailand's national team. Finally, there were other famous German footballers like Rudi Völler, Günter Netzer, Karl-Heinz Rummenigge and Jürgen Klinsmann. In January 2000, for instance, the Kaiser flew to Cameroon, then on to Accra in Ghana, where the Confederation of African Football (CAF) held its congress. This meant Beckenbauer couldn't attend the inaugural FIFA Club World Cup in Brazil, and so Völler went to South America instead.

Down the final stretch, Beckenbauer's schedule became terrifying. He was in Asunción, Paraguay, for the conference of the South American Football Confederation (CONMEBOL), then in Saudi Arabia and Qatar again, while a span of just six days in April saw him spend time in Miami, Costa Rica, Buenos Aires, Montevideo plus Trinidad and Tobago. In May, the Kaiser attended the meeting of the Oceania Football Confederation (OFC) in Samoa, hoping to play some golf with Charles Dempsey. The Glasgow-born septuagenarian would be the single OFC representative on FIFA's executive committee and was supposed to vote for England or South Africa, depending on the results of the first ballots.

From Polynesia, Beckenbauer travelled to Zürich to watch

the tradition-laden annual Blue Stars/FIFA Youth Cup tournament. In early June, he was in Malta, then in Rome, then in southeast Asia to see the game between Thailand and Bayern he had helped arrange. At the National Stadium in Bangkok, a capacity crowd of 20,000 people chanted his name, before the newly crowned Bundesliga champions won the match 2-1. Finally, he travelled back to Europe for Euro 2000 in Belgium and the Netherlands – and of course for the UEFA congress in Luxembourg. 'I'm slowly getting fed up,' the Kaiser said with regal understatement.

Exhaustion set in not before time, because at long last the deciding day, 6 July, was on the horizon. On 2 July, France lifted the European Championship, after Germany had crashed out at the group stage by losing 3-0 to Portugal's reserve team – the worst disaster in more than thirty years for Beckenbauer's once-proud footballing nation. That is why the weekly magazine *Sport Bild* put a photograph of Zinedine Zidane on the cover of its issue dated 5 July. The caption read: 'This is a footballer.' Next to this image was a picture of a Bratwurst in a football kit, with the caption: 'This is a German international.' ('Bratwurst' is German football slang for a useless player.)

The small story on the upcoming ballot, meanwhile, was hidden on page twenty-two, and even that was basically another comment on the Euros, because the magazine said: 'Thanks, Franz, you at least put up a fight' (suggesting the German players had not). *Kicker*, which hit the newsstands on the morning of the vote itself, carried an editorial that was almost defeatist in tone: 'Should the World Cup go to South Africa despite the perfect case for Germany, it will leave a bad taste. Europe will have been shown again that sporting and economic power are not enough to make the difference in sports politics.'

The professional reporters, analysts and columnists had all done their maths. Brazil had already withdrawn a bid that was hopeless to begin with despite having the backing of Nike. Morocco were expected to be eliminated in the first round of the vote, and England in the second, especially after British hooligans had just caused havoc in Brussels and Charleroi. So it would come down to Germany and South Africa in the final round. By most estimates, the Kaiser and his entourage were five votes down. Even a near-miraculous 12-12 draw would not be enough, because in that case the vote of the FIFA president would make the difference. No matter how you looked at it, the German World Cup bid seemed brave but futile.

At seven minutes past two in the afternoon, Sepp Blatter entered the platform in the convention hall at Messe Zürich and walked towards the lectern. He opened an envelope, smiled a sour smile and announced: 'And the winner is – *Deutschland.*' After Beckenbauer had been mobbed like a player who'd just scored the winning goal in a World Cup final, he spoke to the press. 'I'm surprised. I'm not prepared for this because you can't be prepared for this. It was a very close result. We had hoped for this, but we couldn't expect it. We are very, very happy. I guess we had a little luck.'

The Guardian's website reported that 'the key to Germany's shock triumph was a last-ditch deal hatched with the four Asian representatives last night. Sensing that Asian discontent over a disagreement with FIFA president Sepp Blatter about voting rights on the executive committee was still lingering, the Germans exploited the advantage to its maximum.' One of those Asian delegates was the Qatari Mohammed bin Hammam, the other three came from Thailand, Saudi Arabia and South Korea. Of course, their votes were important, but they should have brought the score only to 12-12. However, once England had been eliminated, Charles Dempsey did not give his vote to South Africa in the final round, as the OFC had decided to do in May. Instead, Dempsey abstained. When all was said and done, Beckenbauer had won 12-11. Sorry, that should read Germany.

But what had happened that made Dempsey change his mind? 'I didn't do it lightly,' he explained after the vote. 'I don't make decisions like that lightly. I was under unsustainable pressure.' A few days later, he disclosed a few additional details during a press conference: 'The night before the FIFA meeting, I received a number of calls which disturbed me. One of them was a threatening call. It had also been made clear to me by influential European interests that if I cast my vote in favour of South Africa, there would be adverse effects for OFC in FIFA. I believe that decision was in the best interest of football and in particular those of the OFC.' And that was, by and large, all he would say about the matter until his death in the summer of 2008. Dempsey was asked often enough about that day in Zürich and he always replied at length. But it never became any clearer who had done exactly what to make the elderly gentleman from Maryhill lose his head.

A German satirical magazine called *Titanic* jumped at the chance to generate some headlines and disclosed they had played a prank on FIFA the night before the ballot by sending seven delegates who were expected to vote for South Africa a fake bribe letter. It read: 'In appreciation of your support, we would like to offer you a small gift for your vote in favour of Germany: a fine basket with specialities from the black forest, including some really good sausages, ham and – hold on to your seat – a wonderful KuKuClock [sic]!' Dempsey was one of the seven men who received this note, but since he technically didn't vote for Germany, *Titanic* probably refused him his cuckoo clock.

Most people, though, were convinced that the result of the vote had had nothing to do with bribes, threats, pressure, sausages or ham. With the benefit of hindsight, it suddenly all seemed inevitable. A Swiss paper – not even a German one! – said that 'the shining light Franz Beckenbauer has almost single-handedly made Germany the fourth country to stage World Cup finals for a second time'. Former West Germany manager Jupp Derwall was a tiny bit more reserved, arguing that '30 per cent of this success are down to the people behind Franz Beckenbauer. The other 70 per cent are all his.' Otto Schily, the federal minister of the interior, said that 'Franz Beckenbauer has represented our country just marvellously'. Bernd Hölzenbein, the player who'd found Wim Jansen's leg so inviting back in 1974, probably put it best when he pretended not to be surprised at all. 'If Franz is involved,' he said not even half-jokingly, 'we always win, don't we?'

If Germany hadn't done away with the concept of nobility in 1919, Beckenbauer would have been knighted, if not crowned, on the spot. People were so in awe that some claimed, in total seriousness, that all those cold-hearted power brokers in FIFA's inner circle had been swayed by a poetic eighty-second film which the German bid committee had screened on the day before the vote. Directed by the Austrian artist André Heller, it was called *The Nightmares of Franz Beckenbauer* and showed our hero as he was trying to climb an outsized goal netting or swimming underwater with colourful giant fish. If nothing else, it did represent the Kaiser well, because it was charming in a childish way, a little bit silly and profoundly un-German.

A quarter of a century after he had been regularly booed at German football grounds even though he was undoubtedly the best German footballer – certainly of his generation, probably of all time – Franz Beckenbauer had finally become untouchable. And this was before people knew he could even change the weather to his liking (a little party trick of his that will have to wait until the next chapter). But it wasn't all wine and roses. As soon as the enormity of what Beckenbauer had one way or another achieved sunk in, a good deal of German angst crept up, because there was also the enormity of what lay ahead.

As *Sport Bild*'s Bratwurst cover made clear, the main topic in those months and years was the deplorable state of the German game. In 1998, the DFB had launched the massive Talent Promotion Programme, based on the models of youth development that were up and running in France and the Netherlands. Even though the original programme was ambitious and prohibitively expensive, an updated, improved and even more costly version called the Extended Talent Promotion Programme started as early as 2002.

Everybody knew the nurturing of talent took time – but there was no time. Germany needed to have a halfway competitive team in time for the World Cup on home soil. Was this even possible? There were so many doubters that the joke began making the rounds that winning the bid for the World Cup had been Germany's only chance of taking part in the 2006 tournament in the first place. However, there were a few slim rays of hope. Stephan Beckenbauer, for instance, was now responsible for Bayern Munich's under-17 side, where he had worked with a player called Philipp Lahm. Now there was another really promising kid on his team called Bastian Schweinsteiger. However, the boy was barely sixteen.

Of course, Bayern's senior team didn't really have these problems – or, more precisely, they could work around them by signing strong players from abroad, such as the Swede Patrik Andersson, the French internationals Willy Sagnol and Bixente Lizarazu, and the Brazilian strikers Giovane Élber and Paulo Sérgio. In early March 2001, these players and their German team-mates travelled to Lyon for a game in the Champions League. The French won 3-0. Afterwards, the squad came together for the post-match banquet that was customary on European nights. Once celebrity chef Alfons Schuhbeck had dined the players, the reporters, celebrity fans and other hangers-on, Beckenbauer stood up and grabbed a microphone.

'You can lose a game, that happens,' he said. 'The question is in which manner you lose. What happened today was a disgrace. This bore no resemblance to football. We just stood around watching, there was no physical contact. Like Uwe Seeler's charity XI. It was old-timers' football.' The likes of Oliver Kahn and Stefan Effenberg, not to mention coach Ottmar Hitzfeld, were staring at their plates, sensing that this was turning into the kind of tirade you would fire off behind the closed doors of a dressing room, not in semi-public.

But the Kaiser was warming to his subject. 'I'm sorry I have to say all this, but it's the truth. From the stands, it looked even worse than you may have realised down on the pitch. This was Olympique Lyonnais, not Real Madrid, Barcelona or Manchester United. Yet we were made to look silly. Why? Because the attitude was all wrong. Because we play inadequate football. People may have played like that thirty years ago, but not any more. You cannot keep on playing like that, otherwise we will all have to find another line of work.' After three minutes and thirty-eight seconds of this, he thanked

Schuhbeck and said it had been a nice trip, 'apart from the game'. The speech was followed by a round of applause, though it did not come from any of the players.

It was way past midnight when a few Munich writers invited Hitzfeld over to their table to talk about what had just happened. If they expected him to tear into Beckenbauer for having humiliated the team in front of press people and total strangers, they didn't know him well enough. All Hitzfeld would say was: 'Well, that's just the way Franz is.' Inwardly, he thought back to his very first coaching job in the Swiss town of Zug. The club's president at the time was a man by the name of Werner Hofstetter, who once called his players 'parasites' and came close to grabbing Hitzfeld by the throat. But that had happened in the second division, not in the world's most glamorous club competition. And, of course, Hofstetter was a Swiss building contractor, not one of the most famous football people on the planet.

Ten weeks after the Kaiser's legendary rant, Bayern lifted the Bundesliga title in the most dramatic fashion ever when Andersson tied the final game of the league campaign, away at Hamburg, four minutes into stoppage time and with the last touch of the ball of the entire season. And, a mere four days later, Kahn saved three penalties in the shoot-out against Valencia in Milan to also win the Champions League for the Reds. It was the first time the Munich giants had triumphed in this competition since 1976, when the Kaiser was, to again quote *The Times*' Geoffrey Green, 'strolling at the rear like a boulevardier wandering for his morning aperitif' before telling Franz Roth to let rip.

Was it the Kaiser's acerbic speech in Lyon that had rescued the 2000–01 season for Bayern? Such was his reputation that many fans actually believed this. And who knows, maybe they were right. Heck, even his son was suddenly beginning to show signs of having inherited the Midas touch. Using Schweinsteiger as the holding midfielder in front of a flat back four, Stephan Beckenbauer guided Bayern's under-17 team to the final of the national championship. On 30 June, the Reds demolished rivals Borussia Dortmund 4-0 to win the title in great style. After the game, the boys carried Stephan across the pitch on their shoulders. It would take eight long years for another Bayern Munich coach, a certain Louis van Gaal, to rediscover this position for Schweinsteiger and change the whole course of the player's career.

A few months after this youth match, a lot of money was transferred between banks. According to a dossier compiled by four investigative journalists for *Der Spiegel* magazine in 2016, 6 million Swiss francs was sent in four instalments from an account owned by Robert Schwan and Franz Beckenbauer to a Swiss law firm between late May and early July 2002. Said firm then transferred this money into the bank account of a company in Qatar owned by Mohammed bin Hammam. The dossier in *Der Spiegel* quoted one of those Swiss lawyers, Othmar Gabriel, as saying that the transactions – which would come to cause Beckenbauer a lot of headaches some years down the road – were made by the eighty-year-old Schwan.

After he had sent the fourth instalment, the still supremely fit and healthy Schwan went mountain biking with his fourth wife, Maria, although it was a fiendishly hot summer day. When he was beginning to feel unwell, Maria took him to the hospital, where the doctors informed him that he had suffered a mild heart attack. They asked Schwan to stay for a few days for further tests and surveillance. But, of course, the great white bird told them where to put their stethoscopes and stormed out. 'A heart attack!' he supposedly railed. 'That's what I never wanted. How rotten!' Five days later, on 13 July, he was dead.

The funeral service was held on 17 July at the parish church in Kitzbühel. It was not Beckenbauer who delivered the eulogy but Peter Boenisch, a former editor-in-chief of *Bild* and the founder of *Bravo*, the famous teen magazine. On every seat in the church, there was a funeral card that read: 'Many paths lead to God. One crosses the mountains.'

As he would soon confess in a TV interview, Beckenbauer was so shaken by Schwan's death that he relied on tranquillisers for a while. 'I will miss Robert as a friend and business partner,' he said. 'There is now some work ahead of me. I have to completely change my life.' And he did. Fewer than ten days after the funeral, Franz and Sybille Beckenbauer announced their separation. Soon it was all over town that Heidi Burmester was pregnant again.

And there was another gift for the Kaiser. On 3 September, he got all his money back because Gabriel's law firm transferred the 6 million Swiss francs back into the account he used to share with Schwan. Where did it come from? Had Qatar, for whatever reason, returned the cash? Not according to the research done by *Der Spiegel*. Rather, a 56-year-old businessman had given the law firm 10 million Swiss francs. Six of them went to Beckenbauer, the remaining four were also transferred to the company in Qatar. After ninety-nine days of sending money back and forth, Beckenbauer and Schwan were thus even, while Mohammed bin Hammam had pocketed 10 million. The businessman, meanwhile, was 10 million in the red. His name was Robert Louis-Dreyfus.

LIFE III

Chapter Eleven

Some ten years ago, Sky Germany (formerly known as Premiere) had a peculiar concept for their Champions League live coverage. The station would pair two celebrity pundits, one of whom was more often than not called Franz Beckenbauer, with a journalist. The idea was probably to treat the studio audience and the people watching at home to a fresh face and, ideally, one or two fresh comments.

On a Tuesday in March 2013, I was on the show with Ottmar Hitzfeld and Ruud Gullit. The room where we would watch the games was upstairs, the studio where we were supposed to analyse the action was downstairs. At the beginning of the show, each guest was introduced individually and then casually strolled from the room upstairs down to the studio. To do this, you had to walk down two flights of stairs and then find your way through a short but mazy backstage corridor, while a guy with a Steadicam was walking in front of you to send your likeness across the airwaves.

To make sure that none of us turned the wrong way and lost the cameraman, there was an early-evening dress rehearsal with the set manager, who showed me the way. At one junction, he said: 'This is the spot where Franz Beckenbauer always pretends to turn the wrong way, giving everyone a brief scare.'

'What's he like?' I asked.

'Franz?' The set manager turned around. 'Fantastic guy. The most pleasant person you can imagine. I don't think I know anyone else who treats everybody the same, from the cleaning woman to the presenter of the show. Franz is totally unpretentious.'

This remark made me remember a story a former colleague and friend had told me. In the build-up to the 2006 World Cup, we both worked for a company that created and maintained websites for a number of players, among them various German internationals who would be playing at the tournament. Many weeks before the World Cup, my friend – along with a number of other people – was introduced to Beckenbauer during an official presentaton. It was the first time he had ever met the Kaiser, and all they did was exchange a greeting and a handshake. Two months later, my colleague was sitting in the stands at the stadium in Munich, when he saw Beckenbauer walking towards him, in search of his seat. My friend rose to make it easier for the Kaiser to squeeze past him. Beckenbauer smiled. 'Ah, please remain seated, Mister Kampmann. I can cope.' My friend was unable to reply anything, so bowled over was he by the fact that Beckenbauer had remembered his name.

I guess this is one of the qualities really good politicians, football officials or any other administrators need to possess. But it's still impressive – especially after you talk with Walter Beckenbauer. We were discussing the role Robert Schwan had played in his brother's life, when Walter said:

'You have to remember that one reason why Schwan handled everything for my brother was that Franz was very different when he was twenty, twenty-one. He was shy and totally quiet. He would hardly speak to you. It was really only in New York that he became the person he later was.'

There may have been a period after Schwan's death when the Kaiser was, as he once admitted, 'missing him left, right and centre', but outwardly Beckenbauer had seamlessly grown into his role as the German game's greatest ambassador. Of course, he had been made president of the World Cup organising committee and as such he was touring the country to drum up support and help. In the summer of 2003, Karl-Heinz Rummenigge asked him to be available for another term as Bayern president and of course he said yes. In March 2005, leading DFB officials urged him to succeed his friend Lennart Johansson as UEFA president in 2007 by running against Michel Platini. After a few days of hemming and hawing, the Kaiser agreed to do it. What's one more post?

He was now meeting so many people and talking into so many microphones that sometimes his notorious tongue was a bit too quick, though this was hardly news. As early as 1998, *Der Spiegel* had run a piece by the journalist Klaus Brinkbäumer entitled 'Firlefranz' (a play on words, as *Firlefanz* is German for frippery). It argued that while Beckenbauer might be 'the most powerful man in German football', he was also too often 'talking rubbish' or, more precisely, he was changing his opinion about one thing or another so often 'that he's no longer being taking seriously in the inner circles of sports politics'.

Even Stephan Beckenbauer, in a 1999 interview, said of his father: 'There was a time when I changed the channel the moment he appeared on television, because I felt he couldn't be serious about some of the things he said.' Stephan told this story even before the Kaiser made what is probably his second most famous tasteless quip. In January 2000, the Bayern board sat down with the mayor of Munich to discuss a pressing problem: Bayern's new ground. One option was to remodel the Olympic Stadium into a modern arena, but there was a major hurdle. The ground was a listed building. So Beckenbauer turned to the mayor and said: 'The best thing would be to blow the whole thing up. It must be possible to find a terrorist who can do this job for us.' (It remained his most contentious line only until November 2013, when he was asked a question about Qatar and said something far more embarrassing. But more about this controversy later.)

In February 2003, Beckenbauer presented the World Cup host cities as the chair of the organising committee. Noticing that Frankfurt's ambassador was none other than Bernd Hölzenbein, the Kaiser was gripped by one of his chatty moods. He reminded the audience that he had lost the 1974 cup semi-final with Bayern against Eintracht because 'Bernd dived twice'. Then he looked Hölzenbein in the eye. 'But I guess you made up for that when you went down again later in the summer.' People who were there say Hölzenbein was so upset at the insinuation that his dive had gifted West Germany a penalty in the World Cup final against the Netherlands that Olaf Thon eventually walked over to him and said: 'Bernd, I think one could give this penalty.'

But Hölzenbein couldn't really hold a grudge against Beckenbauer for too long. Nobody could. This was a man who had celebrated his fiftieth birthday back in September 1995 with a party that was not only attended by his then wife Sybille, but also by his ex-wife Brigitte and his ex-mistress Diana. This was another difference between him and his friend Johan Cruyff. No, not the number of women, but the universal popularity. While Cruyff was, in the words of David Winner, 'during his lifetime a difficult and sometimes divisive figure in the Netherlands', the Kaiser appeared to be something like the grand unifying force in Germany.

And one was bitterly needed during those trying years before the World Cup. For health and age reasons, Egidius Braun had not run again for DFB president in 2001. His successor was none other than Gerhard Mayer-Vorfelder, who wasn't exactly Beckenbauer's closest pal. He seemed to get off to a good start when Germany did surprisingly well at the 2002 World Cup. But two years later, the national team collapsed so completely at the European Championship in Portugal that Rudi Völler, another Teamchef because he didn't have any coaching badges, threw in the towel. Two years before the World Cup on home soil, the Germans had no team and no manager.

But they had two DFB presidents. That's because there was now so much pressure on Mayer-Vorfelder that Theo Zwanziger, a 59-year-old lawyer and politician, announced he would run against him at the Bundestag in October 2004. This raised the very real spectre of a governing body at war with itself, just twenty months before hosting a major tournament that was supposed to present a unified Germany to the world. Thus the two parties settled upon an uneasy truce: there would be no infighting for votes because both camps would run the show.

No sooner had this *Doppelspitze* – two men up front – been installed than the German game was overshadowed in the first months of 2005 by a nasty match-fixing scandal involving a number of lower-division referees. This chaos was deplorable while it happened but would prove to have even more dramatic consequences a few years later, when journalists and law enforcement agencies began to investigate suspicious financial transactions. Chief among them a bank transfer dated 27 April 2005.

On this day, the German World Cup organising committee, presided over by Beckenbauer, paid 6.7 million euros into a FIFA account. The transfer was made by Zwanziger and Horst R. Schmidt. According to the reference, the money was meant to cover the German share of the costs for a huge gala to be held at the Olympic Stadium on 7 June 2006, two days before the opening game of the World Cup (provided, of course, nobody would have blown up the venerable monument in the interim).

The Austrian artist André Heller – he of *The Nightmares of Franz Beckenbauer* fame – was already working feverishly on this massive event. He had signed Peter Gabriel and Brian Eno to compose original music for the gala, while the British architect Mark Fisher was supposed to design the stage set. This is why it came as a very big shock to Heller when FIFA cancelled the entire event in mid-January 2006, citing problems with the stadium pitch as the reason. Some people suspected the world governing body had gotten cold feet because only 8,000 tickets had been sold for an event whose budget ran to 25 million euros. Heller said he believed the story about the pitch, adding that 'this won't come cheap for FIFA. We've been working on this for two years.'

However, the fees of Heller, Gabriel, Eno and Fisher were not the reason why the German organising committee never saw their 6.7 million euros again. The money was quite simply gone. On the very day it had reached FIFA back in April 2005, it was redirected into another Zürich account. This one was owned by Robert Louis-Dreyfus. In other words, the former Adidas CEO had also gotten his money back at last.

There are people who say that Beckenbauer called his mother Antonie every day of his adult life that he spent anywhere near a telephone. We can assume that she was particularly happy on 28 October 2003, when Franz's fifth child came into this world. Walter had a boy and a girl, both born in the 1970s. But when Heidi Burmester delivered Francesca, she was the Kaiser's first daughter.

Two years later, Antonie even became a television personality of sorts. On 11 September 2005, her son Franz turned sixty. Luckily, it was a Sunday and so the public-service broadcaster ZDF jumped at the chance to throw a massive birthday party. It was recorded two days before the event and presented by Germany's two most famous television hosts – Thomas Gottschalk and Günther Jauch. Almost 700 selected guests filled one of the largest studios available at the Bavaria Production Services in Munich, with the guests of honour including sporting heroes like tennis icon Boris Becker, former figure skater Katarina Witt and swimmer Franziska van Almsick. Of course, there were also countless footballers on hand, from Gerd Müller to Lothar Matthäus.

But the real star appeared after more than three hours. The two hosts said they had 'a little surprise' for Franz before the 92-year-old Antonie walked on to the stage. The stunned audience rose and gave her a two-minute standing ovation. She cheerfully chatted with Gottschalk and Jauch, telling them that Franz was named Franz because sixty years ago she had hoped she would be delivering a girl she wanted to call Franziska. She also said she couldn't wait 'to follow the 2006 World Cup'. After the show, there was a private party. Antonie stayed until half past two in the morning. 'I'm speechless,' her never-speechless son told the reporters. 'I'd never thought she would be here. Amazing, at her age!' Two days later, almost 6 million viewers tuned in to watch his mother steal his show.

Shortly before Christmas, Antonie suddenly felt very weak. She was taken from her home that was still No. 29 Stauffenbergstrasse to a hospital run by nuns on the other side of the Olympic Park, near Nymphenburg Palace. Franz and Heidi spent more than two hours at her bed every day, even though they had to travel by helicopter from Kitzbühel to beat the traffic. Antonie had to spend Christmas and New Year's Eve at the hospital, but eventually her condition was improving, which is why Beckenbauer travelled to South Africa to film a commercial. But while her younger son was gone, Antonie peacefully passed away on 11 January.

It was really a shame that the lady whom Franz always referred to as the most important woman in his life never got to see the World Cup, because while people think that bringing the tournament to Germany was Beckenbauer's crowning achievement, you could say that his biggest triumph was actually how it all turned out. Let's start with the weather. The three weeks prior to the World Cup were ugly, cold and rainy. A low-pressure area christened Gertrud by the meteorologists and marked by nasty windstorms caused ground frost and snowfall even in low-lying areas. Then, abruptly and as if on cue, the sun came out and temperatures soared. Germans have been calling this kind of weather *Kaiserwetter* since the nineteenth century, which may explain why the country became convinced that Beckenbauer had manipulated the elements. After all, he needed stable conditions because the idea was that he would be flying from game to game. Literally.

The pilot Hans Ostler took Beckenbauer to as many matches in his helicopter as was physically possible – forty-eight out of sixty-four. Ostler says they covered 25,000 nautical miles and spent 100 hours in the air. 'The moment we lifted off, he always had a smile on his face and enjoyed the beautiful landscape and the wonderful weather,' the pilot told *11Freunde* magazine. 'The only thing he didn't want to talk about was football.' Ostler said the duo 'enjoyed the privilege of fools in the airspace', meaning absolutely no rules applied to the Kaiser's helicopter. 'We were more important than the chancellor's aircraft.'

When the DFB had bid for this World Cup, one of the selling points was that a reunified Germany would present itself to the world and show people what a modern, friendly, peaceful country it was, more than six decades after the war. Even the men on the bid committee will not have imagined how thoroughly their dream would come true. As early as 18 June, the BBC's Laura Smith-Spark marvelled: 'Isn't it funny how ten days of football can change so many people's ideas about other nations? I never expected to hear so many voices from around the world say how great the Germans are. I also didn't expect the World Cup to be quite such an international love-in.'

Maybe the biggest wonder of all was that even German football was ready when it counted. After Völler had stepped down in June 2004, no coach worth his salt was willing to go on the suicide mission of taking over the national team. So the then DFB boss Mayer-Vorfelder gave the job to someone who wasn't a coach – but who had played for Stuttgart during his club presidency. Jürgen Klinsmann built a side around talented youngsters, including Stephan Beckenbauer's charges Lahm and Schweinsteiger, and was rewarded with an unexpected third-place finish.

The World Cup was such a smashing success on all levels that it came to be known in Germany as the *Sommermärchen* – the summer (fairy) tale. But if you believe that things couldn't possibly have turned out any better or more perfect for Franz Beckenbauer, you still haven't quite grasped his genius after reading all these pages, because the Kaiser found a way to cap it all off that took even his friends and family by surprise. On 23 June, the sixty-year-old Beckenbauer got married for the third time. His brother Walter served as his best man and was one of only nine people present at the Austrian civil registration office; among them were Heidi and Franz's young children Joel and Francesca. The next day, Beckenbauer saw Germany play a Sweden side starring Henrik Larsson, Freddie Ljungberg and Zlatan Ibrahimović in the round of 16. Some people claimed the Scandinavians were the tournament's most dangerous dark horses. Germany won 2-0.

The *Sommermärchen* was not only the high point of Beckenbauer's stellar career and amazing life, but it was also the pinnacle. It would be downhill from there, first almost imperceptibly, then faster and faster. Maybe the decline began only three days after the World Cup final between Italy and France in Berlin. That was when the 76-year-old Lennart Johansson surprisingly announced he would run for another term as UEFA president after all. The Swede had always been a trustworthy ally of the Germans, which meant that Beckenbauer's own candidature was now no longer an option.

That created a boardroom problem for the DFB. Between 1998 and 2002, when Mayer-Vorfelder was elected a member of FIFA's executive committee, there had been no German on this important body (which, some officials thought, was why the country's World Cup bid had turned into such a nail-biting thriller). Mayer-Vorfelder would leave the committee in 2007 and what then? The UEFA president automatically held a seat on this committee, but now that the Kaiser wouldn't square off against Platini, another vacancy loomed. In September 2006, Theo Zwanziger said: 'It is my wish that Franz Beckenbauer, who is internationally held in the highest esteem, joins the committee in 2007. This is eminently important for us, because he will open all doors.'

Four months later, the DFB suffered a heavy defeat at the UEFA congress in Düsseldorf; despite enjoying the support of the Germans, Johansson was beaten by Platini, who became the new president. But as always, Beckenbauer still won, as he was elected to represent UEFA on FIFA's executive committee. Asked about the body's reputation as an old boys' society, he said: 'This is often depicted in a wrong or misleading way. I think it's really great how stubbornly the older fellows are getting involved. I'm looking forward to being a part of that.' He added he could well imagine 'supporting FIFA's funding projects in Africa. Doing something for the poorest of the poor and furthering those projects is dear to my heart.'

What he didn't know at this point was that one of his jobs in the future would be voting on not one but two World Cup bids. That's because in late 2008, during a meeting in Tokyo, the committee decided to award both the 2018 and the 2022 World Cups on the same day in December 2010. Five years after that infamous vote, an Associated Press wire report about the older fellows Franz had been looking forward to join would open with these words: 'In the history of soccer line-ups, the twenty-four-man FIFA executive committee of 2010 ranks among the all-time worst for bad behaviour.'

*

Despite sinking deeper and deeper into the quagmire of FIFA politics, Franz was still able to enchant everyone he met. In late March 2007, the Dutch writer Marcel Rözer launched his book about Beckenbauer and Cruyff – subtitled *de Keizer en de Verlosser*, the Kaiser and the Saviour – at the Olympic Stadium in Amsterdam, where Ajax used to stage their international games.

Rözer had also made a film about the two players' brothers – Walter Beckenbauer and Henny Cruyff – which is why Franz and Walter chartered an aircraft and travelled from Munich to Amsterdam to attend the event. (Henny and his mother were also there, while Johan was absent.) The former Ajax player Jan Mulder, now a columnist and pundit, presented Franz with a Netherlands shirt bearing the number 5 and the name Beckenbauer. 'It was such a fantastic day,' Rözer remembers. 'Some of my friends were also there. They played football on the pitch of the Olympic Stadium with Franz. Can you imagine that? They still walk around and tell people: You know, we played with Beckenbauer!'

Three months after this cheerful celebration of blood ties, Stephan Beckenbauer won another under-17 title for Bayern. His father had recently admitted on television that in the past he just did not know 'what responsibility for a family means'. He added: 'I was a bad father, because I was always away.' He did care, of course. When Stephan got the offer to join Saarbrücken in 1994, his old club – a small team called Grenchen – demanded 40,000 marks to release the player from his contract. It was a piffling sum, but Saarbrücken refused, so Franz Beckenbauer paid the money himself to give his son a shot at professional football.

However, it didn't really help his very complicated relationship with Stephan, because the son had unfortunately inherited the father's pronounced (though hardly uncommon in men, especially of his generation) problem to talk in earnest about feelings. In the late 1990s, Stephan said he never discussed matters of importance with Franz, because 'in a way our inability to communicate is a taboo subject. We feel awful because we can't really talk, or at least I do. This has changed over the last years, though, and I'm glad about that.'

Franz Beckenbauer had not planned on becoming a father again so late in his life, but – as is often the case – once it happened, he fully embraced his new role the moment he realised it gave him a chance to prove he had learned a lesson. Of course, he couldn't undo a wrong, but this was the next best thing. So he almost became a professional father, doting on Joel and Francesca, and spending a lot more time at home with his family than he had ever done in the previous four decades. Slowly but surely, the Kaiser was sneaking out of the game he loved so much.

In 2009, Beckenbauer stepped down as Bayern president (handing the post over to Uli Hoeness) and also vacated his seat on the limited company's executive board. To be honest, he hadn't really been involved in the club's day-to-day business for quite some time, partly due to his countless other activities and partly because, as the famous 'Firlefranz' article explained, his volatility and tendency to put emotionality before reason often caused more problems than they solved. 'There's nothing left for me to do at Bayern,' the Kaiser explained after the club's AGM in November 2009. 'Three years ago, I allowed myself to be talked into another term, but now it's enough. I helped turn the club into a plc, and I took care of the building of our own stadium. Now we need some younger guys.'

During the meeting, Beckenbauer was also appointed

Bayern's honorary president. Then Karl-Heinz Rummenigge apologised on behalf of the club for the shabby treatment the Kaiser had received back in 1977, when he had to pay 350,000 marks out of his own pocket to be able to leave for New York. In order to make up for this slight, Rummenigge said, Bayern's team would play a friendly against Real Madrid and bill it as Beckenbauer's presidential testimonial. 'Oh,' the Kaiser quipped, 'I was hoping I might get my money back today.'

One year after leaving Bayern's board, he also began to gradually fade out of view as a high-ranking DFB functionary. In March 2010, Zwanziger threatened to step down as president (in connection with yet another refereeing scandal), whereupon some officials suggested Beckenbauer should replace him. But the 64-year-old Kaiser quickly nipped this idea in the bud with a typical joke – 'I'm ten years too young for that' – and instead declared he was going to 'drastically reduce all national and international obligations'.

After the DFB's Bundestag in October 2010, he remained on the board as a 'representative for international tasks', but was no longer officially referred to as a vice-president. Finally, in November 2010, Beckenbauer also announced that he would leave FIFA's executive committee. 'I had and I have a really good time with my colleagues at FIFA and UEFA,' he said, 'and my relationships with Sepp Blatter and Michel Platini are on a very friendly footing. Please bear with me and accept my decision.' As the wire reports added: 'His last official act of importance will be the vote on the 2018 and 2022 World Cup bids on 2 December in Zürich.'

Most observers considered England to be the favourites for 2018, with Spain and Portugal not far behind. The race for 2022 appeared to be more open, as Australia and the USA were level-pegging. However, even before the secret ballot was actually held, there were dark mutterings and suspicions. On 1 December, *Der Spiegel* concluded: 'Corruption, bribery, collusion – the battle for the simultaneous awarding of the World Cups seems to be fought by all available means.'

A major reason for those harsh words was that FIFA's twenty-four-man committee had already been reduced to a twenty-two-man committee. In October, an undercover reporter from the *Sunday Times* had filmed secret footage that showed Reynald Temarii from Tahiti and Amos Adamu from Nigeria offering to sell their votes. Both men were banned by FIFA's ethics committee a mere two weeks before the ballot, meaning there was not enough time to replace them.

The voting procedure began at 1 p.m., local Zürich time. Soon there were the first signs that something was not going quite according to plan. The results were to be announced at 4 p.m., but first that was pushed back by ten minutes, then by another twenty. At 4.18 p.m., the BBC's as-it-happened report noted: 'Some interesting news. FIFA have changed their mind and will reveal all the voting figures – round by round – later on today. So we will get some transparency, no matter what the outcome is for England.' The outcome was not good. At 4.37 p.m., Blatter revealed that the 2018 World Cup would be held in Russia. If this was a bit of a surprise, the word Blatter uttered six minutes later knocked the wind out of almost everybody watching, listening or reading: Qatar.

Equally stunning were the results of the individual rounds of voting. England's bid, widely considered to be excellent, had received only two votes in the first round – fewer than even the joint bid by Belgium and the Netherlands. 'I'm disappointed by how FIFA handled the result after the voting,'

Beckenbauer said two weeks later. 'Seven defeated hosts have been exposed to ridicule, most of all England and Australia. We had been told that neither we nor the public would learn about the exact number of votes. After each round, we were only informed who had been eliminated. And then I hear on the radio who received how many votes.'

While the British media went into overdrive over the 2018 World Cup – the *Daily Mirror* ran with the headline 'Sold', the *Daily Star* said 'What a fix' and the *Daily Mail* announced 'They lied' – the rest of the globe was more shocked by the fact that the 2022 World Cup would be held in a country with no footballing tradition (even no sporting tradition in the Western sense at all) and an inhospitable summer climate, which is why Beckenbauer told a *Bild* reporter only two days after the ballot that FIFA should consider moving the World Cup to the winter. At the time, the Kaiser's remark was ridiculed. The *Frankfurter Allgemeine Zeitung* asked: 'Is Beckenbauer going nuts now? Awarding Qatar the World Cup was a crazy idea to begin with, but that the Kaiser is seriously suggesting to stage the tournament during the winter is taking craziness to new extremes.'

A few years later, I was in Dubai to report on Borussia Dortmund's winter training camp. At the team's posh hotel, I noticed a man in a servant's livery standing next to the door that led out on to the patio. Whenever someone walked towards the door, he opened and then closed it. I strolled over and asked him if this was his job, day in and day out.

'Yes, sir. That's what I do,' he replied. 'Of course, not during the summer.'

'Why not in the summer?' I asked.

He looked at me probingly, trying to find out if I was having him on. Only when he realised my question was serious if stupid did he answer. 'Because nobody ever goes outside in the summer. It's too hot.'

I told him: 'Well, we're going to have a football World Cup in the summer some 250 miles away, in Qatar.'

The man thought for a moment about the politest way to phrase his answer. 'I'm sure that must be some kind of misunderstanding, sir. I can assure you that nobody will play football in the summer here.'

Of course, he and the Kaiser eventually turned out to be right. In March 2015, FIFA decided to play the 2022 World Cup in November and December. However, by that time it had become very obvious that the weather question was actually the smallest problem in connection with those World Cup ballots Beckenbauer had been involved in. Perhaps it was hubris that had made FIFA overlook a simple fact. If South Africa loses a vote under dubious circumstances, many South Africans will be sad, and that's that. But if the same happens to Australia, England and the USA, a great many nosy reporters will start asking questions.

LIFE III

Chapter Twelve

The 2010 ballot was secret and it has remained so. Still, it seems likely that Beckenbauer did not vote for Qatar. For one, when he was asked about a World Cup in the Persian Gulf region very shortly after the ballot, he said: 'I can't say I'm overflowing with happiness.' Also, his good friend and associate Fedor Radmann had worked as an adviser on the Australian bidding team, so it seems certain that's where his vote went for the 2022 tournament.

As regards his vote for 2018, a pretty clear signal was sent out in late May 2012, when Alexey Miller, CEO of the Russian state-owned energy corporation Gazprom, announced during the European Business Congress in Slovenia that the Kaiser would work as a 'sports ambassador' (which is another, nicer sounding word for lobbyist) for the Russian Gas Society. This raised more than a few eyebrows, as Gazprom's reputation in the West was not the best. Going metaphor-crazy, the German weekly *Die Zeit* explained that 'this will be a match of the titans. Either Beckenbauer's image will outshine the gas economy's shadow realm or Gazprom will manage to put even a shining light into the shade.' In the end, it was no contest, because Beckenbauer had begun to run out of luck faster than you could say Amnesty International.

In November 2013, the human rights organisation published a report called 'The Dark Side of Migration' about the situation of the migrant workers who had been recruited to build all those stadiums which Qatar needed for a football tournament but of course didn't have. The report detailed 'widespread and routine abuse across Qatar's construction sector'. This news came in the wake of a *Guardian* article which said the labourers in Qatar 'face exploitation and abuses that amount to modern-day slavery'.

When a television reporter confronted Beckenbauer with those harrowing descriptions, a tight-lipped Kaiser replied by saying he hadn't 'yet seen a single slave in Qatar. They're all running around freely, they aren't in chains or wearing sackcloth. I have no idea where these reports are coming from. I have won a different impression of the Arabic countries, and I think my impression is more realistic.'

Only a couple of days before the Kaiser made this disastrous statement, his son Stephan had caused a much smaller scandal of his own. During an under-12 game in Munich, he had been hurling such abuse at the fourteen-year-old referee (and the boy's father) that neutral witnesses reported the incident to the football authorities. The regional Bavarian federation eventually fined Stephan and his assistant, who happened to be his stepson, twenty euros each.

The two incidents may be entirely unrelated, and there is certainly no excuse for Franz Beckenbauer's outrageous belittlement of the human-rights situation in Qatar. With a good deal of hindsight, though, we know that the Beckenbauers were under a lot of emotional stress at the time. Nobody outside the inner family circle would hear about it for another two years, but at some point in 2013, Stephan had been diagnosed with an inoperable brain tumour.

For his father, who had just discovered or maybe rediscovered his appreciation of family ties, it must have come as a terrible blow. And the timing could not have been any worse, because suddenly allegations and revelations were being made almost daily. At least this would explain, though not excuse, why Beckenbauer also failed to co-operate with FIFA's ethics committee around this time.

Former US attorney Michael J. Garcia had been appointed as the chairman of the investigative chamber of this committee and was looking into the accusations surrounding the 2010 vote. When Beckenbauer repeatedly refused to answer Garcia's questions, FIFA announced in June 2014 that it had banned the German from all football-related activities for ninety days. At first, the Kaiser reacted in a typically irreverent manner, telling Sky Germany: 'I had to look at the date and make sure it wasn't April 1st. I thought it was an April Fools' joke.' But then he must have realised how serious the whole thing was becoming. He explained he was 'not proficient in English, in legal English' and had requested German-language questions. Via Twitter, he also stated that he 'underestimated the case, especially because all these administrative issues are usually handled by my management', a statement that was posted by his agent Marcus Höfl. The ban was lifted two weeks later, but the damage had been done.

While these official investigations and also numerous journalistic probings were going on, Beckenbauer kept hoping against hope that a cure could be found for his son's disease. *Bild* later said that 'he travelled with Stephan to the best specialists', but even a new immunotherapy proved inefficient. In late July 2015, the 46-year-old fell into a coma. For two days, his father, his wife and his three children stayed at his bedside, but Stephan never regained consciousness. On 31 July, he took his final breath. Bastian Schweinsteiger, who had just moved to Manchester United, said on social media: 'I'm deeply saddened by the terrible news about the death of my youth-team coach and mentor Stephan Beckenbauer.'

Years would pass before the Kaiser spoke publicly about losing his son. In 2020, a few days before his seventy-fifth birthday, he granted his former ghostwriter Walter M. Straten and Alfred Draxler, an old journalist friend, one of his now very rare interviews. He said: 'I never had any real problems in my life before. Things were always going well, pushbacks were few and far between. I have never learned to deal with problems, that's why this blow of fate hit me particularly hard. Losing Stephan was the greatest bereavement of my life. I don't know if you can ever come to terms with the death of your child. Probably not.'

Eleven weeks after Stephan passed away, the *Sommermärchen* scandal broke. Until the day in October 2015 when the cover of *Der Spiegel* magazine screamed 'The ruined *Sommermärchen* – Slush funds: The true story of the 2006 World Cup', nearly all the talk had been about the questionable 2010 vote, about how Russia and Qatar became tournament hosts. Now Germans had to look much closer to home. Pictured on the cover were Beckenbauer, incumbent DFB president Wolfgang Niersbach – and Robert Louis-Dreyfus.

The journalists had unearthed those strange money trans-actions dating back to 2002, when Louis-Dreyfus had paid a Swiss law firm 10 million francs, and to 2005, when the DFB sent FIFA the strangely uneven sum of 6.7 million euros for a gala that never took place. At the time, 6.7 million euros exactly equalled 10 million francs. The implication seemed obvious to the investigating journalists: Louis-Dreyfus had given the DFB's organising committee money to buy (at least) the Qatari vote. Three years later, he wanted his money back and got it. 'Why should the German World Cup have been the only one that was clean?' the piece asked. 'It wasn't clean. This changes the images of that summer: the magic was real, but the magicians who conjured up the summer fairy tale were probably conmen after all. And the conmen then became hypocrites.'

Two of the three key figures involved in the 2002 transactions could no longer be held accountable. Louis-Dreyfus had died from leukaemia in 2009, seven years after Schwan had passed away. That left Beckenbauer as the sole man in the centre of the storm. More people, however, were implicated when it came to the 2005 repayment of the loan, or whatever you want to call it, which is why the DFB's top brass, which had never been particularly stable after Egidius Braun stepped down, now came apart at the seams.

Ten days after the *Der Spiegel* exposé, Niersbach's predecessor as DFB president, Theo Zwanziger, defended Beckenbauer with a slightly unfortunate statement. 'This whole thing starts with the rotten FIFA system Franz Beckenbauer had to stumble into so that he would even stand a chance of bringing the World Cup to Germany.' While the other members of the organising committee were denying the existence of slush funds, Zwanziger dragged the next man and the next company into this mess when he presented documents which, he felt, suggested that International Sport and Leisure, Horst Dassler's old company, had bribed Charles Dempsey prior to the 2006 vote.

In November, the attorney general of Switzerland opened criminal proceedings against Beckenbauer, Zwanziger, Niersbach and Horst R. Schmidt in connection with allegations of fraud, criminal mismanagement, money laundering and misappropriation. This didn't become widely known, though, until a year later when police searches were carried out in various locations, one of them being Beckenbauer's Austrian home.

Amid all these whirlwinds of growing accusations, the Kaiser, who had seemingly never stopped talking since he came back from New York as a man of the world, said very, very little. 'I never paid anyone any money to acquire votes to bring the 2006 World Cup to Germany,' he stated. 'And I'm sure that nobody else on the bid committee has done that.' He explained that it was all a long time ago and that he couldn't possibly remember everything he had signed, adding he had rarely actually checked all the documents, invoices or transfer forms he was given. In a television interview, he admitted that he had not even read a single one of the 1,112 pages that made up the German bid book for the 2006 World Cup. 'My conscience is clear,' he concluded.

Niersbach, meanwhile, gave a long-winded explanation for the Louis-Dreyfus millions. He said the organising committee (represented by Beckenbauer) had requested financial assistance from FIFA (represented by Sepp Blatter) to shoulder the costs of the tournament. According to Niersbach, Blatter promised 250 million Swiss francs but first asked for a fee of 10 million Swiss francs to be lodged with FIFA's finance committee. Since the German organising committee didn't have these kinds of funds so early into its existence, Louis-Dreyfus was approached for a loan. Truth be told, this sounded a tad strange even before Blatter told a Swiss newspaper: 'I have never requested money from Beckenbauer or from the DFB. That is just not true.'

In April of 2016, Beckenbauer tweeted photos showing him in China, explaining that he was 'on the trails of Confucius in Qufu, where he lived. The philosopher's teaching accompanies me since many years.' That same month, his old friend Günter Netzer suffered a serious heart attack. This prompted Beckenbauer to have what he thought was a routine cardiological check-up. The doctors told him his heart was only months away from giving in. A few weeks later, the Kaiser underwent coronary bypass surgery.

He had already quit being a pundit for Sky Germany after a quarter of a century, but in the wake of this operation, he almost completely vanished from the public eye. In 2017, his heart was operated on again. In early 2018, he had an artificial hip inserted. In 2019, he suffered a retinal artery occlusion – an obstruction of blood flow in the retina – that left his vision seriously impaired. When Beckenbauer appeared at the annual Kaiser Cup in Bad Griesbach, a charity golf tournament he had launched back in 1987 to raise money for his foundation, many people were shocked at how visibly he had aged in the span of only one year. 'Don't be mad at me if I knock you down because I can't see you,' he joked.

Meanwhile, there were problems an operation or two or three could not fix. In September 2016, it was disclosed that Beckenbauer had been paid 5.5 million euros for being the head of the World Cup's organising committee. There was nothing inherently wrong with that, and nobody would have batted an eyelid about this news eleven months earlier. But the DFB had always given the impression that the World Cup had been a labour of love for the Kaiser. In other words, it was beginning to look as if this *Sommermärchen* thing had never really been what it seemed.

And there were still these other World Cups. In January 2018, whistleblower Bonita Mersiades talked to the German journalist Benjamin Best while promoting her book *Whatever It Takes: The Inside Story of the FIFA Way*. Mersiades, who worked on the Australian World Cup bid, said that 'Radmann received 3.6 million Australian dollars, an enormous sum considering the work he did. What I learned from insiders in world football during my own research was that Beckenbauer got money from Radmann. When I asked Blatter about this, he said: Well, he doesn't do anything without money.'

If she was implying that Beckenbauer had asked for and received money in order to vote for Australia, the Kaiser's reputation was dealt another heavy blow in October 2019 when the Russian website The Insider published documents which, in the words of *Der Spiegel*, 'support the suspicion that Fedor Radmann offered Beckenbauer's vote for sale. As emails explain, 3 million euros up front and another 1.5 million in case of success would give the Russian team Beckenbauer's vote.'

All of this must make it seem to the reader as if Beckenbauer had become a beleaguered, isolated, lonely man. True, you could gain this impression. In late 2016, the weekly celebrity gossip magazine *Bunte* published a photo of Beckenbauer and his wife Heidi with the caption: 'Only his family is still loyal to him.' One year later, a forty-five-minute film titled *The Kaiser's Fall* was shown on public-service television. The opening scenes depicted a car driving through snowy hills on a foggy, cloudy day, while David Bowie's 'Lazarus' was playing in the background, giving the images a sombre, almost funereal atmosphere.

The car, it soon turned out, was headed for Beckenbauer's house in Kitzbühel. The filmmakers were hoping to meet him, but they came away empty-handed, so they talked to neighbours, some of whom said they hadn't seen Beckenbauer in a while. Gunther Latsch, a member of *Der Spiegel*'s investigative team that had broken the *Sommermärchen* story, told the director he had expected Beckenbauer to admit to any wrongdoings 'in his nonchalant way', perhaps explaining that one had to bend the rules a bit in order to be awarded a World Cup. 'I think he would have gotten away with that,' said Latsch. 'People would have forgiven him. I was really surprised he didn't do this.'

What Latsch, and the filmmakers, failed to grasp was that many people seemed to feel there was nothing to forgive. For a very long time, the writers and journalists had been on the Kaiser's side because it was their job to honour his achievements and report on his performances, while many people in the stands found it very hard to relate to him as a person and love him the way they loved other players. But now it was the other way round. Now the media representatives heard the testimonies and looked at the evidence and found the Kaiser wanting, while the man in the street simply chose to ignore all those accusations and continue to hold him in high esteem.

When Bayern hosted Liverpool in the Champions League in March 2019, Sky had a surprise for the viewers at home. During the pre-game coverage, there was an unexpected interview guest. Clad in a long black coat and wearing a dark fedora, Beckenbauer stood in the stands of the Allianz Arena, the construction of which in 2005 had been one of his pet projects as club president. The interview in itself was unremarkable, except maybe for the fact that the Kaiser said he was hoping Jürgen Klopp would one day coach Bayern Munich. What was remarkable was the reaction of the Sky audience. As soon as the interview ended, the people who had been watching from the studio rose as one to give someone who wasn't even there a standing ovation. They were applauding the fact that Beckenbauer was in a good enough shape to make a public appearance and watch his team play. Or maybe they were simply applauding Beckenbauer for being Beckenbauer. As his brother Walter told me: 'This World Cup thing, his health problems, his son's death – he is too good a person to deserve all this.'

In April 2020, the statute of limitations expired on the Swiss court case against Zwanziger, Niersbach and Schmidt. The proceedings against Beckenbauer had been separated from the rest of the case as early as 2019, probably due to medical considerations, although the original statement of the prosecutor's office did not cite any reason. Eventually, Zwanziger, Niersbach and Schmidt would be granted indemnity and compensated for all legal costs.

Ten months after the Swiss had to close their case, FIFA's bribery investigation against Beckenbauer, Zwanziger and Schmidt came to a sudden end as well – also because a statute of limitations had run out. FIFA's ethics judges said the Kaiser had 'invoked his right to silence and refused to provide the investigatory chamber with any written or oral statement' between 2015 and 2018, citing health issues, although – as the governing body poignantly noted – 'his medical condition did not prevent him from attending events, travelling to foreign countries (despite the COVID pandemic), posing for pictures, making speeches, and giving at least three interviews'.

On 11 September 2020, Franz Beckenbauer turned

seventy-five. One day later, he attended the opening of an exhibition dedicated to his life at Bayern Munich's celebrated club museum. It was a fairly low-key affair on account of the COVID pandemic. The list of attendees was short but elite. Günter Netzer, Lothar Matthäus and Andreas Brehme were there, as well as Beckenbauer's wife Heidi and son Joel, plus leading club representatives like Oliver Kahn, Karl-Heinz Rummenigge and Uli Hoeness. The latter made the most emotional speech. While actually fighting back tears, Hoeness said: 'We as Bayern Munich are grateful that we had you – the greatest player this country has ever produced.'

Then everybody dispersed to check out the exhibits. Among the artefacts were some very personal items provided by Beckenbauer himself, such as a couple of annotated books on Confucius and a few vinyl singles from his collection of Tony Christie records. There was also a lone Adidas boot, a right one. If you looked closely you would notice that the leather was particularly worn out on the outside of the shoe.

The Top 40

On 15 March 2007, Mrs Michel was watching people kick a football very gingerly. The forty-year-old executive director of a small but busy communications agency had travelled to Frankfurt to attend a sports sponsorship trade fair on behalf of Deutsche Telekom. In order to draw attention to that company's presentation room, Michel had brought a facility with her that could measure the speed of a football as it travelled through the air.

Gadgets like this one are normally used to find out who has the hardest shot, but on this day Michel had given the competition a twist. She did not want to exclude the young or the old – or indeed most women – by asking them to do something they couldn't, so the idea on this day was to try and kick the ball at a certain speed – forty kilometres per hour (twenty-five miles per hour).

Although this was a smart idea, it soon turned out that shooting at a precise predetermined pace is a very hard thing to do. People kept kicking and kicking without even getting anywhere near the target, which is why the number of attempts per person eventually had to be limited to three and the challenge became to see who would get closest to that speed.

Suddenly Michel noticed a commotion. Somebody was coming her way surrounded by a larger group of people, which had to mean it was a famous person. Being a good PR woman, Michel decided to ask him or her to give the ball machine a try. Then she realised it was Franz Beckenbauer. This was bad news, because she knew that Beckenbauer had a contract with O_2, meaning he would probably not want to be seen at the Deutsche Telekom booth. Still, she felt it couldn't hurt to ask, so she walked over and introduced herself. Without hesitating for even a moment, Beckenbauer agreed to check out the contraption.

A ball was placed on the spot and, while Beckenbauer got ready to shoot, Michel noticed he was wearing patent-leather shoes that were elegant but not ideal for kicking a ball gently. The small crowd that had formed around them held its collective breath as the Kaiser chipped the ball into the makeshift goal.

Instantly, the machine flashed: 40 kph.

For a second, everybody just stared in utter disbelief at the display. Then a tremendous cheer went up that must have rattled the O_2 booth hundreds of metres away.

'I don't believe this,' Michel said. 'This is impossible.'

'Ah,' Beckenbauer said. 'That was just luck.'

INDEX

FB indicates Franz Beckenbauer.